VITAL
SIGNS
1999

VITAL SIGNS 1999

The Environmental Trends That Are Shaping Our Future

Lester R. Brown

Michael Renner

Brian Halweil

Editor: Linda Starke

with

Janet N. Abramovitz
Seth Dunn
Christopher Flavin
Hilary F. French
Gary Gardner
Nicholas Lenssen
Lisa Mastny

Ashley T. Mattoon
Anne Platt McGinn
Molly O'Meara
David M. Roodman
Curtis Runyan
Payal Sampat

W.W. Norton & Company
New York   London

VITAL SIGNS and WORLDWATCH INSTITUTE trademarks are registered in the U.S. Patent
and Trademark Office.

The views expressed are those of the authors and do not necessarily represent those of
the Worldwatch Institute; of its directors, officers, or staff; or of its funders.

The text of this book is composed in Garth Graphic
with the display set in Industria Alternate.

Composition by the Worldwatch Institute; manufacturing by the Haddon Craftsmen, Inc.
Book design by Charlotte Staub.

ISBN 0-393-31893-1 (pbk)

W.W. Norton & Company, Inc.
500 Fifth Avenue, New York, NY 10110
W.W. Norton & Company Ltd.
10 Coptic Street, London WC1A 1PU

1234567890

This book is printed on recycled paper.

CONTENTS

Part One: KEY INDICATORS

Part Two: SPECIAL FEATURES

ACKNOWLEDGMENTS

We are particularly grateful to the W. Alton Jones Foundation and the United Nations Population Fund for their financial support of *Vital Signs*. Over the years, their assistance has helped make this book a popular reference source in some 20 languages—one that in the words of the British newspaper *The Guardian* "makes all other works of reference look trivial."

But *Vital Signs* also draws on the Institute's entire research program, which is supported by a score or more of foundations and individual donors. We thank the Geraldine R. Dodge Foundation, the Ford Foundation, the William and Flora Hewlett Foundation, the Charles Stewart Mott Foundation, the Curtis and Edith Munson Foundation, the David and Lucile Packard Foundation, the Rasmussen Foundation, Rockefeller Financial Services, the Summit Foundation, the Turner Foundation, the Wallace Genetic Foundation, the Wallace Global Fund, the Weeden Foundation, and the Winslow Foundation. In addition, we acknowledge the support of the more than 600 individuals who provided financial support through the Friends of Worldwatch program last year. We are particularly grateful to the members of our Council of Sponsors: Tom and Cathy Crain, Toshishige Kurosawa, Kazuhiko Nishi, Roger and Vicki Sant, Robert Wallace, and Eckart Wintzen, who contribute $50,000 per year to the Institute.

This is the eighth edition of *Vital Signs* and the eighth year that Linda Starke has worked her editing magic to ensure that 50 manuscript drafts written by 16 authors all conform to the same style and length. Many of our authors are by now veterans of *Vital Signs*, but we are joined in this edition by another very talented author, Lisa Mastny. Lisa contributed three pieces and assisted in preparing another one. Alumnus Nick Lenssen continues to pitch in from Boulder, Colorado. And David Malin Roodman, on leave in Viet Nam as a Fulbright Scholar, found time to contribute as well, in addition to providing feedback on colleagues' drafts.

As she did last year, Elizabeth Doherty deftly juggled *Vital Signs* design work with her other responsibilities, which include desktop production of *State of the World*, the Worldwatch Papers series, and our bimonthly magazine, WORLD WATCH. Lori Brown incorporates all the tables and figures in the print version of *Vital Signs* into the Worldwatch Database Disk, and spent long hours revamping and expanding our Web site to make electronic versions of individual *Vital Signs* pieces available for downloading. Lori and Anne Smith keep authors well supplied with books, reports, and other research materials.

We are grateful to them as well as to all the other Worldwatch staffers whose behind-the-scenes work makes this book possible. They include Reah Janise Kauffman, who assists with fundraising and manages some 160 publishing contracts for this and our other publications in more than 30 languages; our operations team of Jim Gillespie, Barbara Fallin, Suzanne Clift, and Sharon Lapier; our communications team of Richard Bell, Mary Caron, Alison Trice, and Amy Warehime; and, last but not least, our publications sales team of Millicent Johnson and Joseph Gravely. Without the hard work of the entire Worldwatch team, we could not publish, market, and disseminate *Vital Signs*.

Authors received comments on drafts or other helpful advice and input from a variety of outside experts. We would like to thank Donald Anderson, Neil Austriaco, Pat Bills, Anthony Burton, Robert J. Coen, Attilio Costaguta, Nigel Griffiths, Ian Heap, Jos Heyman, Bruce Hutton, Frank Jamerson, Clive James, Jessica Jiji, Jeff Kenworthy, Wolfram Koeller, Soren Krohn, Armand Lione, Todd Litman, Angus Maddison, Birger Madsen, Andreas Maurer, Paul Maycock, Peter Newman, Mika Ohbayashi, Maurizio Perotti, Thomas Rabehl, Kent Robertson, José Santamarta, Vladimir Sliviak, Theodore Smayda, Carrie Smith, Andreas Wagner, Mark Whalon, Angelika Wirtz, and Bock Cheng Yeo.

As in previous years, we would like to thank Amy Cherry, Nomi Victor, and Andrew Marasia and their colleagues at W.W. Norton & Company for their continued support, and particularly for converting a manuscript on disk into a printed book within a matter of weeks.

Finally, we note with sadness the untimely death of a long-time member of our Board of Directors: Mahbub ul Haq, a passionate champion of sustainable development and human security for three decades, passed away in July 1998. Through senior positions at the World Bank, the U.N. Development Programme (UNDP), the Society for International Development, the Brandt Commission, and in the government of his native Pakistan, he challenged traditional wisdom about economic growth and "trickle-down" theory. Mahbub was the prime force behind the acclaimed *Human Development Report* published annually by UNDP since 1990. He will be sorely missed. In recognition of his enduring effect on development thinking, we dedicate this edition of *Vital Signs* to Mahbub.

Lester R. Brown
Michael Renner
Brian Halweil

FOREWORD

This is the last edition of *Vital Signs* before the new millennium. Judging by media coverage, this imminent event is arousing rather opposite sets of expectations. Many people look forward to 1 January 2000 for the giddiest and best of New Year's celebrations ever. Others predict doom as the "Y2K bug" makes computer chips malfunction—causing airplanes to fall out of the skies; banks to erase our life savings; communications, transportation, and electricity networks to convulse in paralysis; food to rot before it ever reaches markets; and nuclear missiles to be launched erroneously.

None of these extreme events is likely to come to pass. But there is supreme irony in the fact that some highly educated and talented people—computer programmers—could have gotten the world into such a pickle by way of a relatively minor oversight. Feverishly and single-mindedly writing their computer code in recent decades, programmers apparently did not possess enough foresight and common sense to realize that the year 2000 was just around the corner.

Whatever the true impact of Y2K turns out to be, it is an apt reminder of the unintended results of human inventions and actions. Indeed, after the particular fears about 1 January 2000 are gone, humanity will still confront many other unintended consequences: those arising out of the unsustainable development model that virtually every nation has pursued, in one way or another, since the days of the first industrial revolution some 200 years ago, and particularly since the end of World War II.

Marvelous technological achievements have given us unprecedented power to exploit natural resources, produce ever more sophisticated products, and drive consumerism to new heights. But while we have been able to push back the limits again and again, we have largely overlooked the fact that in the end, we depend on the health and integrity of the natural environment—no matter how dazzling our inventions are. It matters little that computer speed and memory grow at an exponential rate if our croplands and freshwater resources are tapped beyond sustainable levels.

Human ingenuity has always clashed with human arrogance, but in our age it is the fate of the planet that hangs in the balance. The challenge is no longer to produce the next technological breakthrough, but to use our inventions more judiciously and to be wise enough not to use those that are more likely to harm than to benefit us.

In this eighth edition of *Vital Signs*, we again bring together a broad selection of indicators that provide a kaleidoscopic view of a fast-evolving, dynamic world. In addition to such staple issues as grain production, wind power, automobile and bicycle production, international trade and debt, and peacekeeping expenditures, we present this year a large number of topics—14 in all—not covered in previous editions. They are undernutrition and overnutrition, fast-food restaurants, polio, deteriorating male reproductive health, genetically modified crops, pesticide use, algal blooms, biomass energy use, commuting, the role of corporations in the world economy, corruption, unemployment, and the rise of nongovernmental organizations (NGOs).

We encourage readers to compare related trends closely rather than reviewing the contents indicator-by-indicator. This year's *Vital Signs* permits a substantial number of comparisons across several indicators. Those interested in the role of corporations, for instance, may also want to consult the indicators on advertising expenditures and unemployment. Others may want to juxtapose the pieces on corporations and NGOs. Our data on pesticide use may be looked at in conjunction with the information on genetically modified crops, since one aim of genetic manipulation is to create insect-resistant varieties, thus reducing use of the insecticides that may be lowering male sperm counts. Information contained in the indicator on warfare will be useful in conjunction with the pieces on refugee populations and peacekeeping efforts.

In addition to three English-language editions (for North America, Australia, and the United Kingdom/Commonwealth), *Vital Signs* has been published in 20 other languages. It regularly appears in many leading languages, including Chinese, Italian, Japanese, and Spanish, and it has recently been published in Georgian, Persian, Romanian, and Turkish. Information about our foreign publishers is now available on our Web site, at < www. worldwatch.org/foreign/index.html > .

Along with the print version of *Vital Signs*, we continue to provide all the raw data from the book, along with tables and data contained in our other publications, in the Worldwatch Database Disk. And individual *Vital Signs* indicators can now be downloaded from our Web site, at < www.worldwatch.org/ titles/tvs.html > . These are in the popular .pdf format, readable with Adobe Acrobat Reader software.

On behalf of our coauthors, thank you for your interest in *Vital Signs 1999*. Please let us know by e-mail (worldwatch@worldwatch.org), fax (202-296-7365), or regular mail if you have ideas for improving this book or for new indicators we should consider for future editions.

Lester R. Brown
Michael Renner
Brian Halweil
March 1999

Worldwatch Institute
1776 Massachusetts Ave., N.W.
Washington, DC 20036

VITAL
SIGNS
1999

OVERVIEW
An Off-the-Chart Year

Lester R. Brown

Of all the trends that affect us, none is quite as pervasive as temperature. In 1998, Earth's average temperature literally went off the top of the chart we have been using for years in *Vital Signs*. To make room for the new information, we had to extend the vertical axis. (See Figure 1.)

This high temperature, leading to more evaporation and rainfall and contributing to more destructive storms, may have helped push other indicators off the chart as well. For example, weather-related damage worldwide totaled $92 billion in 1998, up some 53 percent from the previous record of $60 billion in 1996. This huge jump not only went off the top of the chart, it went off the page. Indeed, damage in 1998 exceeded the total for the entire decade of the 1980s, even after adjusting for inflation.

Record storms and floods drove some 300 million people from their homes in 1998—more people than live in the United States. Most of these people lived in China's Yangtze River valley, in Bangladesh, and in India. Some were forced from their homes for only a few days, but others left for weeks or months. And some left permanently.

Was this a glimpse of the future as rising atmospheric levels of carbon dioxide (CO_2) from fossil fuel burning lead to a climate that is spiraling out of control? Or was it an aberration, something that happens rarely and may never be repeated? We cannot know for sure, but what we know about climate models suggests that the events of 1998 could be a window on the future, a consequence of failing to rein in carbon emissions soon enough.

ECONOMIC GROWTH SLOWS

The global economy continued to grow in 1998, expanding by 2.2 percent despite the economic turmoil in East Asia, Russia, and Brazil. (See pages 64–65.) This growth, down by half from the 4.2-percent global expansion in 1997, is the slowest since the 1.8 percent registered in 1991.

Among major industrial countries, the United States remained the pacesetter, expanding by 3.6 percent. At the other end of the spectrum, the Japanese economy contracted by 2.8 percent. Growth in France, Germany, and the United Kingdom was in the 2–3 percent range.

In a dramatic shift, several Central European countries moved to the top of the chart, growing by 5–7 percent, among them Bulgaria, Estonia, Hungary, Poland, Latvia, and Lithuania. Meanwhile, several economies in East Asia, the traditional pacesetters, were shrinking, among them Indonesia (–15 percent), Thailand (–8 percent), Malaysia (–8 percent), and South Korea (–7 percent). Offsetting these declines to give Asia a 2.6-percent regional growth rate was China at 7.2 percent and the Indian subcontinent, which, with 1.2 billion people, expanded by roughly 5 percent.

15

Although the global economy continued to expand, international trade declined by nearly 4 percent in 1998, the first drop after 15 years of nonstop expansion. (See pages 68–69.) This was due in part to slumping economies in East Asia, and in part to falling prices for key commodities, importantly oil, grain, and minerals.

While export earnings declined in many developing countries as export prices of primary materials dropped, the external debt of these nations increased. It rose to $2.2 trillion in 1997, the latest year for which figures are available, up from $2.1 trillion in 1996. (See pages 66–67.) And developing countries spent $269 billion servicing their debt, compared with $191 billion in 1990. Contrasting trends in commodity prices and debt mean that developing countries are spending a larger

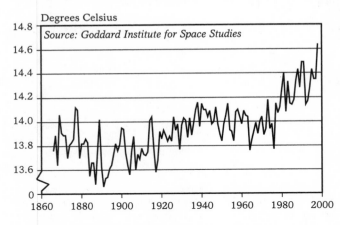

Figure 1: Average Temperature at Earth's Surface, 1866–1998

share of their export earnings servicing their rising debts.

The willingness to forgive the debt of some of the lower-income countries, especially those in Africa, is spreading in the international community. The outright cancellation of debt for countries in Africa could save the lives of 7 million children annually by 2000 and provide 90 million young women with access to basic education. For the United States, this debt forgiveness amounts to

roughly the cost of building two B-2 bombers.

NEW ENERGY ECONOMY EMERGING

In earlier years, the discussion on energy centered on what the new economy would look like. Now we can actually see it emerging. It can be seen in the solar cell rooftops of Japan and Germany, in the wind farms of Spain and Iowa, and in the widely varying growth rates of the various energy sources. While wind use was expanding at 22 percent a year from 1990 to 1998 and photovoltaics at 16 percent per year, the use of oil was growing at less than 2 percent and that of coal was not increasing at all. (See pages 48–49, 52–55, and Table 1.)

The foundation is being laid for the emergence of both wind and solar cells as cornerstones of the new energy economy. World wind generating capacity grew from 7,600 megawatts in 1997 to 9,600 in 1998, an expansion of 26 percent. At the national level, Germany led the way, adding 790 megawatts of capacity, followed by Spain with 380 megawatts, Denmark with 308 megawatts, and the United States with 226 megawatts. In the past, U.S. wind generating capacity was concentrated in California, but in 1998, wind farms began generating electricity in Minnesota, Oregon, and Wyoming, broadening the new industry's geographic base.

Within the developing world, India—the unquestioned leader now with more than 900 megawatts of generating capacity—expects that some 14 domestic companies will be manufacturing new high-tech wind turbines within the next five years, setting the stage for phenomenal growth. China could double its national electricity generation from wind alone. With the help of the Dutch, China began operation in 1998 of its first commercial wind farm, a 24-megawatt project. Inner Mongolia, which is within easy transmission distance of the industrial centers in northern China, could become the Saudi Arabia of wind energy early in the next century.

With the costs of generation dropping from $2,600 per kilowatt in 1981 to $800 in 1998, wind power is fast becoming one of the world's cheapest sources of electricity, undercutting coal in some locations. Once cheap electricity is available from the wind, it can be used to electrolyze water and produce hydrogen, an ideal way of storing and transporting wind energy.

In 1998, sales of solar cells, the silicon-based semiconductors that can convert sunlight into electricity, jumped 21 percent, reaching 152 megawatts. This growth marked the sharp competition emerging among major industrial countries in the solar cell market as the world looks for clean energy sources that will not destabilize the climate. The United States maintained the lead, at 54 megawatts of solar cell sales. Japan was close behind with 49. Europe was third at 30.

In Japan, nearly 7,000 rooftop solar systems were installed in 1998. The new coalition government in Germany announced the goal of 100,000 solar roofs in that country. In response, Royal Dutch Shell and Pilkington Solar International launched a joint venture to build the world's largest solar cell manufacturing facility in Germany. Italy joined in with a goal of 10,000 solar rooftops.

The growth in oil use in 1998 slowed to less than 1 percent because of the global economic slowdown. The actual decline in coal production in 1998, which came somewhat as a surprise, was largely due to an estimated drop of 7 percent in China. This was apparently tied in part to the abandonment of subsidies and in part to the imposition of a tax on the use of high-sulfur coal. There is now

TABLE 1. TRENDS IN GLOBAL ENERGY USE, BY SOURCE, 1990–98[1]

ENERGY SOURCE	ANNUAL RATE OF GROWTH (percent)
Wind power	22.2
Solar photovoltaics	15.9
Geothermal power	4.3
Hydroelectric power[1]	1.9
Oil	1.8
Natural gas	1.6
Nuclear power	0.6
Coal	0

[1] 1990–97 only.
SOURCE: See pages 48-55.

growing evidence that world coal use may be about to peak and begin a long-term decline.

The burning of natural gas, the cleanest of the three fossil fuels, increased by 1.6 percent in 1998. Carbon emissions per unit of energy produced are scarcely half those of coal. Because it is less polluting, natural gas has become increasingly popular as a fuel for power generation as well as for residential and industrial use.

The near zero growth in nuclear power generation in 1998 was largely because the power source once described as "too cheap to meter" has now become too costly to use. (See pages 50–51.) The issue is no longer simply whether it is economical to build nuclear power plants but—given the high operating costs—whether it makes economic sense to continue using those already built.

Wherever a competitive market exists for electricity, no one invests in nuclear reactors. Only in countries where electrical generation remains a monopoly—where costs are simply passed on to consumers—is there any interest in building these plants. Only five new plants were started in 1998: two in India, two in South Korea, and one in Japan. The long-term decline is projected to start within the next few years, with world nuclear generating capacity falling by half by 2020.

Within the fossil fuel industry, firms such as British Petroleum and Royal Dutch Shell are publicly acknowledging that a new energy economy is emerging and they are investing heavily in it. In a remarkable speech in early 1999, Mike Bowlin, chairman and CEO of ARCO, a leading U.S. oil company, said, "We've embarked on the beginning of the last days of the age of oil." He went on to say that the challenge now was to convert the carbon-based world energy economy into one that was based on hydrogen and other forms of energy.

CLIMATE CHANGE ACCELERATES

As noted earlier, Earth's temperature in 1998 went off the top of our usual chart. (See pages 58–59.) The one-year increase of nearly a fifth of a degree Celsius (a third of a degree Fahrenheit) was much larger than anyone had anticipated.

The record-high temperature in 1998 had many effects. Among other things, it increased the rate of glacial melting. New scientific studies published in 1998 show an acceleration of the melting of ice, particularly in high altitudes and polar regions. This is evident in the shrinkage of the outer limits of ice in the summer in the Arctic, in New Jersey–size chunks breaking off from the Antarctic ice cap, and in the melting of glaciers in Greenland, in the Andes, and on the Qinghai-Tibetan Plateau. If the melting of recent years continues, it will one day lead to the inundation of many densely populated coastal cities, shrinking the habitable land area at a time when world population will still be increasing.

Another consequence of higher temperatures is more evaporation. The more water goes up, the more comes down. Exactly where it will land is not always clear. Higher temperatures also mean more heat radiating from surface waters in the tropics and subtropics, creating more powerful storms. Hurricanes George and Mitch, each with sustained winds in excess of 180 miles per hour, were two of the most powerful storms ever to come out of the Atlantic. Mitch, which took 11,000 lives, was the deadliest Atlantic storm

in 200 years. (See pages 74–75.)

The most devastating single weather-related event was the flooding of the Yangtze River basin, one of the worst floods in China's history. It racked up $30 billion in damage, enough to lower China's overall economic growth rate.

FOOD: A FALSE SENSE OF SECURITY

With world grain prices in early 1999 at the lowest level in two decades, there is a tendency to relax on the food front—to assume that the world's food production capacity is more than adequate to satisfy future needs. Unfortunately, future world food supplies may be less secure now than at any time in recent history. (See pages 30–31).

The recent drop in grain prices was largely due to declining demand for grain in several East Asian countries in 1998. When economies that were growing at 8 percent annually just two years ago suddenly shrank by 6–15 percent in 1998, the demand for grain fell.

In addition, the depreciation of currencies in several countries in Southeast Asia, Russia, and Brazil made it more difficult for these grain importers to obtain the supplies they need. Currency devaluations have raised the price of imported food products, making them more costly and leading, literally, to a belt-tightening by consumers.

More fundamentally, a substantial fraction of the world's current grain harvest is based on the unsustainable use of resources, primarily land and water. Between 1980 and 1998, Kazakhstan, which once produced and exported more grain than Australia, has lost half of its grainland as a result of wind erosion. In the 1950s, as part of the Soviet Virgin Lands project, agriculture was extended onto grassland that should never have been plowed. It is unclear how much of the land remaining under the plow will eventually be abandoned because of erosion and other forms of degradation.

The other major source of unsustainable

output is the overpumping of groundwater. The availability of powerful diesel and electrical water pumps in recent decades has enabled farmers throughout the world to tap underground water supplies. Unfortunately, in the major food-producing countries heavily dependent on irrigation—China and India— and in North Africa and the Middle East, water tables are falling. (See pages 44–45.) A report by a joint Sino-Japanese research team indicates that water tables are falling almost everywhere in China that the land is flat. Under the north China plain, which produces 40 percent of China's grain harvest, water tables are falling by an estimated 1.5 meters (roughly 5 feet) a year.

The International Water Management Institute (IWMI) reports that in India the withdrawal of underground water for the country as a whole is now double the rate of aquifer recharge. Once overpumping leads to aquifer depletion, irrigation water supplies will be reduced to the rate of aquifer recharge. If current pumping is double the rate of recharge, then the water supply will be cut in half. IWMI estimates that aquifer depletion could reduce India's grain harvest by 25 percent. In a country adding 18 million people a year, this is not a pleasant prospect.

Aside from aquifer depletion in major food-producing countries, the diversion of irrigation water to cities is also taking a toll. In the southwestern United States, where virtually all the available water is now being used, the expanding demand for water for cities can be satisfied only by diverting water from agriculture.

No one knows what share of the world's grain harvest is based on the unsustainable use of resources, but we do know there are cutbacks ahead. Thus far, the countries that have experienced cutbacks either because of cropland degradation or aquifer depletion are smaller nations, such as Kazakhstan and Saudi Arabia. In the future, larger countries will face cutbacks as well.

It takes 1,000 tons of water to produce 1 ton of grain. As water becomes scarce and countries are forced to divert irrigation water

to cities and industry, they will import more grain. As they do so, water scarcity will be transmitted across national borders via the grain trade. Aquifer depletion is a largely invisible threat, but that does not make it any less real.

RESTRUCTURING THE PROTEIN ECONOMY

The world relies mainly on five sources for its high-quality protein: beef, pork, poultry, fish, and soybeans. Historically, societies have depended heavily on beef and fish for animal protein, both of which are produced largely by natural systems: rangelands and oceanic fisheries.

As the demand for animal protein has soared throughout the last half-century, the production of both beef and fish has climbed. (See pages 34–37.) But by 1980 the world's rangelands were being pushed to their sustainable limits and beyond. By 1990, a similar situation existed for oceanic fisheries. As these limits were reached, they led to changes in the structure of the world protein economy. With the potential for expanding cattle grazing and the fish catch constrained by natural limits, future growth in protein supplies could be achieved only by feeding grain. To get more beef, cattle had to be put in feed lots. To get more seafood, fish had to be put in ponds. In both cases, they had to be fed. They then began to compete with pigs and chickens for feed.

At this point, the relative efficiency of converting feed into protein becomes a prime consideration. With cattle in the feedlot requiring seven pounds of grain per pound of additional live weight and hogs requiring nearly four pounds, the advantage has shifted to poultry, which require just over two pounds of grain per pound of meat, and fish, which require less than two pounds of feed per pound of additional live weight. More efficient conversion by poultry and fish translates into lower prices. As a result, world poultry production has been expanding rapidly, averaging 5.2 percent annually from 1990 to 1998, overtaking that of beef in 1995. (See Table 2.)

Fish farming has been expanding at an even faster rate, from 7 million tons in 1984 to 28 million tons in 1997. From 1990 to 1997 it has grown 11.6 percent a year. By 2015, fish farming output could overtake that of beef. At that point, the consumption of both poultry and farmed fish would be greater than that of beef.

Closely related to the growth in the demand for animal protein—beef, pork, and poultry—has been growth in the demand for soybeans for use as a protein supplement in feed rations. By including a relatively minor amount of soybean meal with grain and feed rations, the efficiency of grain use can be increased dramatically, perhaps even doubled in some situations. This helps explain why world soybean production has climbed from 17 million tons in 1950 to 155 million tons in 1998, a ninefold increase. (See pages 32–33.) Despite the high quality of soybean protein, less than one tenth of the world harvest is consumed directly as food, and most of that in three countries—China, Japan, and Indonesia.

As world population continues to grow and incomes continue to rise, the demand for high-quality protein will also increase, putting ever more pressure on Earth's natural systems and resources.

TABLE 2. WORLD PRODUCTION OF PROTEIN, BY SOURCE, 1990–98

SOURCE	ANNUAL RATE OF GROWTH (percent)
Aquaculture[1]	11.6
Poultry	5.2
Soybeans	5.1
Pork	3.4
Oceanic fish catch	1.3
Beef	0.3

[1]1990–97 only.
SOURCE: See pages 32–37.

THE MOBILITY FACTOR

In 1998, world production of cars fell 2 percent as the economy faltered. While Europe expanded output by 6 percent and North America declined by 1 percent, the biggest drops came in Asia at 11 percent and Latin America at 17 percent. (See pages 82–83.) Despite this, world sales exceeded the number of vehicles scrapped, expanding the global fleet from 498 million vehicles to 508 million.

Bicycle production dropped from 99 million in 1996 to 94 million in 1997, the last year for which data are available. (See pages 84–85.) The big drop came in China, the world's leading manufacturer, where output declined by 20 percent as a result of a buildup of excess capacity and excessive inventories.

In many Asian cities, bicycles account for half of all trips taken. In western countries that strongly support bicycle use, such as the Netherlands and Denmark, up to 30 percent of trips taken in some cities are by bicycle.

While the production of cars and bicycles was declining, air travel continued to increase, rising 2 percent in 1998. (See pages 86–87.) This growth was down from the 6 percent of the year before, largely because of the economic slump in Asia. Now accounting for nearly 5 percent of world oil consumption, future growth in air travel is projected to be rapid.

ELECTRONIC LINKAGES MULTIPLY

Over the last year, the number of phones linked by line to the global network, the number of cellular phones in use, and the number of Internet connections all increased dramatically, tying more and more people into a global electronic network. (See pages 92–95.)

This growing linkage was facilitated by the launching of 140 satellites in 1998, most of them commercial communication satellites. (See pages 90–91.) The rapid growth in commercial communication satellite launches in the 1990s along with heavy investments in cable, both long distance and local, is linking more and more of the world's people together electronically. Satellite launches, once dominated by government military satellites, have now been eclipsed by the launching of communications satellites by private corporations.

In 1997, the latest year for which data are available, the number of lines linking telephones to the global phone network increased to 781 million, up from 741 million the year before. This continues a four-decade trend of 4–7 percent annual growth in phone connections. Impressive though this growth is, it was overshadowed by the growth in cellular phones, which jumped from 144 million in 1996 to 214 million in 1997, a gain of 48 percent. Thus nearly two thirds of the worldwide growth in new telephones is in those linked by radio waves rather than those linked by more-traditional phone lines. For people in developing countries who once had to wait years to get a phone installed, the immediate availability of cellular phones is a godsend.

Growth in the number of lines linking host computers to the Internet increased to 43 million in 1998, up from 30 million the year before. This translated into an estimated 147 million people worldwide having access to the Internet. The United States, with 76 million individuals linked to the Internet, accounted for half of the world total. Japan was a distant second with 10 million users, followed by the United Kingdom and Germany with 8 million and 7 million, respectively. The share of national populations on the Internet varies widely among the world's most populous countries. In the United States, it is 1 in 4; in China, 1 in 800; and in India, 1 in 2,100. In Africa, just 1 in 4,000 individuals is linked to the Internet.

The data for telephones and Internet use indicate that the world is electronically divided into haves and have-nots. The good news is that new models are evolving to increase access. In Bangladesh, for example, cellular phones are being sold to villagers who then sell calls to their neighbors as needed. Thus one phone can give 1,000 villagers access to a phone system in much the same way that pay phones in low-income urban neighborhoods

have traditionally done.

In some countries, the number of individuals linked to the Internet is growing by leaps and bounds. The 1.6 million Internet users in China at the end of 1998, which was double the number in 1997, is expected to rise dramatically in the next few years. One set of projections shows the number of Internet users exceeding the number of car owners there by 2002.

Which contributes more to mobility: access to the Internet or ownership of an automobile? For someone interested in visiting the great museums of the world, the Internet obviously provides more mobility. And for someone needing to do some shopping, the Internet offers more goods than any one shopping center could possibly provide. As the information economy continues to expand, we may redefine not only mobility, but many other dimensions of progress as well.

The Internet today serves as a major information resource, a way of communicating with others, and a shopping mart. Last year, $33 billion was spent ordering products and services on-line, nearly triple the 1997 level. In fact, you may be reading this book either in hard-copy format or after downloading it from the Worldwatch Web site.

SMOKING TREND REVERSED

Spreading awareness of the effects of smoking on health contributed to a drop in world cigarette production in 1998 to 5.61 trillion, down from 5.64 trillion in 1997. (See pages 108–09.) Marking the second straight annual decline, this fall may indicate something even more fundamental—the reversal of a half-century of growth in the number of smokers in the world.

Cigarette production has fallen in the last few years in both China and the United States, the two biggest manufacturers. In China, production dropped from the historic high of 1.74 trillion cigarettes in 1995 to 1.68 trillion in 1998, a decline of more than 3 percent. In the United States, where both cigarette smoking and exports are falling, production dropped from 758 million in 1996 to 716 million in 1998, down nearly 6 percent.

Worldwide cigarette production per person in 1998 fell by 2 percent from the preceding year, continuing a decade-long trend. After peaking in 1990 at 1,027 cigarettes per person, output fell to 948 per person in 1998, a drop of almost 8 percent or nearly 1 percent a year. This follows a trend in the United States, where the number of cigarettes smoked per person fell from 2,940 in 1981 to 1,739 in 1998—a drop of 41 percent.

The principal reason for declining cigarette use is a spreading awareness worldwide of smoking's devastating effect on health. Prominent among the diseases linked with cigarette smoking are cardiovascular disease, including both heart attacks and strokes; several forms of cancer, most notably lung cancer; and various respiratory illnesses, including emphysema, bronchitis, and pneumonia.

The number of smoking-related deaths in the United States is estimated at 400,000 per year, more than eight times the number of automobile fatalities. Worldwide, the World Health Organization (WHO) projects that the number of smoking-related deaths will increase from today's 3 million a year to 10 million over the next generation as smoking spreads in developing countries.

The changing fortunes of the tobacco industry are evident in its landmark agreement in the United States to pay the 50 state governments collectively a total of $251 billion over the next 25 years—nearly $1,000 for every American—to compensate for the Medicare costs of treating smoking-related illness. In addition, the U.S. Department of Justice plans to file a lawsuit to recover federal Medicare costs associated with smoking. Six other national governments—Bolivia, Guatemala, the Marshall Islands, Nicaragua, Panama, and Venezuela—have also filed suits in U.S. courts against the U.S. tobacco industry to recover the costs of treating smoking-related illnesses.

Some 35 years have passed since the first U.S. Surgeon General's Report on Smoking and Health was published, putting the issue on the public agenda. With the United States leading the way, the world appears to be crossing a threshold on smoking. In early 1999, WHO announced that it would seek a worldwide ban on tobacco advertising and was considering seeking a similar ban on smoking in public.

RISE IN LIFE EXPECTANCY SLOWING

Global life expectancy in 1998 reached 66 years, up from 65.8 in 1997. (See pages 100–01.) But this annual gain of 0.2 years is far lower than the average gain of 0.6 years in the 1950s and early 1960s. Gains in life expectancy are becoming more difficult in many industrial countries, possibly because of emerging biological constraints. Beyond this, the world is facing the rising mortality associated with the spread in cigarette smoking over the last few decades and with the HIV epidemic. Indeed, these latter two sources of rising mortality threaten to reverse the rising life expectancy trend of the last half-century.

New HIV infections in 1998 total an estimated 5.8 million and deaths from the virus totaled 2.5 million. (See pages 102–03.) Both trends have risen every year since 1980, when data were first gathered, and they are expected to continue to do so in the absence of a major effort by governments to mobilize quickly to contain the epidemic. Indeed, this epidemic could claim more lives in the early part of the next century than World War II did in this one.

The highest infection rates are in Africa, where in several countries 20–25 percent of the adult population is HIV-positive. Without a dramatic advance in developing a low-cost treatment for the disease, countries like Botswana, Namibia, Zambia, and Zimbabwe will lose one fifth to one fourth of their adult populations within the next decade.

HIV now has a foothold in India and China, which together contain more than a third of the world's people. In India, where some 4 million people are infected, this comes to roughly 1 percent of the adult population. In China the virus can now be found in every province. Centers of dissemination of the virus include sex workers, intravenous drug users, and contaminated blood supplies.

Cigarette smoking, which has spread rapidly in developing countries over the last few decades, now claims an estimated 3 million lives annually, a bit more than AIDS over the last few years. Encouragingly, deaths from smoking or from AIDS can be controlled by behavioral changes.

Another trend that is reducing life expectancy is the expanding world automobile fleet, which is associated with 885,000 fatalities from accidents each year. Beyond this, automobiles contribute to the urban air pollution that takes a heavy toll on human life. Although global data are not available, those available for China indicate that air pollution from coal burning, industry, and automobiles killed nearly a million people a year in cities there from 1994 to 1996. (See pages 128–29.) The World Bank estimates that this fatality level could be reduced by close to one fifth by satisfying even the most modest air quality standards.

Children whose developing lungs are particularly vulnerable suffer the most from air pollution. For children, breathing the air in cities with the worst air pollution, such as Beijing, Calcutta, Mexico City, Shanghai, and Tehran, is equivalent to smoking two packs of cigarettes a day.

The principal source of premature death in the world is one of longer standing—malnutrition. The world today is plagued with two nutrition problems: the more traditional undernutrition, and a growing share of the world's population who are overnourished and overweight. (See pages 146–47.) The effects of these two forms of malnutrition are essentially the same: increased susceptibility to illness, reduced life expectancy, and lowered productivity. The toll from undernutrition is concentrated in infants and children, whereas overnutrition finds its victims later in life. Thus undernutrition has a much greater effect on life expectancy.

The latest WHO estimates indicate some 6 million people are dying from undernutrition each year, or 17,000 per day. Some 830 million people are estimated to be undernourished and underweight, compared with 600 million who are overweight.

Among the more populated developing countries, the highest percentages of children under five who are underweight are found in Bangladesh (56 percent), India (53 percent), and Ethiopia (48 percent). This helps explain why infant mortality rates continue to be so high in these countries. At the same time, a similar share of adults are overweight in the leading industrial countries. For the United States, 55 percent of the population is overweight. In Russia the figure is 54 percent, and in Germany, 50 percent.

Among the more exciting gains on the health front in recent years has been worldwide progress in eradicating polio, once a feared disease. (See pages 104–05.) Since 1988, when WHO launched an eradication campaign, the number of new polio cases reported each year has dropped from over 35,000 to less than 4,000—a fall of nearly 90 percent. This impressive achievement has put the United Nations on the verge of its biggest success on the health front since it led the effort that successfully eradicated smallpox some 20 years ago.

POPULATION GROWTH CONTINUES

In 1998, world population increased by 78 million, roughly the equivalent of another Germany. (See pages 98–99.) Nearly all these 78 million people were born in the developing world, since population growth has come to a near standstill in much of the industrial world. Population has stabilized in some 32 countries, including Japan and most of Western and Eastern Europe. In another group of countries—which includes China and the United States, the world's first and third largest countries—fertility has fallen to the replacement level of 2.1 children per woman or less. This group of countries contains some 40 percent of the world's people.

In its biannual update of population numbers and projections released in late 1998, U.N. demographers reduced the projected population for 2050 by some 500 million. Roughly two thirds of this decline was due to falling fertility, but unfortunately one third was due to rising mortality, largely the result of the HIV epidemic, especially in sub-Saharan Africa.

Another trend that could affect population growth over the longer term is a fall in one of the most vital of vital signs: male sperm counts. (See pages 148–49.) In the United States, sperm counts per milliliter of semen have dropped from 120 million in 1940 to just under 50 million in 1988. Counts in the European countries for which records exist indicate a similar decline there, though it started more recently. The principal explanation for this is the so-called endocrine disruption hypothesis, namely that chemicals in the environment act as "environmental estrogens." The presence of these imitators of this basic female hormone may adversely affect male sexuality.

Analysis of this issue is handicapped by a lack of reliable historical data on sperm counts and research on the health effect of the various estrogen-mimicking chemicals. In an effort to rectify this, a study of sperm counts has been launched in nine cities in the United States, Europe, and Japan.

Sperm counts have not yet dropped in any country to the point where they are measurably affecting fertility. If they do continue to decline, however, they will begin to have this effect. One of the difficulties with environmental estrogens is that they are long-lasting and do not readily disintegrate.

WAR AND PEACE

After five consecutive annual declines, the number of wars in the world increased in 1998, climbing from 25 to 31. (See pages 112–13.) Except for Serbia's Kosovo province, all the armed conflicts are in developing countries and nearly all are taking place within countries. Many of these conflicts are fought with small-caliber arms, a category of weapons that is now widely available in the international weapons market. (See pages 154–55.) Among the costliest ongoing wars in terms of human lives lost are those in Afghanistan, Algeria, Sri Lanka, and Sudan. One of the most recent ones is the insurrection against the Kabila regime in the Democratic Republic of Congo (formerly Zaire), a conflict that has drawn six neighboring countries into the fray.

On the plus side, the number of nuclear warheads worldwide declined from 39,800 in 1996 to 36,100 in 1997. (See pages 116–17.) Of these, roughly 20,000 are actively deployed, 14,000 are awaiting dismantlement, and the remainder are held in reserve. Since peaking in 1986, the global nuclear arsenal has declined by 48 percent. Most of the nuclear warheads are held by Russia (23,000) and the United States (12,000). The other three longstanding nuclear powers—France, China, and the United Kingdom—have just over 1,000 warheads combined.

U.N. peacekeeping expenditures have declined to a projected $852 million in fiscal year 1999, down from $992 million a year earlier. (See pages 114–15.) The largest missions are now those in Lebanon (with some 4,500 personnel) and Bosnia (close to 2,000). At the end of 1998 there were roughly 1,000 peacekeepers at each of five other peacekeeping sites—Cyprus, the Golan Heights, the Iraq/Kuwait border, Angola, and the Central African Republic.

TRENDS TO WATCH

Over the last half-century, farmers in both industrial and developing countries have come to rely heavily on pesticides. Unfortunately, in a situation that has many parallels with the spreading resistance of human disease organisms to antibiotics, plant insects and diseases are evolving a resistance to pesticides. (See pages 124–25.) Since 1950, the number of insects resistant to insecticides has grown from a negligible level to more than 500. Some 230 crop diseases and 220 weeds are now resistant to pesticides.

One response to the growing resistance to chemical control is efforts to breed crops that themselves are resistant to various insects and diseases. Increasingly this involves transferring a resistance gene from other species. Between 1996 and 1998, the area planted to these "transgenic crops" increased from 1.7 million to 27.8 million hectares. (See pages 122–23.) Most of the transgenic crops planted in 1998 consisted of soybeans and corn. Of these, roughly 70 percent were designed to tolerate a specific herbicide, allowing farmers to eradicate weeds without damaging the crop.

While the use of transgenic crops is spreading rapidly in the United States, Argentina, and Canada, resistance to this trend is building in Europe and in many developing countries. The opposition to genetically modified crops stems from several concerns, including the possibility that genes could jump to other plants, such as wild relatives, which could lead to the disruption of natural ecosystems. In addition, consumers in some countries are worried about the possible effects of eating the products of plants that have been modified with genes from other species.

Another agricultural trend of growing concern is the increased nutrient content of coastal waters resulting from fertilizer runoff in agricultural regions. Augmented by urban sewage discharge in some situations, this results in huge algal blooms, which, as they die and decay, deplete the oxygen content in the water, leading to the death of fish. (See pages 126–27.) Each summer, for example, nitrogen and phosphate washing from farmlands in the Mississippi Valley enter the Gulf of Mexico, creating a massive algal bloom covering some 16,000 square kilometers. As the blooms die off, this area—roughly the size of New Jersey—is so deprived of oxygen that no fish survive.

These destructive algal blooms are now found in the Adriatic, Baltic, and Black Seas and, increasingly, in the coastal regions of developing countries, such as in the seas around China. They affect not only coastal fisheries, but also fish farms in coastal waters.

On the demand side of the food equation, recent social trends are driving more and more people to fast-food restaurants. As the increases in single-person households, single-parent families, and working women have combined to reduce the time available to prepare food, more and more meals are eaten out—a large share of them in fast-food restaurants such as McDonald's, Pizza Hut, or Kentucky Fried Chicken. Since 1950, the number of fast-food outlets has increased from nil to 100,000. (See pages 150–51.) McDonald's—the world leader, with 23,000 restaurants—typically opens five new restaurants somewhere in the world each day.

Although this dramatic growth in fast-food restaurants makes eating more convenient, it is also altering diets. While health experts are emphasizing the importance of increasing the share of fruits and vegetables in the diet, fast-food restaurant offerings are high in refined starch and saturated fats, thus increasing the risk of obesity, coronary heart disease, high blood pressure, diabetes, and several forms of cancer.

A final set of trends to keep an eye on involves the rapidly changing roles of the public and private sectors worldwide. Large corporations have emerged as powerful players in most national economies. And transnational corporations—those operating in more than one country—are a strong force behind global economic integration. (See pages 136–37.) In 1970, there were some 7,000 transnational corporations. Today, there are nearly 54,000. Due to their size and massive reach, the power and influence of the largest transnationals rival or surpass those of many national governments.

While corporations have augmented economic activity in ways that governments have not been able to, over the last half-century another institution has evolved—the non-governmental organization (NGO)—in response to gaps left by government in meeting social needs, including adequate and equitable provision of health care, education, food, shelter, and environmental protection.

Since mid-century there has been an incredible surge in the number, diversity, and influence of NGOs worldwide, one that has invigorated the public sector by supplementing the role of governments. (See pages 144–45.) Growing from under 1,000 in 1956, the number of international NGOs now tops 20,000.

These nonprofit organizations are participating in decisionmaking and policy-setting contexts that were once the exclusive domain of governments and corporations. And because of their unique position outside of the market and the state, NGOs can pressure businesses and governments to reform their practices or refocus their resources. (See pages 138–39.) In other cases, NGOs have even proved more successful than corporations or governments at addressing the social and environmental challenges now threatening humanity.

It is unclear what the relationship between corporations, governments, and NGOs will be in the future. Nonetheless, as the mix of power and responsibilities among them evolves, the shifting economic and political architecture has the potential to influence the direction of virtually all the trends described in this book.

Part **ONE**

Key Indicators

Food
Trends

Grain Harvest Drops   Lester R. Brown

In 1998, the world grain harvest totaled 1.85 billion tons, down 30 million tons from 1997—a drop of nearly 2 percent.[1] (See Figure 1.) With world population growing by some 78 million in 1998, the per capita grain supply dropped to 312 kilograms, down from 321 kilograms the preceding year.[2] (See Figure 2.) This 3-percent decline marked the continuation of a per capita trend that has been under way since 1984.[3]

The 30-million-ton drop in the world grain harvest in 1998 was due largely to severe drought and heat in Russia on top of an overall deterioration of that country's economy.[4] The Russian wheat harvest dropped from the unusually good harvest of 44 million tons in 1997 to 27 million tons in 1998, a decrease of 39 percent.[5] For coarse grains, half of which are accounted for by barley, production dropped from 41 million tons to 19 million tons—a fall of more than one half.[6]

The precipitous harvest decline in Russia, plus a slight one in India, more than offset modest gains by two other major grain producers, the United States and the European Union.[7] China's grain harvest, the largest of any country, was essentially unchanged from the year before.[8]

Among the big three grains—wheat, rice, and corn—the drop in the wheat harvest was the largest.[9] (See Figure 3.) The 1998 harvest of 586 million tons was 23 million tons below the 1997 record.[10] The principal contributor to the drop of nearly 4 percent was Russia.[11]

The world rice harvest also dropped in 1998, falling to 378 million tons from 384 million tons the year before.[12] This nearly 2 percent drop was largely the result of severe flooding in China's Yangtze River basin.[13] For rice, an irrigated crop, and therefore one whose production is remarkably stable compared with either wheat or corn, 1998 saw the first production falloff in 12 years.[14]

While production of the two food grains was dropping, that of corn—the world's overwhelmingly dominant feedgrain—climbed from 574 million tons in 1997 to a record 597 million tons in 1998, a gain of 4 percent.[15] The corn harvest exceeded the wheat harvest

in 1998, marking only the fourth time in history that this has occurred.[16] The first time was in 1979, but with the corn harvest exceeding wheat in three of the last five years, we may be entering a time when more corn than wheat is routinely produced.[17]

With overall grain production, there has been a loss of momentum. After the big jump that occurred in 1996, as a result of the dismantling of the U.S. farm commodity programs and the return to production of a large area of highly productive land, there has been little or no growth.[18]

Despite the 30-million-ton drop in the world grain harvest in 1998, grain prices are at their lowest level in more than a decade.[19] The reason lies not on the supply side, which weakened substantially, but on the demand side, which weakened even more. Economies in East Asia that have been growing by an average of 8 percent a year for several years suddenly shrank by that much in 1998.[20] Since this region had been the world's most dynamic grain market, the world grain supply-demand balance was altered sharply. In more normal times, a production drop of 1.7 percent and a population increase of 1.4 percent would lead to rising, not falling, grain prices.

In addition to falling incomes in a number of East Asian countries, depreciating currencies in the region made imported grain much more costly.[21] Falling incomes and rising food prices in countries such as Indonesia reduced overall grain consumption.[22] With strong growth in grain consumption replaced by decline, the world grain market weakened substantially.

In largely rural societies, grain production per person is an indicator of not only food availability but also economic progress. The grain harvest of 312 kilograms per person in 1998 is down from the all-time high in 1984 of 342 kilograms.[23] If world population continues to grow as projected, this trend is likely to continue, raising the possibility that the number of people in the world who are undernourished will increase from the current 828 million.[24]

WORLD GRAIN PRODUCTION, 1950–98

YEAR	TOTAL (mill. tons)	PER PERSON (kilograms)
1950	631	247
1955	759	273
1960	824	271
1965	905	270
1966	989	289
1967	1,014	291
1968	1,053	296
1969	1,063	293
1970	1,079	291
1971	1,177	311
1972	1,141	295
1973	1,253	318
1974	1,204	300
1975	1,237	303
1976	1,342	323
1977	1,319	312
1978	1,445	336
1979	1,410	322
1980	1,430	321
1981	1,482	327
1982	1,533	333
1983	1,469	313
1984	1,632	342
1985	1,647	339
1986	1,665	337
1987	1,598	318
1988	1,549	304
1989	1,671	322
1990	1,769	335
1991	1,708	319
1992	1,790	329
1993	1,714	310
1994	1,761	314
1995	1,712	301
1996	1,870	324
1997	1,875	321
1998 (prel)	1,845	312

SOURCES: USDA, *Production, Supply, and Distribution,* electronic database, February 1999; USDA, "World Grain Database," unpublished printout, 1991; USDA, FAS, *Grain: World Markets and Trade,* February 1999.

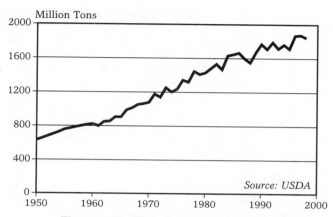

Figure 1: World Grain Production, 1950–98

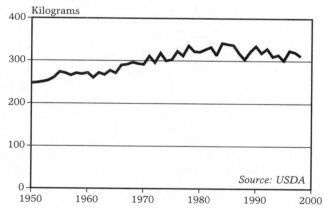

Figure 2: World Grain Production Per Person, 1950–98

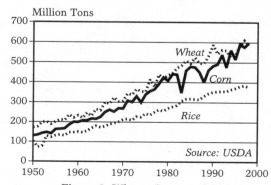

Figure 3: Wheat, Corn, and Rice Production, 1950–98

The world soybean harvest of 155 million tons in 1998 was the second largest on record, trailing only 1997, with 156 million tons.[1] (See Figure 1.) The harvest per person, which peaked at a record of close to 27 kilograms in 1997, dropped to just over 26 kilograms in 1998.[2] (See Figure 2.)

The demand for soybeans is a sentinel indicator of oilseed supply and demand, as soybeans account for half the world harvest of oilseeds.[3] (The other half consists largely of cottonseed, peanuts, sunflowers, rapeseed, and coconuts.)

During the 1990s, the demand for soybeans has grown by 5 percent a year, increasing by nearly half between 1990 and 1998.[4] This robust growth reflects rapid increase in demand for soybean oil and meal, since only small quantities are consumed whole as beans.

As incomes rise in low-income countries, one of the first dietary shifts is a rise in cooking oil use. There have been impressive rises during the 1990s in vegetable oil consumption in both China and India, countries that together contain 2.3 billion people.[5]

When soybeans are crushed, they typically yield 18 percent oil and 82 percent meal.[6] Although almost all the oil is used for direct human consumption, the meal provides protein supplements in the diets of livestock and poultry. Hogs, poultry, beef and dairy cattle that are on feed, and farmed fish typically depend on soybean meal in their diets.

Although the soybean originated in China, it has found a welcome home in the United States, where the value of the harvest now exceeds that of wheat.[7] The United States produced roughly half of the 1998 world crop of 155 million tons.[8] Brazil produced just under a quarter, and Argentina and China most of the rest.[9]

Production of soybeans has been declining in China in recent years.[10] As the nation has made an all-out effort to maintain self-sufficiency in grain, it has sacrificed soybean production. As a result, the harvest dropped from 16 million tons in 1994 to 13.5 million tons in 1998.[11] Over the last four years, China has gone from being a small net exporter of soybeans to the world's largest importer of soybeans, meal, and oil.[12]

Since 1950, the world soybean harvest has expanded from 17 million tons to 155 million tons, a staggering ninefold increase.[13] By comparison, during the same period, the oceanic fish catch—another major source of high-quality protein—expanded from 19 million tons to 94 million tons, a fivefold gain.[14] And while the fish catch has been leveling off during the 1990s, the soybean harvest continues to climb.

How long this rapid growth can continue remains to be seen. While growth in the grain harvest has come overwhelmingly from raising land productivity, that of the soybean harvest has come more from expanding the area planted.[15] With the soybean area doubling over the last 25 years, part of the growth has come by converting grainland to soybeans.[16]

Most of the world's exports of soybeans, meal, and oil come from the western hemisphere, while Europe, North Africa, the Middle East, and Asia are the principal importers, with most of the meal going to Europe and most of the oil going to Asia.[17]

The principal exporter of whole soybeans is the United States, accounting for 23 million tons of the 39 million tons traded in 1998.[18] The United States is not only the world's breadbasket, it has become its bean basket as well. Among importers, the leaders are Japan, the Netherlands, China, and Germany.[19]

The pattern with soybean meal exports is somewhat different, with both Argentina and Brazil actually edging out the United States.[20] The largest soybean meal importer in the world today is China, followed by France and Germany.[21]

With soybean oil, Argentina leads both the United States and Brazil on the export side of the equation. Among importers, China ranks first here too, at 1.75 million tons—far more than any other country.[22]

Barring a major global recession in the years ahead, world soybean production and exports are both likely to continue increasing, driven by the rising demand for oil for human consumption and meal for livestock and poultry consumption.

WORLD SOYBEAN PRODUCTION, 1950–98

YEAR	TOTAL (mill. tons)	PER PERSON (kilograms)
1950	17	6.5
1955	19	7.0
1960	25	8.2
1965	32	9.5
1966	36	10.7
1967	38	10.8
1968	42	11.7
1969	42	11.7
1970	44	11.9
1971	47	12.5
1972	49	12.7
1973	62	15.9
1974	55	13.6
1975	66	16.1
1976	59	14.3
1977	72	17.1
1978	78	18.0
1979	94	21.4
1980	81	18.2
1981	86	19.0
1982	94	20.3
1983	83	17.7
1984	93	19.5
1985	97	20.0
1986	98	19.9
1987	104	20.6
1988	96	18.8
1989	107	20.7
1990	104	19.7
1991	107	20.0
1992	117	21.6
1993	118	21.3
1994	138	24.6
1995	125	22.0
1996	132	22.8
1997	156	26.6
1998 (prel)	155	26.1

SOURCES: USDA, *Production, Supply, and Distribution,* electronic database, February 1999; USDA, FAS, *Oilseeds: World Markets and Trade,* February 1999.

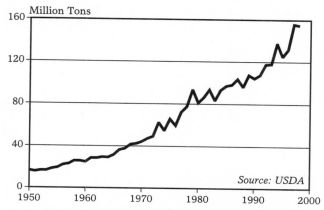

Figure 1: **World Soybean Production, 1950–98**

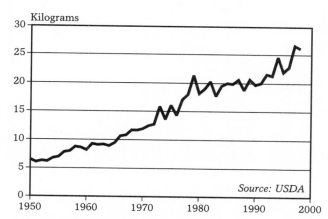

Figure 2: **World Soybean Production Per Person, 1950–98**

Meat Production Growth Slows   Lester R. Brown

World meat production in 1998 totaled 216 million tons, up 2.4 percent from the 211 million tons of 1997.[1] (See Figure 1.) Meat production per person continued to rise, but much more slowly, going from 36.1 kilograms in 1997 to 36.4 in 1998, a gain of 1 percent.[2] (See Figure 2.)

Growth in output of the three leading meats ranged widely in 1998. (See Figure 3.) Beef output remained essentially the same as in 1997 at 54 million tons.[3] But production of pork expanded by 3.5 percent to 91 million tons, further widening the excess over beef and, for the first time in years, growing faster than poultry.[4]

Beef production is growing at a snail's pace in part because the world's rangelands are being pushed close to their limits or beyond, so additional gains must now come largely in feedlots.[5] Here the relatively inefficient conversion of grain into meat by cattle compared with pigs or chickens gives the latter a strong advantage.

In Argentina, a major beef producer and exporter, the expansion of grain production in recent years has come in part from plowing up some of the country's better rangelands, forcing cutbacks in cattle numbers.[6] Indeed, Argentina's cattle herd in 1998 was the smallest in 25 years.[7]

In Russia, the herd liquidation under way for the last eight years as the country's inefficient producers lost out to imports may finally be ending.[8] China, meanwhile, continues to push ruminant production, including sheep and goats as well as cattle, partly as a way of using large supplies of crop residues, including the wheat straw, rice straw, and corn stalks that are so abundant in villages.[9]

Beef trade is down as the economies of key importers, like South Korea and Russia, actually shrank in 1998.[10] In South Korea, where the devaluation of the won raised the price of imported beef, consumption has fallen 12 percent and the import beef market has virtually collapsed.[11] In Russia, as the shrinking economy is reducing purchasing power, the devaluation of the ruble has led to a suspension of beef imports.[12]

Japan, where imports account for two thirds of total beef consumption, is one exception to this trend.[13] Here both consumption and imports are continuing to rise, reflecting a westernization of the diet.[14]

Growth in pork production in 1998 was concentrated in the United States, the European Union, and China.[15] The growth in China, which went from 42.5 million tons to 44 million tons, is still 85 percent backyard production.[16] Although larger commercial operations are expanding rapidly, they account for a minor share of pork output.[17]

In Europe, the Netherlands—one of the region's larger producers—is facing potentially unmanageable problems in disposing of hog manure.[18] As a result, the industry is facing a government-imposed requirement to reduce the pig herd 25 percent by the year 2000.[19] In Russia, the production and consumption of pork declined in 1998, continuing a trend of the 1990s.[20]

The production of poultry, the fastest growing source of meat in many developing countries, has slowed markedly as financial turmoil has dampened demand in key countries, such as Indonesia.[21] After expanding at 5 percent or so per year for more than a dozen years, growth in production was cut more than half in 1998.[22] Poultry output, which surpassed beef in 1995 for the first time and which was gaining on pork, actually lost ground to the latter in 1998.[23]

In 1998, production of poultry continued to expand in both the United States and China, the two leading producers, which together account for nearly half of world poultry output.[24] The two big importers—Russia and China, including Hong Kong—are both cutting back imports, contributing to an actual decline in world poultry trade.[25] After growing at double-digit rates for many years, world poultry exports declined in 1998.[26]

In looking ahead, there is more uncertainty in the world meat market today than at any time in recent years. It is quite possible that the slowdown in growth of production in 1998 could deepen in 1999.

WORLD MEAT PRODUCTION, 1950–98

YEAR	TOTAL (mill. tons)	PER PERSON (kilograms)
1950	44	17.2
1955	58	20.7
1960	64	21.0
1965	81	24.2
1966	84	24.4
1967	86	24.5
1968	88	24.8
1969	92	25.4
1970	97	26.2
1971	101	26.7
1972	106	27.4
1973	105	26.8
1974	107	26.6
1975	109	26.6
1976	112	26.9
1977	117	27.6
1978	121	28.2
1979	126	28.8
1980	130	29.2
1981	132	29.2
1982	134	29.0
1983	138	29.4
1984	142	29.7
1985	146	30.1
1986	152	30.8
1987	157	31.3
1988	164	32.2
1989	166	32.0
1990	171	32.5
1991	173	32.2
1992	175	32.1
1993	177	32.1
1994	187	33.3
1995	197	34.7
1996	206	35.7
1997	211	36.1
1998 (prel)	216	36.4

SOURCES: FAO, *1948–1985 World Crop and Livestock Statistics* (Rome: 1987); FAO, *FAO Production Yearbooks 1988–1991* (Rome: 1990–1993); USDA, FAS, *Livestock and Poultry: World Markets and Trade*, October 1998.

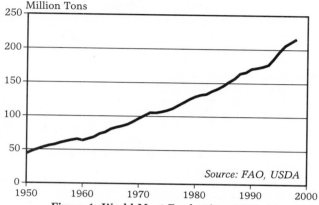

Figure 1: World Meat Production, 1950–98

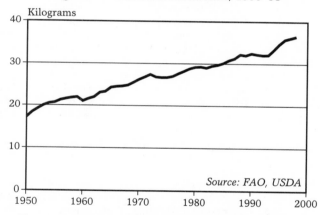

Figure 2: World Meat Production Per Person, 1950–98

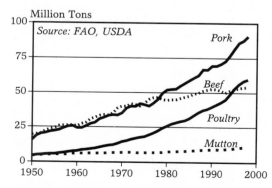

Figure 3: World Meat Production, by Type, 1950–98

The world fish catch from marine and inland waters fell slightly to 93.7 million tons in 1997, the latest year for which global data are available.[1] (See Figure 1.) Although world supplies dropped by 1 percent from the all-time high in 1996, per capita supplies declined by 2.4 percent to 16 kilograms per person.[2] (See Figure 2.)

Preliminary reports for 1998 indicate an even steeper decline due to a strong El Niño, which brought warmer waters to the western coast of South America. Chile's landings of anchoveta (Peruvian anchovy)—the world's number one species by volume caught—plummeted by 73 percent in 1998, while those of Chilean jack mackerel, which ranks third, dropped by 47 percent.[3] These two stocks accounted for 14 percent of world marine catches in 1996, the latest year for which species catch data are available.[4] The 1997–98 season for the global fish meal and oil industries was the worst ever on record, with production expected to drop by more than half.[5]

An estimated 73 percent of the world's major fishing areas and 70 percent of the world's major fish species are at peak production or in decline.[6] After a record catch of 5.4 million tons in 1988, landings of Japanese pilchard fell by 92 percent in just eight years, to 0.4 million tons.[7]

Landings of the most commercially valuable species have dropped by one fourth since 1970.[8] To maintain landings, fishers now capture less valuable species, such as pollock and hake, which account for a growing share of the global catch.[9] This trend cannot continue indefinitely unless fishing is reduced. The barndoor skate, for instance, is now quickly fading to extinction as a result of indiscriminate trawling.[10]

Depleting fisheries has ripple effects throughout the marine food chain. In Alaska, for example, pollock catches have nearly tripled since 1986.[11] But since the late 1970s the population of Steller sea lions, which feed on pollock, has plummeted by 90 percent in western Alaska.[12] In 1990, the National Marine Fisheries Service designated the species as threatened under the Endangered Species Act, and in May 1997 the designation was changed to endangered, an even more serious category.[13] Loss of sea lions has deprived killer whales of their primary source of food. In turn, the whales are now eating sea otters, a leaner and bonier mammal. And as a result, sea otter populations have declined by 90 percent since 1990, triggering a surge in their prey, sea urchins.[14]

In 1997, there was a 10-percent escalation in piracy and armed robberies directed toward ships, many of them fishing vessels.[15] Most attacks occurred in national waters of the South China Sea, the Indian Ocean, and off East and West Africa and South America.[16] Illegal fishing is still found in the North Pacific, where three Chinese fishing trawlers using driftnets—which were banned from use in international waters in 1992—were apprehended by Russian and U.S. fisheries enforcement officers in May 1998.[17]

A growing problem is the practice of registering a vessel in a country that is not member to a particular treaty, thus allowing the owner to fly a "flag of convenience" and evade responsibility. Between 1991 and 1995, an estimated 13 percent of the vessels added to the global fleet were registered in Honduras and Liberia, two leading "flag of convenience" nations.[18] None of the 195 vessels were built in these countries, nor are they owned by companies based there.[19] Such arrangements complicate efforts to crack down on overfishing. For instance, Korean- and Taiwanese-owned trawlers are registered in Oman and fish illegally in Pakistani waters.[20]

To address some of these concerns, the U.N. Food and Agriculture Organization has organized high-level consultations on the issues of fishing capacity and seabird and shark mortality. Nonbinding action plans were approved in February 1999.[21] Even before then, with salmon populations dropping to dangerously low levels, all seven members of the North Atlantic Salmon Conservation Organization agreed to shut down commercial salmon fishing in the region for 1998.[22] Unless depleted stocks are allowed to recover, fishers worldwide face a similar prospect.

WORLD FISH CATCH, 1950–97

YEAR	TOTAL (mill. tons)	PER PERSON (kilograms)
1950	19	7.5
1955	26	9.5
1960	36	12.0
1965	49	14.7
1966	53	15.4
1967	56	16.0
1968	56	15.9
1969	57	15.8
1970	58	15.7
1971	62	16.5
1972	58	15.1
1973	59	15.0
1974	63	15.6
1975	62	15.3
1976	65	15.5
1977	63	15.0
1978	65	15.2
1979	66	15.1
1980	67	15.0
1981	69	15.3
1982	71	15.4
1983	72	15.3
1984	78	16.3
1985	79	16.3
1986	85	17.1
1987	85	16.9
1988	89	17.4
1989	89	17.2
1990	86	16.3
1991	85	15.9
1992	86	15.8
1993	87	15.8
1994	93	16.5
1995	93	16.4
1996	95	16.4
1997	94	16.0

SOURCES: FAO, *Yearbook of Fishery Statistics: Catches and Landings* (Rome: various years); 1990–97 data from FAO, Rome, e-mail, 19 November 1998.

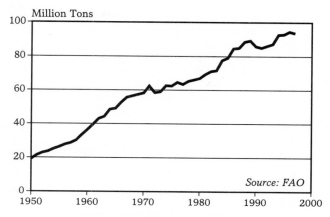

Figure 1: World Fish Catch, 1950–97

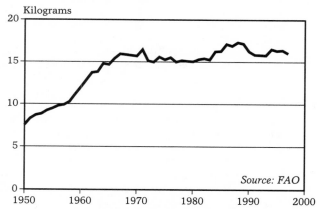

Figure 2: World Fish Catch Per Person, 1950–97

Grain Stocks Down Slightly   Lester R. Brown

World carryover stocks of grain in 1999 are estimated at 313 million tons, the equivalent of 62 days of consumption.[1] (See Figures 1 and 2.) Down from 64 days in 1998, this is the third lowest level in 25 years.[2] The only years since 1974 that were lower were 1996 at 53 days and 1997 at 58 days.[3]

World grain stocks go up when production exceeds consumption, and of course they go down when the opposite occurs. In each of the last two years, world grain production exceeded consumption by roughly 35 million tons, leading to two consecutive annual increases in stocks.[4] In 1998, consumption rose from 1,842 million tons to 1,856 million tons.[5]

Defined as the amount of grain in the bin when the new harvest begins, the level of carryover stocks is the most sensitive of all food security indicators. While few of those living in affluent societies ever think about grain stock levels, for the billion poorest people in the world, having enough grain to make it to the next harvest is often a major preoccupation.

In an unusual situation, Russia faces this concern in 1999.[6] With its 1998 grain harvest reduced by some 39 percent due to severe heat and drought and economic mismanagement, it has turned to the outside world for help, requesting food aid from both the European Union and the United States.[7]

Among the big three grains, stocks of wheat and rice—the world's principal food staples—were both down, while those of corn—the principal grain fed to livestock and poultry—were up.[8] Wheat carryover stocks in 1999 at 78 days are expected to be the third lowest on record, exceeded only by the 70 days each year in 1996 and 1997.[9]

Rice stocks are down to 42 days of consumption, matching the all-time low in 1973.[10] Although the 1998 rice harvest was down from 1997, consumption rose again, marking the twenty-sixth consecutive year of increasing world rice consumption.[11]

Corn stocks are up quite a bit in 1998, climbing from 86 million tons in 1997 to 98 million tons in 1999, a gain of 14 percent.[12]

Consumption and production of corn both increased in 1998, but production increased more.[13]

As a general matter, wheat and corn stocks need to be higher than those of rice simply because with most of the rice crop irrigated, year-to-year variability in the harvest rarely exceeds 2 percent.[14] With wheat and corn, both of which are largely rain-fed, worldwide year-to-year swings of 10 percent are not uncommon.[15]

Normally when carryover stocks drop below 60 days of consumption, prices become highly volatile and can easily double from one year to the next, as they did when wheat prices jumped from $1.90 per bushel in 1972 to $3.81 in 1973.[16] To maintain price stability in world markets and to cushion the effects of a poor harvest, world carryover stocks of at least 70 days are needed.

The role of carryover stocks of grain in ensuring food security has become even more important during the late 1990s since the United States dismantled its agricultural commodity supply management programs, which paid farmers to set aside part of their cropland each year. In 1995, the last year before the program was dismantled, U.S. farmers were paid to idle just over 7 million hectares.[17] Assuming average grain yields, this land could produce, when returned to production, roughly 35 million tons of grain—enough to feed the world for seven days at the current consumption rate of 5 million tons per day.[18] Without this major reserve, the world is in a much more vulnerable position in the event of a poor harvest.

No one knows what the future will bring, but we do know that there is little cropland remaining that can easily be brought under production and there is little additional irrigation capacity that can be easily developed. In addition to these land and water constraints, record high temperatures in recent years and more extreme climate events could combine to undermine food security as the world enters the twenty-first century.

WORLD GRAIN CARRYOVER STOCKS, 1961–99[1]

YEAR	STOCKS (mill. tons)	(days use)
1961	203	90
1962	182	81
1963	190	82
1964	193	83
1965	194	78
1966	159	62
1967	189	72
1968	213	79
1969	244	87
1970	228	77
1971	193	63
1972	217	69
1973	180	56
1974	191	56
1975	199	61
1976	219	66
1977	279	79
1978	277	77
1979	326	85
1980	315	81
1981	288	72
1982	307	77
1983	356	88
1984	305	73
1985	366	85
1986	434	100
1987	466	104
1988	405	89
1989	314	70
1990	297	64
1991	339	72
1992	326	69
1993	363	76
1994	318	66
1995	306	63
1996	255	53
1997	291	58
1998	324	64
1999 (prel)	313	62

[1]Data are for year when new harvest begins.
SOURCES: USDA, *Production, Supply and Distribution,* electronic database, February 1999; USDA, FAS, *Grain: World Markets and Trade,* February 1999.

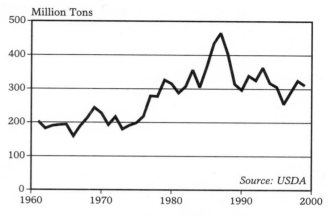

Figure 1: World Grain Carryover Stocks, 1961–99

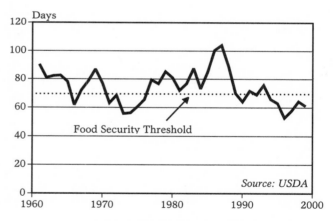

Figure 2: World Grain Carryover Stocks as Days of Consumption, 1961–99

Agricultural Resource Trends

Grain Area Declines
Brian Halweil

Global grain harvested area shrank to 684 million hectares in 1998, a drop of more than 6 million hectares or 1 percent from 1997.[1] (See Figure 1.) Since the historic high in 1981, grain harvested area has declined 48 million hectares, a 7-percent drop.[2] And grain area harvested per person—at 0.12 hectares—has plummeted to half the 1950 level.[3] (See Figure 2.) In contrast to the rest of agricultural history, the near tripling in production since 1950 has come largely from yield increases, rather than from bringing more land under the plow.

Grain harvested area indicates the acreage of land reaped each year. (Land that yields two crops in one year is counted twice.) Grains provide more than half the calories and protein eaten directly by humans as well as the feedgrain for meat, milk, and egg production.[4] Planted on roughly half the world's cropland, grains serve as a proxy for trends in all crops.[5]

Wheat area declined by nearly 2 percent in 1998, rice area barely changed, and corn area rose 2 percent, spurred by rising global feedgrain demand.[6] But wheat dominates global grain acreage with 225 million hectares.[7] At 150 million hectares, rice area edges out corn's 140 million hectares.[8]

The area planted to grain each year tracks closely with grain prices: a brief jump in those spurred grainland expansion in 1996, though historically low prices since then have driven land out of production.[9] Price supports, input subsidies, and other policies affect production throughout the world.[10]

In addition to these year-to-year fluctuations, nonfarm uses, crops other than grain, and land degradation permanently consume grainland at a dizzying pace. From the Middle East to the Far East, swelling cities and industry often squeeze agriculture from scarce land.[11] And soybean area worldwide has tripled since 1950, steadily replacing grain on some of the best cropland.[12]

By reducing yields, declining land quality can have the same negative effects as declining quantity. Worldwide, according to a 1990 U.N. assessment, 38 percent of cultivated area has been damaged to some degree by agricultural mismanagement since 1950, with higher levels of degradation in Latin America and Africa.[13] Severe and prolonged land degradation, including soil erosion, nutrient depletion, and desertification, will ultimately remove land from cultivation. Various sources suggest that present losses range from 5 million to 12 million hectares per year.[14]

Once grain area per person drops below a certain level, a nation can lose its ability to feed itself. In Japan, South Korea, and Taiwan, as grain area per person plummeted and incomes soared, grain imports as a share of total consumption have soared from 20 to 70 percent since 1960.[15] In Pakistan, Ethiopia, Iran, and other nations where area per person is already a fraction of the world average, projected population doublings or triplings do not bode well for food security.[16]

Since the best cropland is already under the plow throughout most of the world, substantial future increases will likely come at a cost.[17] For example, of the land available for expansion in developing nations—where nearly all the global potential exists—more than 65 percent suffers from yield-lowering soil and terrain constraints.[18] Moreover, over half of the potential area lies under forests or in protected natural areas that provide vital ecosystem services.[19]

Efforts to expand cropland into areas that are too steeply sloped, too arid, or otherwise ill suited for cultivation are often short-lived: conversion of fragile pastureland in Kazakhstan to grain production in the 1950s, for instance, yielded such severe erosion that half the land has been abandoned since 1980, with further losses expected.[20] (See Figure 3.)

All the cropland previously idled under the U.S. commodity supply management programs has been returned to production, as has nearly all land idled in Europe under similar programs.[21] Nonetheless, some uncultivated, arable land remains in parts of sub-Saharan Africa and South America, where a lack of infrastructure, high agricultural taxes, inequitable land distribution, and other unfavorable policies keep large tracts out of production.[22]

WORLD GRAIN HARVESTED AREA, 1950–98

YEAR	AREA HARVESTED (mill. hectares)	AREA PER PERSON (hectares)
1950	587	0.23
1955	639	0.23
1960	639	0.21
1965	653	0.20
1966	655	0.19
1967	665	0.19
1968	670	0.19
1969	672	0.18
1970	663	0.18
1971	672	0.18
1972	661	0.17
1973	688	0.18
1974	691	0.17
1975	708	0.17
1976	717	0.17
1977	714	0.17
1978	713	0.17
1979	711	0.16
1980	722	0.16
1981	732	0.16
1982	716	0.16
1983	707	0.15
1984	711	0.15
1985	715	0.15
1986	709	0.14
1987	685	0.14
1988	688	0.14
1989	694	0.13
1990	694	0.13
1991	692	0.13
1992	694	0.13
1993	685	0.12
1994	686	0.12
1995	682	0.12
1996	703	0.12
1997	690	0.12
1998 (prel)	684	0.12

SOURCE: USDA, *Production, Supply, and Distribution*, electronic database, Washington, DC, February 1999.

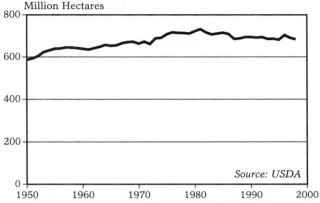

Figure 1: World Grain Harvested Area, 1950–98

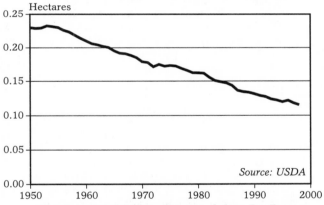

Figure 2: World Grain Harvested Area Per Person, 1950–98

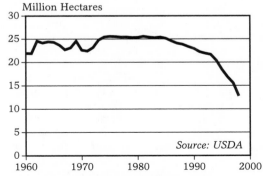

Figure 3: Grain Harvested Area in Kazakhstan, 1960–98

World irrigated area rose by 4 million hectares in 1996, the last year for which global data are available.[1] (See Figure 1.) The 1.7-percent increase over 1995 is the largest increase this decade, but it still runs well behind the peak growth rates of the 1970s.[2] The reported growth may reflect statistical adjustments to national data as much as actual changes in physical area, but it is consistent with the relatively slow growth worldwide since the early 1980s.

Expansion of irrigated area peaked in the mid-1970s at 2.3 percent per year, but has slowed this decade to 1.4 percent.[3] On a per capita basis, the slowdown is more marked: after peaking in 1978, irrigated area per person fell more than 4 percent by 1988.[4] It recovered a bit around 1990, and has been roughly stable in the 1990s at 45.8 hectares per thousand people—the same as in 1974 and 3.5 percent below its peak.[5] (See Figure 2.)

Nearly all the expansion in 1996 was reported in developing countries. Asia, with 70 percent of world irrigated area, saw the fastest growth—some 2.4 percent.[6] India alone registered a 3-million hectare expansion, accounting for 75 percent of the global increase.[7] Irrigated area in Africa and Latin America remained virtually unchanged, while industrial countries experienced a slight contraction.[8] The biggest losers were countries in transition, whose irrigated area declined by 1.1 percent in 1996, the sixth straight year of decline.[9]

Irrigated area is important because it is especially productive land. Some 40 percent of the world's food comes from the 17 percent of global cropland that is watered artificially.[10] Irrigation is credited with more than half of the growth in agricultural output between the mid-1960s and the mid-1980s, and its importance is expected to grow in coming decades.[11] By one estimate, the share of the world's crop water provided by irrigation as opposed to rainfall may need to rise from 28 percent today to 46 percent in 2025.[12]

Despite its growing importance, irrigation faces a host of challenges, the most critical being water availability. Signs of shortages are already apparent. Several major agricultural regions pump groundwater faster than it is recharged by rainfall, an unsustainable practice that could well curtail output once aquifers are depleted or become too expensive to pump. The International Water Management Institute (IWMI) estimates that Indian grain production could fall by 25 percent when it finally brings groundwater withdrawals into line with the rate of recharge.[13] Other major agricultural regions that rely on overpumped groundwater include the north China plain (which produces some 40 percent of China's grain), the southern U.S. Great Plains, and most of the Middle East and North Africa.[14]

One reason for rapidly falling water tables is that groundwater has become easy to extract. Inexpensive pumps have dramatically increased the capacity of poor farmers to get to groundwater.[15] Today, India irrigates more land using small pumps than through all surface irrigation systems combined.[16] But ease of access carries a stiff price: aquifers are being pumped at about twice the rate of recharge in India, causing water tables to fall some 1–3 meters a year.[17]

Other threats to irrigation include salination, the gradual salt buildup that occurs on irrigated land as water evaporates, and waterlogging, the saturation of cropland as percolating irrigation water raises the level of water tables. Salination is severe enough on an estimated 10 percent of world irrigated area to reduce crop yields; losses from salination offset some of the gains in irrigated area that are achieved each year.[18]

As population growth and prosperity drive up food demand in coming decades, the pressure to expand irrigation is likely to increase. To meet projected crop water requirements in 2050, irrigation capacity may need to more than triple, a quantity equal to the annual flow of 24 Nile Rivers.[19] But the water may not be available where it is needed. IWMI estimates that more than a billion people will be living in countries facing absolute water scarcity by 2025.[20]

WORLD IRRIGATED AREA, 1961–96

YEAR	TOTAL (mill. hectares)	PER PERSON (hectares per thousand)
1961	139	45.0
1962	141	44.9
1963	144	44.9
1964	147	44.8
1965	150	44.9
1966	153	44.9
1967	156	44.8
1968	159	44.9
1969	164	45.1
1970	167	45.2
1971	171	45.3
1972	174	45.2
1973	180	45.8
1974	183	45.8
1975	189	46.3
1976	194	46.7
1977	198	47.0
1978	204	47.4
1979	207	47.4
1980	209	47.1
1981	213	47.1
1982	215	46.6
1983	216	46.2
1984	221	46.4
1985	224	46.2
1986	225	45.8
1987	227	45.3
1988	230	45.1
1989	236	45.5
1990	241	45.8
1991	245	45.9
1992	248	45.7
1993	252	45.7
1994	255	45.7
1995	259	45.6
1996	263	45.8

SOURCES: FAO, *FAOSTAT Statistics Database*, Rome; USDA, *Agricultural Resources and Environmental Indicators* (Washington, DC: 1996–97).

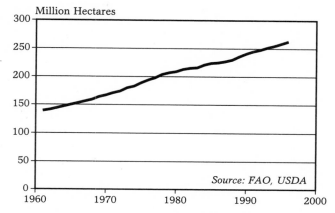

Figure 1: World Irrigated Area, 1961–96

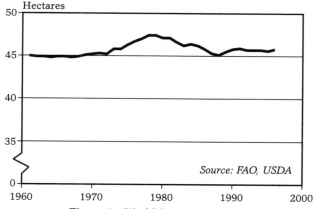

Figure 2: World Irrigated Area Per Thousand People, 1961–96

Energy
Trends

Growth in Fossil Fuel Burning Slows   Christopher Flavin

Growth in the use of fossil fuels in 1998 fell to the lowest rates since the early 1990s. (See Figure 1.) Use of oil increased by a meager 0.8 percent in 1998, while coal use actually fell 2.5 percent.[1] With China's coal burning now declining, along with that of most industrial countries, use of coal—the most environmentally damaging fossil fuel—is likely near its historical peak.

Growth in the use of oil, which accounts for 30 percent of world energy use, was held back by a 3.5-percent decline in Japan in 1998, and by slower growth throughout Asia.[2] The stronger economies of Europe and North America, on the other hand, continued to expand their use of oil, particularly in the United States, where ever-larger sports utility vehicles are driving gasoline use up.

The combination of slower demand growth and a major increase in Iraq's oil production, under a humanitarian sales program supervised by the United Nations, drove oil prices in 1998 to the lowest levels (measured in real inflation-adjusted dollars) since the 1973 Arab oil embargo, more than a quarter-century ago.[3] (See Figure 2.) The average oil price of $12 per barrel in 1998 represented an 80-percent decline in real oil prices since the peak levels of the 1980s.[4]

Although low oil prices were a boon to consuming industries, they created considerable havoc for producers—both governments and companies. The severe economic crises that rocked exporters Indonesia and Russia in 1998, for example, were caused in part by falling oil prices, which greatly reduced foreign exchange earnings.[5]

At the corporate level, falling prices cut sharply into revenues, lowering the profits of the world's largest oil company—Royal Dutch Shell—by half, and driving share prices down.[6] One publication described 1998 as the year that "will live in infamy for oil producers."[7] One consequence of falling prices was a wave of mergers as the major oil companies sought to reduce costs by consolidating and laying off redundant workers. Early in the year, British Petroleum joined with U.S.-based Amoco, and at the end of 1998 two U.S.

giants, Exxon and Mobil, tied the knot.[8]

Although low oil prices signal a temporary glut in world oil markets, they may in fact bring the next crisis closer, reducing investment in marginal areas where oil prices of $12 per barrel are insufficient to cover costs.[9]

Natural gas markets were steadier than oil markets in 1998, as gas use grew by 1.6 percent, including a strong rebound in Europe, coupled with slower growth in crisis-plagued Asia.[10] Natural gas remains a popular fuel for power generation, as well as for industrial and residential use, propelled by the fact that it is the least polluting of the fossil fuels. Major gas discoveries in China's Tarim Basin in 1998 may help clear the air in one of the world's most polluted countries.[11]

The weakest of the fossil fuels in 1998 was the dirtiest of the three. Coal saw its first decline since the collapse of the Soviet coal industry in the early 1990s.[12] The use of coal dropped both in the European Union and Russia, while the United States saw modest growth estimated at 1.7 percent.[13]

But the big surprise of 1998 was China, the world's leading coal burner, where use of the fuel fell 7 percent, continuing a slowdown that began in 1997.[14] Although the cause of the decline is uncertain, the government has reduced its coal subsidies in recent years, and China's transportation infrastructure may be showing the strains of moving such vast quantities of this solid fuel, chiefly by rail.[15]

The shift in China's coal markets may portend a broader transition. A growing number of energy analysts and industry officials now argue that energy markets are beginning the inevitable long-run shift away from fossil fuels. In a remarkable speech in Houston in early 1999, Mike Bowlin, Chairman and CEO of the ARCO oil company said, "We've embarked on the beginning of the Last Days of the Age of Oil." Bowlin went on to say that the world is moving "along the spectrum away from carbon, and headed toward hydrogen and other forms of energy."[16]

WORLD FOSSIL FUEL USE, BY TYPE, 1950–98

YEAR	COAL	OIL	NATURAL GAS
	(mill. tons of oil equivalent)		
1950	1,043	436	187
1955	1,234	753	290
1960	1,500	1,020	444
1965	1,533	1,485	661
1966	1,559	1,591	721
1967	1,480	1,696	774
1968	1,554	1,849	847
1969	1,601	2,025	928
1970	1,635	2,189	1,022
1971	1,632	2,313	1,097
1972	1,629	2,487	1,150
1973	1,668	2,690	1,184
1974	1,691	2,650	1,212
1975	1,709	2,616	1,199
1976	1,787	2,781	1,261
1977	1,835	2,870	1,283
1978	1,870	2,962	1,334
1979	1,991	2,998	1,381
1980	2,021	2,873	1,406
1981	1,816	2,781	1,448
1982	1,878	2,656	1,448
1983	1,918	2,632	1,463
1984	2,001	2,670	1,577
1985	2,100	2,654	1,640
1986	2,135	2,743	1,653
1987	2,197	2,789	1,739
1988	2,244	2,872	1,826
1989	2,269	2,914	1,909
1990	2,241	2,958	1,945
1991	2,186	2,955	1,980
1992	2,167	2,980	1,983
1993	2,157	2,953	2,011
1994	2,168	3,011	2,017
1995	2,200	3,235	2,075
1996	2,275	3,325	2,179
1997	2,293	3,396	2,175
1998 (prel)	2,236	3,423	2,210

SOURCE: Worldwatch estimates based on UN, BP, DOE, EC, Eurogas, PlanEcon, IMF, and LBL.

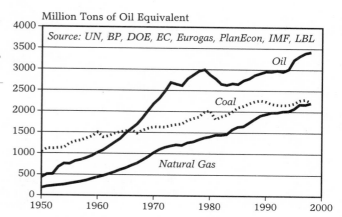

Figure 1: World Fossil Fuel Use, by Type, 1950–98

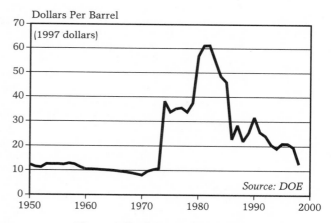

Figure 2: Real Price of Oil, 1950–98

Nuclear Power Declines Slightly Nicholas Lenssen

Between 1997 and 1998, total installed nuclear generating capacity declined for only the second time since the 1950s. The decline was just 175 megawatts, to 343,086 megawatts.[1] (See Figure 1.) Since 1990, global capacity has risen only 4.4 percent.[2]

Even though capacity is likely to rise marginally in the next year or two, it will almost certainly decline thereafter as the construction pipeline dries up and the closure of older, uneconomic, and politically unpopular reactors accelerates. A few governments still support nuclear power, but the number is dwindling with each passing year.

Construction started on five reactors in 1998 (see Figure 2)—two each in India and South Korea, and one in Japan—bringing the total being built to 33, with a combined capacity of 25,018 megawatts.[3] Of these, 14 may never be completed.[4]

Three new reactors—two in South Korea and one in the Slovak Republic—were connected to the grid in 1998, and two reactors—one each in the United States and Japan—were permanently closed.[5] This brings to 94 the number of reactors that have been retired after an average service life of less than 18 years.[6] (See Figure 3.) By the end of 1998, 429 reactors were operating—one less than five years earlier.[7]

In Western Europe, only one reactor is still under construction: the French reactor, Civaux 2, was scheduled to open in 1998, but a design fault delayed the opening until 1999.[8]

Political changes in Europe have set the stage for a shift away from nuclear power. The new German government of Socialist and Green parties has a goal of phasing out the country's 19 nuclear power reactors.[9] The debate is now focused on how quickly this will happen.

Sweden's government held fast to its 1994 decision to begin shutting down the country's reactors—and won reelection in 1998.[10] However, the owner of the first reactor targeted, Sydkraft, has taken the government to court and delayed closure until at least 1999.[11]

In Belgium, the government has convened an expert commission to study reorienting the country's electricity supply away from nuclear power, and it has canceled a contract for reprocessing nuclear fuel in France.[12] Even in France, some officials have called for less dependence on nuclear power.[13]

North America also appears close to abandoning its existing nuclear plants, though this is due to the high cost rather than the unpopularity of nuclear power. The gradual opening of electricity markets to competition led to another U.S. closure in 1998, the Millstone 1 plant in Connecticut, and more are expected.[14]

Asia still remains the last region of growth for nuclear power, though the pace continued to slow in 1998. South Korea has the world's most active construction program, but economic difficulties—and political reforms—are taking a toll even while construction started on two more reactors at Ulchin. The country's economic crisis depressed demand growth and drove up the costs of financing capital-intensive nuclear projects.[15] And the 1998 election of President Kim Dae Jung led to additional cutbacks in the country's plans.[16]

Elsewhere in Asia, Japan approved the construction of a new nuclear power plant for the first time in 10 years, at Higashidori in Aomori.[17] It was partly offset by the closure of a reactor, Tokai I.[18]

China currently has three operating nuclear reactors and six under construction, with probably overly ambitious plans to build some 50 additional reactors by 2020.[19] Meanwhile, India launched construction on a new project—its first since 1990.[20] India's new coalition government, led by the Hindu nationalist Bharatiya Janant Party, more than doubled the budget for nuclear power in 1998.[21] Still, nuclear energy only supplies 2 percent of the country's power.[22]

Construction projects are frozen in both Russia and Ukraine as funds for work have dried up.[23] Ukraine remains hopeful, though, that it will be able to obtain western money to complete two stalled projects in a controversial exchange for closing the final operating reactor at the Chernobyl station.[24]

WORLD NET INSTALLED
ELECTRICAL GENERATING CAPACITY
OF NUCLEAR POWER PLANTS,
1960–98

YEAR	CAPACITY (gigawatts)
1960	1
1961	1
1962	2
1963	2
1964	3
1965	5
1966	6
1967	8
1968	9
1969	13
1970	16
1971	24
1972	32
1973	45
1974	61
1975	71
1976	85
1977	99
1978	114
1979	121
1980	135
1981	155
1982	170
1983	189
1984	219
1985	250
1986	276
1987	297
1988	310
1989	320
1990	328
1991	325
1992	327
1993	336
1994	338
1995	340
1996	343
1997	343
1998 (prel)	343

SOURCE: Worldwatch Institute database,
compiled from the IAEA and press reports.

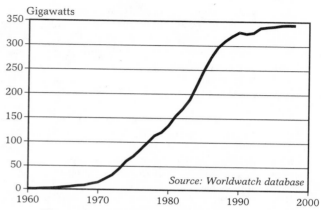

Figure 1: World Electrical Generating Capacity of
Nuclear Power Plants, 1960–98

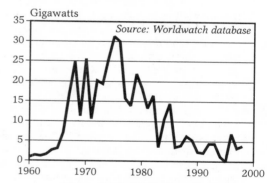

Figure 2: World Nuclear Reactor
Construction Starts, 1960–98

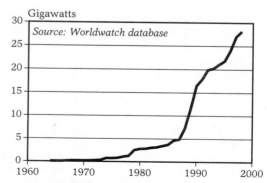

Figure 3: Cumulative Generating Capacity
of Closed Nuclear Power Plants, 1964–98

Wind Power Blows to New Record   Christopher Flavin

The world added 2,100 megawatts of new wind energy generating capacity in 1998.[1] This is a new all-time record, and 35 percent more capacity than was added in 1997. The new wind turbines pushed overall wind generating capacity worldwide to 9,600 megawatts at the end of 1998—double the capacity in place just three years earlier.[2] (See Figures 1 and 2.)

These wind turbines will generate an estimated 17 billion kilowatt-hours of electricity in 1999—worth $1.2 billion, and enough to meet the needs of 3.4 million homes.[3] Wind power has become one of the most rapidly expanding industries, with sales of roughly $2 billion in 1998.[4] The wind industry is creating thousands of manufacturing jobs.

The 1998 boom in wind energy was led by Germany, which added 790 megawatts, pushing its wind energy capacity over 2,800 megawatts.[5] (See Figure 3.) Germany's wind industry, which is only seven years old, is now producing more than 1 percent of the nation's electricity, and has reached 11 percent in the northernmost state of Schleswig-Holstein.[6]

Spain also emerged as a major player in 1998. The nation added 380 megawatts of wind power, pushing its overall capacity up 84 percent to 830 megawatts.[7] In the northern industrial state of Navarra, 20 percent of electricity already comes from wind turbines, most of them manufactured in local assembly facilities that employ hundreds of workers in the area around Pamplona.[8]

Wind power installations grew rapidly in the United States in 1998, with some 226 megawatts of new capacity added in 10 different states.[9] The surge in U.S. wind investment, the largest since 1986, was spurred by efforts to take advantage of a wind energy tax credit scheduled to expire in June 1999. The largest projects are a 107-megawatt wind farm in Minnesota, one of 42 megawatts in Wyoming, and one of 25 megawatts in Oregon.[10]

Denmark continued as a leader in the global wind power industry, adding 308 megawatts of capacity.[11] Some 1,400 megawatts of wind power now generate more than 8 percent of the country's electricity.[12] And Denmark's wind companies export heavily, accounting for more than half the new wind turbines installed worldwide in 1998.[13] Danish companies have formed joint venture manufacturing companies in nations such as India and Spain. Altogether, the Danish wind industry had gross sales of just under $1 billion in 1998—roughly equal to the combined sales of the nation's natural gas and fishing industries.[14]

The developing world could benefit most from further growth of the wind industry. India is the leader so far, with more than 900 megawatts of wind power in place, but wind development has slowed dramatically there in the last two years due to suspension of generous tax breaks enacted in the mid-1990s.[15] In response, the Ministry of Non-Conventional Energy Sources introduced new wind energy incentives, and projects that 14 domestic manufacturers will be building large wind turbines in India within five years.[16]

China is a potential wind superpower—with a resource large enough to double its current electricity supply, which comes mainly from coal. Unlike India, China has not yet established a solid legal basis for a sustained wind power industry, but with the help of foreign aid, a growing number of wind projects have been installed, including the first commercial wind farm, a 24-megawatt Dutch project opened in July 1998.[17]

The dramatic growth of wind power in the 1990s stems from the introduction of supportive government policies in countries such as Germany and Spain. Most important to date are laws that guarantee access to the grid for wind generators at a legally set price for the electricity they produce.

Larger turbines, more efficient manufacturing, and careful siting of wind machines have brought wind power costs down precipitously—from $2,600 per kilowatt in 1981 to $800 in 1998.[18] New wind farms have now reached economic parity with new coal-based power plants. And as the technology continues to improve, further cost declines are projected, which could make wind power the most economical source of electricity in many countries.

WORLD WIND ENERGY GENERATING CAPACITY, TOTAL AND ANNUAL ADDITION, 1980–98

YEAR	TOTAL (megawatts)
1980	10
1981	25
1982	90
1983	210
1984	600
1985	1,020
1986	1,270
1987	1,450
1988	1,580
1989	1,730
1990	1,930
1991	2,170
1992	2,510
1993	2,990
1994	3,680
1995	4,820
1996	6,115
1997	7,630
1998 (prel)	9,600

YEAR	ANNUAL ADDITION (megawatts)
1980	5
1981	15
1982	65
1983	120
1984	390
1985	420
1986	250
1987	180
1988	130
1989	150
1990	200
1991	240
1992	340
1993	480
1994	720
1995	1,294
1996	1,290
1997	1,566
1998 (prel)	2,100

SOURCES: Preliminary figure based on sources in leading countries; BTM Consult, *International Wind Energy Development: World Market Update 1997* (March 1998).

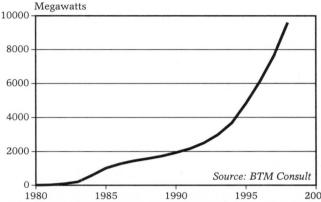

Figure 1: World Wind Energy Generating Capacity, 1980–98

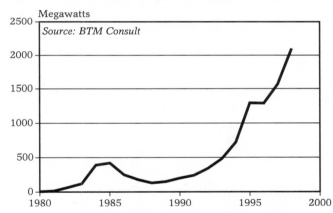

Figure 2: Annual Addition to World Wind Energy Generating Capacity, 1980–98

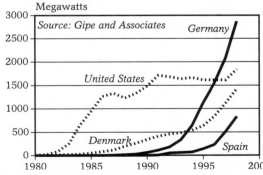

Figure 3: Wind Generating Capacity in Germany, the United States, Denmark, and Spain, 1980–98

Solar Cells Continue Double-Digit Growth   Molly O'Meara

Shipments of solar photovoltaic (PV) cells neared 152 megawatts in 1998, up 21 percent from 1997.[1] (See Figure 1.) Sales of these silicon-based semiconductors, which turn sunlight directly into electricity, have grown an average 16 percent a year in the 1990s.[2]

The United States remained the world's largest PV producer in 1998, with 54 megawatts.[3] Japan shipped 49 megawatts, led by Kyocera, which surpassed Siemens, a German-owned company in the United States, to become the world's top PV seller.[4] Europe produced 30 megawatts.[5] Other countries with growing solar industries include Australia, India, China, and Taiwan, with combined production of 19 megawatts.[6]

Solar cells, which unlike most energy technologies are lightweight and modular, are competitive for many applications. About half the world market for PVs is for remote nonresidential power supply: highway signals, radios, and water pumps and purification systems.[7] Another 20 percent goes to small devices such as calculators and watches.[8]

Electrical generation for individual buildings accounts for the remaining 30 percent of PVs.[9] Solar cells have long been the most economical power source in remote parts of the developing world.[10] But in areas served by electric lines, solar power is still two to five times more expensive than grid power.[11]

Some industrial-country governments have strengthened support for PVs in the 1990s to stimulate further cost reductions. Installation of grid-connected rooftop systems has exploded as a result.[12] (See Figure 2.) And in 1998 the average factory price for solar cells dropped below $4 per watt.[13] (See Figure 3.)

Japan's rooftop program has prompted the current boom. Between 1994 and 1998, some 12,000 customers took advantage of that government's cash subsidy for PVs.[14] The government broadened the program in 1998, allowing customers to buy larger systems and to make more than one purchase, and permitting housing projects and businesses to apply for the subsidy.[15] More than 6,800 systems were installed in 1998.[16]

In the past two years, the European Union and the United States have each announced Million Roofs programs, which include solar heating as well as solar electric systems, to be completed by 2010 (although half the European program involves roofs in developing countries).[17] Germany, Switzerland, Norway, and the Netherlands have long-standing solar incentives in place, and Italy recently joined the club with a five-year 10,000 Roofs program.[18] Germany plans to launch the largest effort to date, a 100,000 Roofs Program expected to spur installation of 300 megawatts of PVs over six years.[19]

More than 70 percent of solar cells produced in the United States continue to be sent abroad.[20] The new initiative to boost U.S. sales will rely on partnerships between the federal government and electric utilities, nonprofit organizations, and state and local governments.[21] Proposed policy changes include a federal tax credit for 15 percent of the cost of a new system.[22]

Solar-powered buildings are becoming easier to build, as PVs are now directly integrated into roofing shingles, tiles, and even window glass.[23] A Japanese company offers a predesigned home that can be assembled in eight hours, complete with a solar roof.[24] Technological advances hold promise for such applications. The newer "thin film" cells, unlike conventional crystalline cells, do not need to be rigidly encased and can be made into large, flexible sheets ideal for incorporating into building materials.[25]

Certification and financing mechanisms are developing to boost the rooftop market.[26] In 1998, parallel global efforts to verify the quality of PV systems and to certify solar technicians and training courses gained momentum.[27] A key financial incentive available in Japan, Switzerland, and half of the states in the United States is "net metering," in which electric companies purchase electricity produced by individual solar rooftops at the same price they charge consumers. Other new tools include the solar loans offered by a large U.S. mortgage corporation and several Japanese banks.[28]

WORLD PHOTOVOLTAIC SHIPMENTS, 1971–98

YEAR	SHIPMENTS (megawatts)
1971	0.1
1975	1.8
1976	2.0
1977	2.2
1978	2.5
1979	4.0
1980	6.5
1981	7.8
1982	9.1
1983	17.2
1984	21.5
1985	22.8
1986	26.0
1987	29.2
1988	33.8
1989	40.2
1990	46.5
1991	55.4
1992	57.9
1993	60.1
1994	69.4
1995	78.6
1996	88.6
1997	125.8
1998 (prel)	151.7

SOURCE: Paul Maycock, *PV News,* various issues.

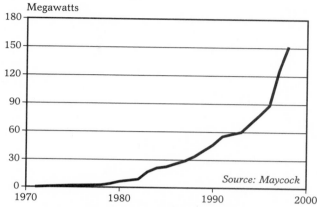

Figure 1: World Photovoltaic Shipments, 1971–98

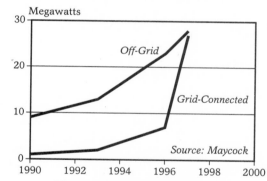

Figure 2: PVs in Buildings, Grid-Connected and Off-Grid, 1990–97

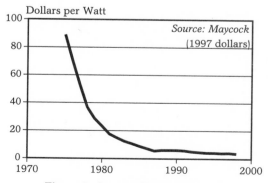

Figure 3: Average Factory Price of Photovoltaic Modules, 1975–98

Atmospheric
Trends

The average temperature of the atmosphere at Earth's surface jumped dramatically to a new high of 14.57 degrees Celsius in 1998, according to NASA's Goddard Institute for Space Studies.[1] (See Figure 1.) The increase of 0.17 degrees was unusually large, particularly given the fact that it immediately followed a new record set the previous year.[2]

Although the El Niño warming of the tropical Pacific exacerbated the temperature rise, particularly in the first half of 1998, it did not fully explain it.[3] The rapid warming of the last 25 years is greater than that of any period since the beginning of instrumental temperature measurements.[4] NASA scientists believe that the accelerated buildup of greenhouse gases in the atmosphere is the best explanation for the warming.[5]

The global average surface temperatures released by NASA are based on thousands of measuring devices scattered around the world for the broadest possible coverage. The figures are adjusted to take account of local effects, such as the heating up of urban areas.[6]

The data gathered for 1998 indicate that the greatest temperature increases occurred over continents, while the air over the oceans, which warm more slowly, showed less of an increase. The greatest temperature increases occurred at high latitudes, which is consistent with the effects of increased greenhouse gas concentrations as predicted by computer models. North America saw some of the largest temperature rises in 1998—the highest temperatures in 40 years, and close to those of the Dust Bowl year of 1934.[7]

One indirect measure of climate change is loss of ice in high-altitude and polar regions. Scientists reported accelerated melting of glaciers in many parts of the world last year—in the Arctic and Antarctic, as well as in many mountainous regions such as the Andes and the Qinghai-Tibet plateau.[8] A new study published in early 1999 indicates that the huge Greenland ice sheet has been shrinking rapidly, losing nearly 1 meter (3 feet) just since 1993 in some areas.[9]

A report published in the journal *Nature* in 1998 used tree rings and lake sediments to push the temperature record back a full 600 years—and came to the conclusion that the last decade of soaring temperatures represents the warmest seen during that entire period.[10]

The higher temperatures of 1998 were accompanied by unusually severe weather in many parts of the world.[11] Scientists also reported that the warmer ocean temperatures led to massive, unprecedented damage to the world's coral reefs, which they link specifically to global warming and the stronger El Niños it has spawned.[12]

In earlier years, some scientists questioned the reliability of the surface temperature record by pointing to seemingly contradictory satellite-based microwave measurements of temperatures high in the atmosphere.[13] But this slender straw was swept away in 1998 by a report in *Nature* by scientists Frank Wentz and Matthias Schabel.[14] It demonstrated that the satellite data were skewed by the failure to account for the predictable gravity-induced decay in the orbits of the satellites. Once this is corrected, the satellite data correspond more closely to the ground-level measurements.

The sharp jump in temperatures in 1998 was accompanied by the largest jump in the global concentration of carbon dioxide (CO_2) since data were first collected.[15] (See Figure 2.) Although CO_2 concentrations have risen throughout this century—due primarily to fossil fuel combustion—they increased last year by much more than usual, nearly 3 parts per million (ppm), to 366.7 ppm.[16] (See Figure 3.)

The increase in CO_2 concentrations in 1998 appears to have been an indirect outgrowth of the temperature rise. Scientists monitoring the CO_2 data attribute the rise in part to the extensive burning of tropical forests that accompanied the strong 1997–98 El Niño, which released hundreds of millions of tons of carbon.[17] Although a single year of data is inadequate to establish a trend, the accelerating rise in CO_2 concentration presents the risk of a positive feedback loop if rising temperatures lead to a runaway greenhouse effect.[18]

GLOBAL AVERAGE TEMPERATURE, 1950–98, AND ATMOSPHERIC CONCENTRATIONS OF CARBON DIOXIDE, 1960–98

YEAR	TEMPERATURE (degrees Celsius)	CARBON DIOXIDE (parts per mill.)
1950	13.84	n.a.
1955	13.91	n.a.
1960	13.96	316.8
1965	13.88	319.9
1966	13.96	321.2
1967	14.00	322.0
1968	13.94	322.9
1969	14.03	324.5
1970	14.02	325.5
1971	13.93	326.2
1972	14.01	327.3
1973	14.11	329.5
1974	13.92	330.1
1975	13.94	331.0
1976	13.81	332.0
1977	14.11	333.7
1978	14.04	335.3
1979	14.08	336.7
1980	14.18	338.5
1981	14.30	339.8
1982	14.09	341.0
1983	14.28	342.6
1984	14.13	344.2
1985	14.10	345.7
1986	14.16	347.0
1987	14.28	348.8
1988	14.32	351.3
1989	14.24	352.8
1990	14.40	354.0
1991	14.36	355.5
1992	14.11	356.3
1993	14.12	357.0
1994	14.21	358.9
1995	14.38	360.9
1996	14.32	362.7
1997	14.40	363.8
1998 (prel)	14.57	366.7

SOURCES: Surface Air Temperature Analyses, Goddard Institute for Space Studies, New York, 26 February 1999; Scripps Institution of Oceanography, August 1998 and January 1999.

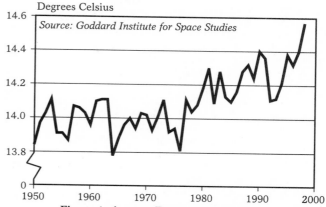

Figure 1: Average Temperature at Earth's Surface, 1950–98

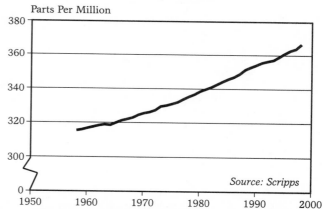

Figure 2: Atmospheric Concentrations of Carbon Dioxide, 1958–98

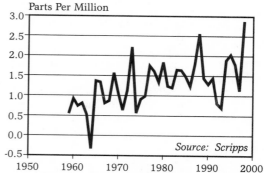

Figure 3: Annual Increase in Atmospheric Concentrations of Carbon Dioxide, 1958–98

Carbon Emissions Dip

Seth Dunn

Global emissions of carbon from fossil fuel combustion fell 0.2 percent in 1998, to just below 6.4 billion tons.[1] (See Figure 1.) Despite the drop, the annual total was the second highest on record.[2] Human activity has now added more than 200 billion tons of carbon to the atmosphere since 1950.[3]

Among industrial nations, responsible for 45 percent of global carbon emissions, output increased 8.1 percent between 1990 and 1998.[4] (See Figure 2.) The United States, the world's leading emitter with 23 percent of the overall total, saw output rise 11.8 percent between 1990 and 1998.[5] In the European Union, output rose only 3.1 percent—due mostly to declines in Germany, the United Kingdom, and France.[6] Carbon emissions in Japan shot up 5.9 percent during this period.[7]

In former Eastern bloc countries, which account for 14 percent of emissions, output fell 32.5 percent between 1990 and 1998.[8] In Russia and the Ukraine, output has fallen 28 and 44 percent, respectively, due mostly to the region's economic downturn.[9] Under the 1997 Kyoto Protocol to the U.N. Framework Convention on Climate Change, industrial and former Eastern bloc nations are committed to collectively cutting carbon and other greenhouse gas emissions 5.2 percent below 1990 levels between 2008 and 2012.[10] As of 1997, the overall carbon output from these countries was 4.7 percent below 1990 levels.[11]

Developing countries hold a 41-percent share of global carbon emissions, and saw a 39.1-percent rise in output between 1990 and 1998.[12] But the convergence of industrial and developing-country shares masks major disparities in historical and per capita rates.[13] Industrial and former Eastern Bloc nations remain responsible for 75 percent of the carbon emitted into the atmosphere since 1950.[14] The average emissions of 1 American equal those of 7 Chinese, 24 Nigerians, 31 Pakistanis, or hundreds of Somalis.[15] The richest fifth of the world accounts for 63 percent of emissions; the poorest fifth contributes just 2 percent.[16]

The burning of coal, oil, and natural gas releases carbon into the atmosphere, where it reacts with oxygen to form carbon dioxide (CO_2). These activities are understood to be enhancing the widely established greenhouse effect, by which CO_2 and other gases trap thermal radiation that is emitted from Earth's surface and would otherwise escape into space, causing atmospheric temperatures to rise.[17] Since preindustrial times, atmospheric CO_2 levels have risen 32.5 percent, from 276.7 to 366.7 parts per million in 1998—their highest point in 160,000 years.[18] (See Figure 3.)

Scientists project that a doubling of preindustrial atmospheric CO_2 concentrations would raise surface temperatures 1–3.5 degrees Celsius over the next century, leading to a broad array of adverse impacts on human health, socioeconomic, and natural systems.[19] A November 1998 article in *Science* added further evidence of human-induced climate change, accounting for the natural influences of sunspots and volcanic events and still detecting a significant "human fingerprint."[20]

New research also sheds light on the limited capacity of oceans and terrestrial ecosystems to serve as "sinks," cycling carbon out of the atmosphere.[21] Recent studies suggest that rising surface temperatures may over time greatly diminish the CO_2-absorbing ability of both oceans and forests.[22] While warming appears to be increasing carbon uptake in North America, recent El Niños have caused Amazon forests, normally CO_2 sponges, to release large amounts of carbon.[23]

Carbon sinks, emissions trading, and a "clean development mechanism" for carbon-saving projects were the focus of the first round of climate talks since the Kyoto pact, held in November 1998 in Buenos Aires.[24] More than 160 nations adopted a "plan of action," with a two-year deadline, for setting rules on these issues.[25] In addition, Argentina announced it would voluntarily commit to limiting its greenhouse gas emissions, and the United States became the protocol's sixtieth signatory.[26] But as a series of articles in *Nature* observed, carbon-cutting strategies have yet to address the need for major energy innovation and adaptation measures.[27]

WORLD CARBON EMISSIONS FROM FOSSIL FUEL BURNING, 1950–98

YEAR	EMISSIONS (mill. tons of carbon)
1950	1,609
1955	2,009
1960	2,520
1965	3,068
1966	3,222
1967	3,334
1968	3,501
1969	3,715
1970	3,986
1971	4,143
1972	4,306
1973	4,538
1974	4,545
1975	4,518
1976	4,777
1977	4,910
1978	4,950
1979	5,229
1980	5,156
1981	4,984
1982	4,947
1983	4,933
1984	5,098
1985	5,271
1986	5,453
1987	5,575
1988	5,799
1989	5,892
1990	5,946
1991	6,021
1992	5,928
1993	5,896
1994	6,034
1995	6,212
1996	6,316
1997 (est)	6,394
1998 (prel)	6,381

SOURCES: Worldwatch estimates based on ORNL, BP, DOE, EC, Eurogas, PlanEcon, IMF, and LBL.

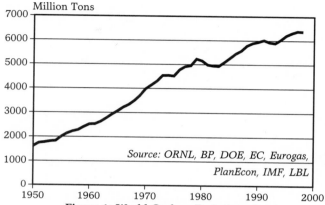

Figure 1: World Carbon Emissions from Fossil Fuel Burning, 1950–98

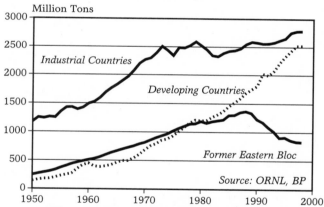

Figure 2: Carbon Emissions from Fossil Fuel Burning, by Economic Region, 1950–98

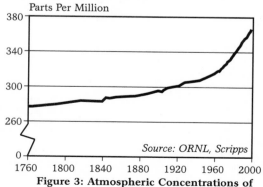

Figure 3: Atmospheric Concentrations of Carbon Dioxide, 1764–1998

Economic Trends

Global Economic Growth Slows
Lester R. Brown

The global economy continued to grow in 1998, expanding by 2.2 percent despite the economic turmoil in East Asia, Russia, and Brazil.[1] This growth, down by nearly half from the 4.2-percent global expansion in 1997, is the slowest since the 1.8 percent registered in 1991.[2]

The slower growth in 1998 stands in contrast to the last several years, when the global economy was growing easily twice as fast as population.[3] Thus the rise in average global income last year was nominal. The change in income per person among countries varied more widely than ever before, ranging from a drop of 17 percent in Indonesia and 10 percent in Thailand to a climb of 10 percent in Georgia and 6.6 percent in Ireland.[4]

Using the purchasing power parity method of aggregating gross national product data among countries instead of the traditional market exchange rate method, the global economic output of 1998 totaled $39.3 trillion.[5] (See Figure 1.) Per person this comes to $6,638, up from $6,583 in the preceding year—the smallest gain since early in the decade.[6] (See Figure 2.)

Among the major industrial countries, the United States remained the pacesetter, expanding by 3.6 percent.[7] At the other end of the spectrum, the Japanese economy contracted by 2.8 percent.[8] Growth in the major countries in Europe was somewhat slower than in the United States—3.0 percent in France, 2.7 percent in Germany, 2.6 percent in the United Kingdom, and 1.3 percent in Italy.[9]

Some of the world's most dynamic economies in 1998 were in Central and Eastern Europe.[10] Poland, Latvia, Lithuania, and Estonia each expanded by roughly 6 percent.[11] Bulgaria and Hungary grew at 5 percent.[12] In contrast, Romania declined by 6 percent, its second consecutive decline.[13]

The Central Asian and Trans-Caucus region also chalked up impressive economic gains in 1998. Demonstrating a strong recovery, the region was led by rates of roughly 6–8 percent in Armenia, Azerbaijan, and the Kyrgyz Republic.[14]

Asia recorded 2.6-percent growth in 1998, well below Africa's 3.6-percent growth. Some countries are still expanding at a steady rate, such as India at 4.7 percent, with similar rates in Pakistan and Bangladesh. In East Asia, however, the International Monetary Fund (IMF) estimates that contrary to official claims of 8-percent growth, China's economy likely grew only 7.2 percent in 1998.

Economic conditions vary widely within Asia. Several economies in the region are shrinking, including Indonesia (–15 percent), Thailand (–8 percent), Malaysia (–8 percent), and South Korea (–7 percent).[15] Other economies continued to expand. Taiwan and Viet Nam each grew at roughly 4 percent.[16]

After lagging for many years in its development, Africa registered 3.6-percent growth in 1998, a rate somewhat faster than the growth of its population.[17] Several countries were in the 5–7 percent category, including Cameroon, Côte d'Ivoire, Ghana, Morocco, Sudan, Tunisia, and Uganda.[18]

In the Middle East, a region whose economy suffered from low oil prices, economic growth averaged only 3.3 percent in 1998, the slowest of any region.[19] Egypt at 5 percent and Turkey at just over 4 percent were among the stronger economies there.[20]

Aside from the slowdown in global economic growth itself, perhaps the most distinguishing feature of 1998 is the difference in performance of regions compared with a few years ago. For example, Asia, the regional pacesetter in economic growth for many years, dropped from the average of close to 8 percent to 2.6 percent.[21] Meanwhile, some of the world's highest national growth rates were recorded in Africa and Eastern Europe.[22]

What lies ahead? In late 1997, the IMF estimated the 1998 growth would be at 3.5 percent and it actually came in at 2.2 percent.[23] This year, the IMF's October 1998 growth estimate for 1999 of 2.5 percent was lowered to 2.2 percent by December.[24] With Asia's economy projected to expand by 4.3 percent in 1999 as recovery in the region continues, the prospects for achieving this global rate of growth are encouraging.

GROSS WORLD PRODUCT, 1950–98

YEAR	TOTAL (trill. 1997 dollars)	PER PERSON (1997 dollars)
1950	6.4	2,503
1955	8.1	2,912
1960	10.0	3,275
1965	12.7	3,795
1966	13.4	3,921
1967	13.9	3,986
1968	14.6	4,119
1969	15.5	4,258
1970	16.2	4,381
1971	16.9	4,465
1972	17.7	4,585
1973	18.9	4,794
1974	19.3	4,811
1975	19.6	4,785
1976	20.5	4,936
1977	21.4	5,062
1978	22.3	5,181
1979	23.0	5,261
1980	23.5	5,276
1981	24.0	5,292
1982	24.2	5,261
1983	25.0	5,320
1984	26.1	5,465
1985	27.0	5,557
1986	27.9	5,650
1987	28.9	5,754
1988	30.1	5,900
1989	31.0	5,974
1990	31.6	5,993
1991	31.8	5,927
1992	32.1	5,902
1993	33.0	5,971
1994	34.3	6,115
1995	35.5	6,245
1996	37.0	6,412
1997	38.5	6,583
1998 (prel)	39.3	6,638

SOURCES: Worldwatch update of Angus Maddison, *Monitoring the World Economy 1820–1992* (Paris: OECD, 1995); updates and deflator indexes from IMF, *World Economic Outlook* tables.

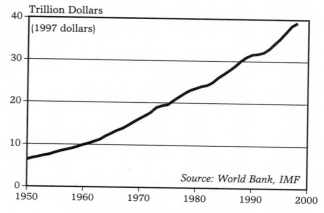

Figure 1: Gross World Product, 1950–98

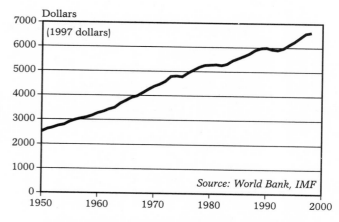

Figure 2: Gross World Product Per Person, 1950–98

Third World Debt Still Rising　　　　　Lisa Mastny

The indebtedness of developing countries rose to $2.2 trillion in 1997, the latest year for which figures are available—up from $2.1 trillion in 1996.[1] (See Figure 1.) Some 52 percent of this was owed to commercial creditors, 31 percent to other governments, and 17 percent to multilateral creditors, including the International Monetary Fund (IMF) and the World Bank.[2]

Developing countries spend a large share of their annual export revenues servicing their growing debts—diverting scarce resources from other vital investments. In Kenya, for instance, some 25 percent of government revenue is spent on debt service payments, compared with 6.8 percent on education and 2.7 percent on health.[3] In total, developing countries paid $269 billion in debt service in 1997, up from $191 billion in 1990.[4] (See Figure 2.)

The debt burden can also have serious implications for the environment. As governments seek to obtain the foreign investment and hard currency needed to service debts, they may tap the natural wealth in their countries to generate commodities for export—cutting trees for timber and clearing land for cash crops.[5]

Another way to measure the severity of the debt burden is to compare the level of indebtedness to a nation's gross national product (GNP). From this perspective, the debt situation has grown considerably worse in areas such as sub-Saharan Africa, where in 1997 debtor countries owed an amount equal to more than 70 percent of the region's annual income. (See Figure 3.) Latin America, in contrast, has seen an improvement in its debt situation over the past decade, with debt levels now equaling only around 38 percent of the region's GNP.

Although the debt burden has eased in some countries, in much of the developing world the money will likely never be repaid. With this in mind, bilateral creditors have rescheduled debt payments by lowering interest rates or extending due dates, and some have even canceled debts. For example, between 1990 and 1997 the U.S. government forgave $2.3 billion—about 37 percent—of loans to the world's most indebted countries.[6]

In 1996, the World Bank and the IMF launched the Highly Indebted Poor Countries (HIPC) Initiative, the first effort to include all creditors in addressing the repayment problems of the 40 most indebted nations. Its goal has been to reduce the debts of these countries—some $214 billion, or 9 percent of total developing-country debt—to "sustainable" levels, enabling governments to make payments on time and without rescheduling.[7]

But the HIPC Initiative has been criticized for doing "too little, too late."[8] To qualify for relief, countries must not only face an unmanageable debt burden, they must also establish a six-year record of economic reform through structural adjustment programs—which often impose strict conditions such as currency devaluation, cuts in government spending, and privatization of industry.[9] These conditions, critics argue, put economic priorities above social needs and penalize nations that are unprepared to implement rigid reforms.[10]

As of late 1998, only 10 of the 40 designated highly indebted countries had been considered under the HIPC Initiative, and only 7 were actually deemed eligible for debt relief.[11] Mozambique has been promised nearly $3 billion in relief over time—the equivalent of more than 70 percent of its 1997 GDP. But its accumulated debt is so large that it will likely still spend as much on debt servicing as on health and education combined.[12] Thus, while the initiative expects to deliver some $20 billion in total debt relief, it is unclear whether this will lead to genuine social progress in the world's poorest nations.[13]

Alternatively, the outright cancellation of debt payments in these countries could lead to investments that in Africa alone would save the lives of 7 million children per year by 2000 and provide 90 million females with access to basic education.[14] And forgiving this debt would cost industrial nations relatively little—for the United States, roughly the equivalent of two B-2 bombers, or the accounting errors in one year of the Pentagon's budget.[15]

EXTERNAL DEBT AND DEBT SERVICE
OF ALL DEVELOPING COUNTRIES,
1971–97

YEAR	DEBT	DEBT SERVICE
	(bill. 1997 dollars)	
1971	277	32
1972	312	37
1973	354	46
1974	405	52
1975	493	56
1976	566	62
1977	707	76
1978	827	103
1979	973	133
1980	1,115	169
1981	1,171	178
1982	1,260	190
1983	1,313	172
1984	1,319	180
1985	1,428	186
1986	1,533	190
1987	1,701	187
1988	1,646	206
1989	1,668	193
1990	1,720	191
1991	1,746	183
1992	1,776	182
1993	1,899	187
1994	2,015	203
1995	2,119	238
1996	2,134	267
1997	2,171	269

SOURCE: World Bank, *Global Development Finance 1998*,
electronic database, Washington, DC, 1998.

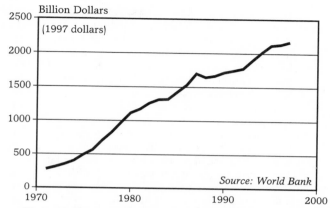

Figure 1: External Debt of Developing Countries, 1971–97

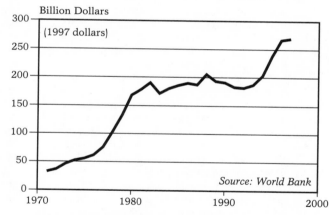

Figure 2: Developing-Country Debt Service, 1971–97

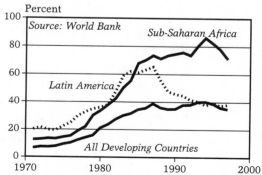

Figure 3: Developing-Country Debt as Share of
Gross National Product, 1971–97

World exports of goods declined 3.8 percent in 1998, falling to $5.4 trillion in value (in 1997 dollars), according to preliminary International Monetary Fund estimates. (See Figure 1.)[1] This was a sharp reversal from the 8.4-percent growth rate recorded the previous year.[2] The decline can be traced largely to lower demand in Japan and other parts of East Asia as a result of the region's economic slump.[3]

Sharply declining commodity prices over the last few years have cut steeply into the export earnings of many countries, particularly those in the developing world. The World Bank estimates that between October 1997 and October 1998, fuel prices fell by 26 percent, agricultural prices by 18 percent, and metals and minerals by 16 percent.[4] The price drops had several causes, including stagnating demand as a result of the economic crisis as well as an oversupply of some commodities. This oversupply was due in part to the flooding of markets by goods made cheap by depreciating currencies in crisis-ridden countries.[5]

Growth in trade has generally outpaced overall economic growth for the past 250 years. An important exception was the period between 1913 and 1950, when two World Wars and the Great Depression brought international commerce nearly to a standstill. But the downturn reversed by 1950.[6] Between 1950 and 1997, exports increased 15-fold, while the world economy expanded sixfold.[7] While exports of goods accounted for only 6 percent of the gross world product in 1950, by 1997 this figure had climbed to 15 percent.[8] (See Figure 2.) In 1998, however, exports dropped to 14 percent of the world economy.[9]

The growing volume of world trade over the last half-century has led to burgeoning international transport. Measured by weight, the amount of merchandise shipped internationally grew 10-fold between 1948 and 1998—to 5,064 million tons.[10] Transporting this cargo requires the equivalent of some 1.6 billion barrels of oil annually—slightly more than used each year in th entire Middle

East.[11] Though far more goods are sent by ship than air, the volume of international air freight has also increased rapidly in recent years, climbing from just 6 million tons in 1970 to 24 million tons in 1997.[12] Air transport is far more energy-intensive than shipping: it takes nearly 50 times as much energy to carry a ton of goods a given distance by air as it does by boat.[13] Yet merchandise sent by ship uses nearly nine times as much energy overall due to the far larger volume.[14]

The composition of world trade by economic sector has shifted substantially during the postwar period. Agricultural products accounted for some 47 percent of all exports of goods in 1950; by 1997, their share had fallen to 11 percent.[15] Manufactured goods, on the other hand, increased from 38 percent of exports in 1950 to 74 percent in 1997.[16] Mining products, including nonferrous metals and fuel, account for most of the remainder. Their share of the total has remained relatively stable.[17]

Recent decades have seen rapid growth in international commerce in commercial services, such as tourism, transportation, and banking. According to the World Trade Organization, world exports of such services grew from $467 billion in 1980 to $1.3 trillion in 1997 (in 1997 dollars)—an average annual rate of some 6 percent.[18] (See Figure 3.) In 1997, services accounted for nearly a fifth of total world trade.[19]

The rapid growth of world trade since 1950 was no accident. Rather, it was the deliberate result of tariff and quota reductions through eight rounds of trade negotiations pursued under the General Agreement on Tariffs and Trade (GATT).[20] Last year was GATT's fiftieth anniversary. (It was transformed into the World Trade Organization in 1993.) In November 1999, trade ministers will gather in the United States, where they are likely to launch a "millennium round" of global trade talks.[21] Reconciling efforts to further free international trade with the growing urgency of preserving the ecological integrity of the planet merits a prominent place on their agenda.

WORLD EXPORTS OF GOODS AND EXPORTS AS SHARE OF GROSS WORLD PRODUCT, 1950–98

YEAR	EXPORTS (trill. 1997 dollars)	SHARE OF GROSS WORLD PRODUCT (percent)
1950	0.4	6
1955	0.5	6
1960	0.7	7
1965	1.0	8
1966	1.0	8
1967	1.1	8
1968	1.2	8
1969	1.4	9
1970	1.5	9
1971	1.6	9
1972	1.7	10
1973	2.0	10
1974	2.0	11
1975	2.0	10
1976	2.2	11
1977	2.3	11
1978	2.4	11
1979	2.6	11
1980	2.6	11
1981	2.6	11
1982	2.5	10
1983	2.4	10
1984	2.7	10
1985	2.8	10
1986	2.8	10
1987	3.0	10
1988	3.2	11
1989	3.5	11
1990	3.7	12
1991	3.8	12
1992	4.0	12
1993	4.2	13
1994	4.6	13
1995	5.0	14
1996	5.2	14
1997	5.6	15
1998 (prel)	5.4	14

SOURCE: IMF Statistics Division, e-mails, 25 January and 4 March 1999.

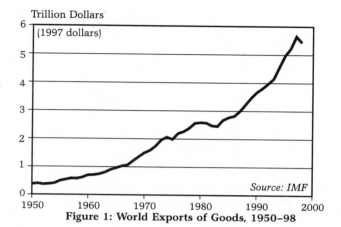

Trillion Dollars

Figure 1: World Exports of Goods, 1950–98

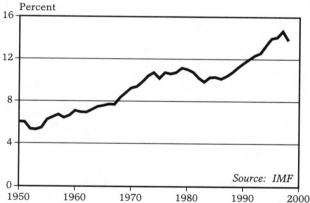

Percent

Figure 2: Exports of Goods as Share of Gross World Product, 1950–98

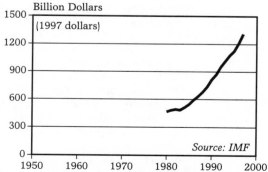

Billion Dollars

Figure 3: World Exports of Commercial Services, 1980–97

World Ad Spending Climbs   Payal Sampat

Worldwide, a record-breaking $413 billion—more than 1 percent of global economic output—was spent on advertising in 1998.[1] (See Figure 1.) Since mid-century, advertising expenditures have swelled ninefold, growing one third faster than the global economy.[2] (All data are in 1997 dollars.) On average, $70 worth of advertisements appeared per person in 1998, almost four times the figure for 1950.[3] (See Figure 2.)

Advertising's power to persuade has made it a primary vehicle to promote consumer spending. Resource-intensive consumption, however, has serious implications for environmental and human health. For example, automobiles, the planet's most heavily marketed product—4 of the world's 10 top-spending advertisers are auto companies—are also among the fastest-growing emitters of carbon, a contributor to human-induced climate change.[4] And of public health concern is the aggressive marketing of cigarettes and junk food worldwide: tobacco giant Philip Morris and fast-food vendors McDonald's and Coca Cola, for instance, are also among the world's top 10 advertisers.[5]

The United States has historically dominated world advertising, absorbing three fourths of ad budgets in 1950 and almost half of the total—some $199 billion—today.[6] In this period, U.S. ad spending grew nearly sixfold.[7] (See Figure 3.) The next three major spenders—Japan, the United Kingdom, and Germany—together accounted for another one fourth of global budgets in 1998.[8]

In recent years, ad expenditures have skyrocketed in the Third World, growing fourfold in developing Asia and 5.6-fold in Latin America in the last 10 years.[9] In 1998, 8 of the top 20 spenders were developing nations, whereas a decade earlier, just 3 were.[10] Brazil leads this group, with $8.7 billion spent on ads in 1998.[11] Colombia, where ad budgets grew 15-fold between 1988 and 1998, spends more on advertising relative to its gross domestic product—2.5 percent in 1995—than any other nation.[12]

Mexico, another fast-emerging ad market, spent $7 billion on ads in 1998, up 22 percent from 1997; India and China each expanded their ad budgets by 12 percent in 1998.[13] This growth kept developing-country ad budgets buoyant in 1998, despite shock waves sent by the global financial crisis. Ad spending plummeted in nations at the epicenter of the crisis, however, falling by 20 percent in Malaysia, by almost 30 percent each in Thailand and Indonesia, and by 42 percent in Russia.[14]

While commercial advertising dates back at least 2,000 years, when it was first recorded in Chinese literature, the scale, diversity, and wide reach of advertising this century is unprecedented.[15] Today the average American adult is exposed to 254 advertisements daily, transmitted through a range of media.[16] More than 40 percent of these are television commercials; another 45 percent are print ads.[17] Like television advertising in its early days—surging 40-fold in the United States between 1950 and 1998—advertising on the Internet is growing rapidly.[18] By one estimate, spending on Internet advertising worldwide is projected to jump 10-fold between 1998 and 2003, to $15 billion.[19]

Social marketing campaigns, although a tiny fraction of global ad budgets, have been successful in many parts of the world in getting people to change their behavior in line with various societal goals. Within the first six months of initiating a child immunization ad campaign in the Philippines, for example, vaccination rates rose by 14 percent.[20] Aggressive anti-smoking campaigns and bans on televised cigarette ads in several industrial countries have helped reduce their per capita cigarette use.[21]

In many parts of the world, advertisers finance commercial media to a considerable extent: in the United States, ads cover more than 60 percent of the cost of periodicals, 70 percent of newspapers, and almost 100 percent of radio and network television costs.[22]

WORLD ADVERTISING EXPENDITURES, 1950–98

YEAR	TOTAL (bill. 1997 dollars)	PER PERSON (1997 dollars)
1950	45	18
1955	70	25
1960	87	29
1965	113	34
1966	120	35
1967	121	35
1968	123	35
1969	128	35
1970	127	34
1971	132	35
1972	137	36
1973	151	38
1974	150	37
1975	145	35
1976	155	37
1977	165	39
1978	185	43
1979	196	45
1980	203	46
1981	201	44
1982	198	43
1983	204	44
1984	215	45
1985	224	46
1986	252	51
1987	285	57
1988	310	61
1989	316	61
1990	328	62
1991	322	60
1992	332	61
1993	329	60
1994	351	63
1995	383	67
1996	394	68
1997	398	68
1998 (prel)	413	70

SOURCE: McCann-Erickson, letter to author, 6 January 1999.

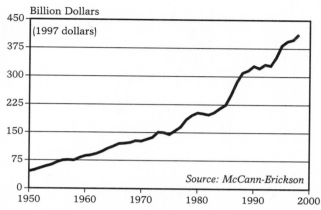

Figure 1: World Advertising Expenditures, 1950–98

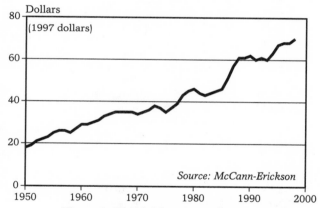

Figure 2: World Advertising Expenditures Per Person, 1950–98

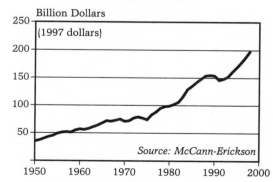

Figure 3: U.S. Advertising Expenditures, 1950–98

U.N. Finances Decline Further   Michael Renner

The approved regular budget for the United Nations amounted to almost $1.3 billion in 1998.[1] In nominal terms, this represents continued growth from past years, but taking inflation into account, budgets have been flat since 1995.[2] (See Figure 1.) Actual expenditures, meanwhile, declined 19 percent (after inflation) during this time.[3]

The regular budget supports headquarters in New York; offices in Geneva, Vienna, and Nairobi; and the operations of five regional commissions. The U.N.'s specialized agencies and other organs, funded separately from the regular budget, had a combined budget of $9.5 billion in 1997 (the most recent year available), a decline in real terms of 6 percent since 1992.[4] (See Figure 2.)

The United Nations has spent the past decade mired in financial crisis. Collectively, its member states have failed to make payments for the budgets they approve.[5] At the end of 1998, they owed $413 million in regular budget payments. Still, this is 29 percent below the record $585 million in 1995.[6] (See Figure 3.)

During the past few years, most members' payment habits actually improved dramatically. During 1998, 117 countries paid their regular budget dues before the end of the year, up from only 75 countries in 1994.[7] A total of 32 member states fully met their 1999 obligations by paying up at the beginning of the year, compared with 22 for 1998.[8] The number of states that owed more than a year's worth of assessments decreased from 75 in 1994 to 49 in 1997, while the number that made no payments at all fell from 39 to 17.[9]

Of 68 states with outstanding arrears in 1998, 53 owed less than $1 million each.[10] Another 13 owed $1–10 million each.[11] Brazil, the second-largest debtor, is $31 million behind in its payments.[12] The single largest contributor, the United States, is also the largest debtor: at $313 million, it accounted for 76 percent of all arrears.[13] Since 1980, the United States has on average paid about 90 percent of the money it owes, compared with an average of 99 percent for all other U.N. members combined.[14]

The United States is now the only U.N. member that withholds legally owed payments for national policy reasons.[15] And it is currently the only permanent member of the Security Council to be in arrears on regular budget dues.[16]

Since the early 1980s, the United States has paid late (in October, for assessments due in January) and has withheld portions of its dues to express dissent on some specific policies and to impose broader reform measures unilaterally.[17] During 1998, Congress provided roughly adequate funding to cover current-year U.S. dues. But a congressional deal to pay off a large portion of arrears unraveled due to controversial abortion politics linked to the arrears plan.[18]

Being the leading deadbeat has not come without cost. In November 1996, the United States lost its seat on a key U.N. budget committee, a decision reaffirmed in November 1998.[19] And a U.S. demand that its share of the regular budget be reduced from 25 to 22 percent, and eventually to 20, was rejected.[20] The United States only narrowly avoided losing its vote in the General Assembly in late 1998, when it made a last-minute payment.[21]

As a consequence primarily of U.S. delinquency, the United Nations now runs out of cash near the end of each summer; for several years it has run negative year-end cash balances. These deficits grew to a record $197 million in 1996.[22]

In past years, the United Nations has been able to cover its operating expenses only by borrowing money from peacekeeping operations—deferring reimbursements due to countries that contribute troops and equipment to these missions. But this is a fast-disappearing option as peacekeeping budgets are shrinking dramatically.[23] In addition to regular budget arrears, members owe about $1.6 billion for specialized agency budgets.[24]

UNITED NATIONS REGULAR BUDGET, 1971–98

YEAR	AMOUNT (mill. 1997 dollars)
1971	598
1972	614
1973	649
1974	768
1975	702
1976	843
1977	792
1978	1,003
1979	924
1980	983
1981	898
1982	1,002
1983	961
1984	1,001
1985	968
1986	1,003
1987	973
1988	974
1989	951
1990	998
1991	1,145
1992	1,124
1993	1,120
1994	1,155
1995	1,225
1996	1,132
1997	1,112
1998	1,255

SOURCES: Global Policy Forum Web site, various pages; U.N. General Assembly, November 1998.

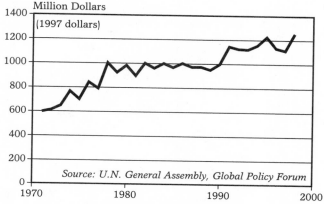

Figure 1: United Nations Regular Budget, 1971–98

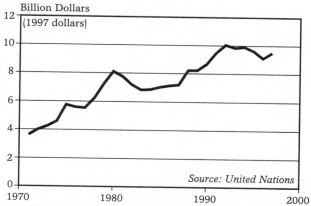

Figure 2: Budgets of U.N. Agencies and Organs, 1971–97

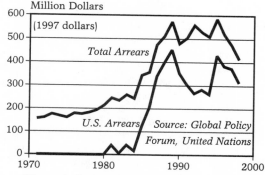

Figure 3: Arrears on Regular U.N. Budget, 1971–98

Weather-Related Losses Hit New High　　Seth Dunn

Economic losses from weather-related natural disasters reached $92 billion in 1998, according to the Germany-based Munich Reinsurance Company.[1] (See Figure 1.) This exceeded by 53 percent the previous annual record of $60 billion, set in 1996, and the inflation-adjusted weather-related damages during the entire decade of the 1980s.[2] As many of the disasters hit poor, uninsured regions, insured losses totaled only $15 billion—still a fourth-highest total.[3] (See Figure 2.) In comparison to the 1960s, during the 1990s the number of natural catastrophes tripled, while economic costs increased ninefold and insured costs, 15-fold.[4]

The human toll of these weather-related disasters was also severe. At least 41,000 lives were lost in storms, heat waves, fires, floods, and drought.[5] In addition, an estimated 300 million people were displaced from their homes by weather-related events.[6]

The remarkably strong and prolonged 1997–98 El Niño, dominated by warm, dry weather, contributed to the record.[7] The United States and Canada endured a powerful ice storm—the strongest in Canadian history—and suffered $2.5 billion in economic losses, $1.1 billion in insured losses, and 23 deaths.[8] Spring and summer heat waves and forest fires in the United States added another 130 deaths and $4.3 billion in damages.[9]

Further loss came with a subsequent and pronounced La Niña phase, which was associated with exceptionally heavy rainfall in Asia.[10] The economically costliest event of 1998 was the extended summer flooding of China's Yangtze River basin, causing $30 billion in economic losses and 3,656 deaths.[11] A tropical cyclone ravaged the Indian province of Gujarat, killing some 10,000 and leaving $1.7 billion in economic losses.[12] India and Bangladesh were both swamped by delayed, severe monsoon flooding, which killed an estimated 4,500 people, displaced 55 million, and left $5 billion in damages.[13]

El Niño and La Niña also influenced an unusually late, active, and destructive hurricane season. Japan was hit by Typhoon Vicki, which killed 18 people and left $1.5 billion in economic losses.[14] Hurricane Georges swept through the United States and several Caribbean nations, delivering some $10 billion in total damages and $3.3 billion in insured losses—the largest of the year—and taking an estimated 4,000 lives.[15] The largest loss of life occurred with Hurricane Mitch, the deadliest Atlantic storm in two centuries, which dumped an average of nearly 65 centimeters of rain on Central America in the space of a week.[16] Mitch killed more than 11,000 people, displaced 3 million, and caused at least $5 billion in economic losses.[17]

Many disasters hit regions made increasingly vulnerable due to human activity. The Yangtze River basin has seen a half-century of rampant clear-cutting of upstream slopes, which buffer against runoff. In September 1998 the Chinese government acknowledged a human hand in the floods' severity, announcing a ban on the logging of old-growth forest in the upper watershed.[18] Central America, one of the world's most deforested regions, is losing 48 hectares of forest cover per hour, increasing the risk of flooding and mudslides.[19] Honduran officials are considering a 10-year logging moratorium.[20]

The upward trend in weather-related disasters has occurred in tandem with a rise in global average surface temperatures, which scientists observe may increase the frequency and intensity of extreme events, including the wind speed of tropical storms.[21] Recent research suggests a potential feedback, as more intense storms roil oceans and cause them to release heat-trapping carbon dioxide into the atmosphere.[22]

Gerhard Berz, a geoscientist with Munich Re, believes continued climate change will almost inevitably yield increasingly extreme natural events and large catastrophic losses.[23] This may make some vulnerable regions uninsurable, particularly low-lying islands and coastal regions in or along the Caribbean, Indian, and Pacific Oceans.[24] Andrew Dlugolecki of the U.N. Environment Programme's insurance initiative is "quite certain that there are some areas which will be unprotectable and may disappear."[25]

ECONOMIC LOSSES FROM WEATHER-RELATED NATURAL DISASTERS WORLDWIDE, TOTAL AND INSURED, 1980–98

YEAR	TOTAL LOSSES (bill. dollars)
1980	2.8
1981	13.2
1982	3.3
1983	9.4
1984	3.4
1985	7.1
1986	9.3
1987	12.9
1988	4.2
1989	12.0
1990	17.9
1991	30.9
1992	40.2
1993	24.2
1994	23.9
1995	39.9
1996	61.1
1997	30.0
1998 (prel)	92.0

YEAR	INSURED LOSSES (bill. dollars)
1980	0.1
1981	0.6
1982	1.5
1983	4.4
1984	1.5
1985	2.8
1986	0.4
1987	5.8
1988	1.0
1989	5.6
1990	11.9
1991	9.2
1992	25.1
1993	5.7
1994	1.9
1995	9.3
1996	9.2
1997	4.5
1998 (prel)	15.0

SOURCES: Munich Re, "Weather-Related Natural Disasters 1998" (9 February 1999); Munich Re database.

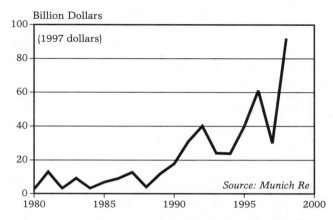

Figure 1: Economic Losses from Weather-Related Natural Disasters Worldwide, 1980–98

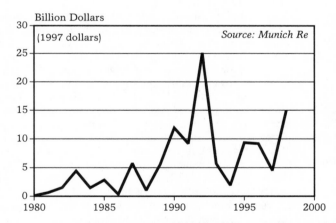

Figure 2: Insured Losses from Weather-Related Disasters Worldwide, 1980–98

Roundwood Production Levels Off

In 1997, according to the U.N. Food and Agriculture Organization, global production of roundwood—the logs that become fuel, lumber, paper, and other wood products—reached 3.36 billion cubic meters.[1] Since 1983, production has exceeded 3 billion cubic meters every year, more than double the amount harvested in the 1950s.[2] (See Figure 1.) The relentless upward trend in production has leveled off since 1990, however, in large part because production in the former Soviet Union plummeted from a peak of 386 million cubic meters in 1990 to just 111 million cubic meters by 1997, due to the economic transition.[3]

About 55 percent of the roundwood cut today is used directly for fuelwood and charcoal, with the other 45 percent becoming "industrial roundwood"—the logs that are cut into lumber and panels for construction purposes or ground into pulp to make paper.[4]

Developing countries produce about 90 percent of wood cut directly for fuel.[5] (See Figure 2.) In 1996, about 47 percent of the world's fuelwood was produced in India, China, Indonesia, Brazil, and Nigeria.[6] Yet these figures understate the importance of wood fuel in industrial countries. In many nations, wood byproducts (such as chips and sawdust) are burned to fuel the lumber and paper mills. These secondary sources add close to 300 million cubic meters of wood to the 173 million consumed directly for fuel in industrial countries.[7] In the United States, for example, while only 18 percent of wood is harvested directly for fuel, when residues are included the proportion used for energy is actually 27 percent.[8]

Five countries produced about 57 percent of the world's industrial roundwood harvest in 1996.[9] The United States, Canada, and Russia have remained among the top five producers for at least 40 years, while China and Brazil joined this group in the 1970s.[10] Together, the top 10 (which includes Sweden, Finland, Malaysia, Germany, and Indonesia) account for about 71 percent of production.[11] While tropical forests receive the most public attention, temperate and boreal forests actually account for 83 percent of the total volume of industrial roundwood produced.[12]

A disproportionate share of the world's industrial roundwood is consumed in industrial nations. (See Figure 3.) In fact, 77 percent of the world's timber harvested for industrial purposes is used by the 22 percent of the world's population who live in these nations.[13] Although developing nations have been increasing their share of consumption in recent decades, they are still well below the levels found elsewhere. Indeed, consumption per person in industrial nations is 12 times higher than in developing ones.[14] Fuelwood is the only wood product that developing nations use more of, and even then their consumption per person is less than twice that in industrial nations, despite the fact that it is the dominant industrial and household energy source in some developing nations.[15]

Production of some wood products has grown more quickly than others in recent decades. Paper now accounts for the largest single share of industrial wood use. Paper production has grown by 189 percent since 1965.[16] Directly or indirectly (through the use of mill residues), paper production accounted for 40 percent of industrial roundwood use in 1993.[17] Sawnwood, the lumber used for construction and so forth, accounted for 29 percent of production in 1995, down from 34 percent in 1965.[18] Sawnwood production increased by only 11 percent since 1965.[19] On the other hand, production of wood panels such as plywood jumped 248 percent in that time, now accounting for 10 percent of production, up from 4 percent in 1965.[20]

Wood products originating in well-managed forests are increasingly available, although still only a small portion of the market. By the end of 1998, nearly 11 million hectares in 27 countries had been certified by the Forest Stewardship Council (FSC, the largest and most credible third-party certifier), double the area of a year earlier.[21] FSC certification can help ensure consumer confidence and improve market access for timber from well-managed forests around the world.

WORLD PRODUCTION OF ROUNDWOOD, 1950–97

YEAR	TOTAL (mill. cubic meters)
1950	1,421
1955	1,496
1960	1,753
1965	2,232
1966	2,289
1967	2,322
1968	2,362
1969	2,401
1970	2,459
1971	2,488
1972	2,503
1973	2,584
1974	2,608
1975	2,575
1976	2,681
1977	2,701
1978	2,784
1979	2,873
1980	2,920
1981	2,920
1982	2,918
1983	3,030
1984	3,140
1985	3,167
1986	3,253
1987	3,342
1988	3,397
1989	3,449
1990	3,447
1991	3,343
1992	3,279
1993	3,277
1994	3,301
1995	3,348
1996	3,358
1997 (prel)	3,359

SOURCE: FAO, *FAOSTAT Statistics Database*, Rome.

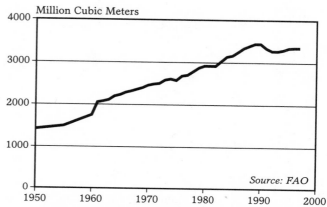

Figure 1: **World Roundwood Production, 1950–97**

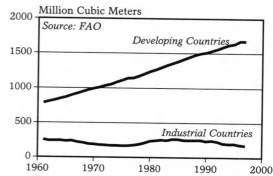

Figure 2: **Fuelwood and Charcoal Production, 1961–97**

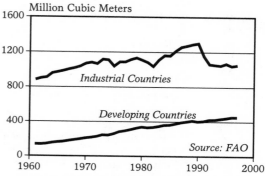

Figure 3: **Industrial Roundwood Production, 1961–97**

Paper Production Inches Up — Ashley T. Mattoon

According to preliminary figures from the U.N. Food and Agriculture Organization (FAO), world production of paper and paperboard rose from approximately 282 million tons in 1996 to 298 million tons in 1997.[1] (See Figure 1.) Since 1950, production has increased more than six times and per capita consumption has leapt from approximately 18 kilograms to 51 kilograms.[2] By 2010, production is projected to reach 396 million tons and per capita use will be nearly 58 kilograms.[3]

The United States, Japan, and China are the world's leading paper producers, accounting for 31, 11, and 9 percent, respectively, of total world production.[4] These three countries are also the world's leading consumers, each using about the same proportion as they produce.[5] Industrial nations use the lion's share of the world's paper—close to 75 percent in 1996—and will continue to do so well into the future.[6] But consumption is growing at a faster rate in developing nations, and by 2010 these countries are expected to use almost 33 percent, up from 15 percent in 1980.[7]

Differences in per capita consumption are even more pronounced. (See Figure 2.) Per capita consumption in industrial countries was roughly 160 kilograms in 1996, compared with 17 kilograms in developing nations.[8] In the United States, the per capita figure is over 330 kilograms per year, while in more than 20 African nations it is less than 1 kilogram per year.[9]

International trade in pulp and paper has increased gradually in recent decades. In the 1960s roughly 16 percent of the world's production of wood pulp and 17 percent of its paper and paperboard production were traded internationally.[10] Today, these figures are 21 and 26 percent.[11] Together these products represent close to 44 percent of the total value of world forest products exports.[12]

Last year was a dramatic one for the paper industry, as consolidation trends accelerated and the industry struggled with weakened Asian markets. Several significant mergers occurred, including that of Sweden's Stora and Finland's Enso—a multibillion-dollar union that displaced International Paper as the world's largest paper and board supplier.[13] Asia has been the fastest-growing market in recent years—increasing by about 10 percent annually.[14] In 1998, however, demand for paper and board in the region was expected to fall by 2–3 percent, the first decline since 1981.[15]

About 40 percent of the world's industrial wood harvest is used to make paper.[16] This virgin wood fiber represents approximately 55 percent of the total fiber inputs for paper.[17] The sources of this wood fiber are old-growth forests, primarily in boreal regions (17 percent); secondary forests (54 percent); and tree plantations (29 percent).[18] North America and Scandinavia have long been the world leaders in wood pulp production, but the role of countries such as Brazil, Chile, Indonesia, and South Africa is expanding with the proliferation of fast-growing plantations.[19]

Recycling has seen a major upsurge in the last two decades, rising from 23 percent of fiber supply in 1970 to 36 percent today.[20] FAO predicts that by 2010, recycled paper will account for over 45 percent of the fiber supply for paper.[21] Although this will reduce demand for wood pulp, consumption will continue to rise about 1 percent a year due to increases in population and per capita consumption.[22]

Nonwood fibers constitute close to 9 percent of the total fiber supply for paper.[23] Two main types are used for paper: agricultural residues from crops such as wheat and rice, and crops grown specifically for pulp, such as kenaf and industrial hemp. Developing nations account for 97 percent of the world's nonwood pulp production and use.[24]

Aside from raw material use, the paper industry has many other environmental impacts. In the United States, for example, the industry ranks third in the release of toxic chemicals (behind the chemical and primary metals sectors).[25] In addition, paper and paperboard account for more than 38 percent of the municipal solid waste generated in the United States, and 30–40 percent in Europe.[26]

WORLD PAPER AND PAPERBOARD PRODUCTION, 1961–97

YEAR	PRODUCTION (mill. tons)	PER PERSON (kilograms)
1961	78	25
1962	81	26
1963	86	27
1964	92	28
1965	98	29
1966	105	31
1967	106	30
1968	114	32
1969	123	34
1970	126	34
1971	128	34
1972	138	36
1973	148	38
1974	150	37
1975	130	32
1976	147	35
1977	152	36
1978	160	37
1979	169	39
1980	170	38
1981	171	38
1982	167	36
1983	177	38
1984	190	40
1985	193	40
1986	203	41
1987	215	43
1988	228	45
1989	233	45
1990	240	46
1991	243	45
1992	245	45
1993	252	46
1994	277	49
1995	282	50
1996	282	49
1997 (prel)	298	51

SOURCE: FAO, *FAOSTAT Statistics Database*, Rome.

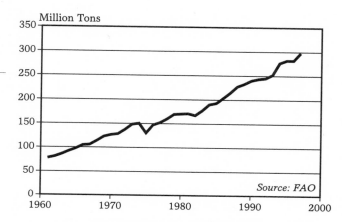

Figure 1: World Paper and Paperboard Production, 1961–97

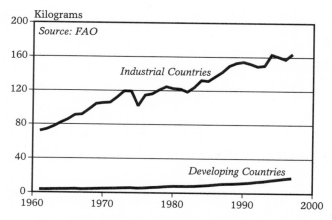

Figure 2: Consumption of Paper and Paperboard Per Person, Industrial and Developing Countries, 1961–97

Transportation Trends

Worldwide passenger car production fell 1.9 percent in 1998, to approximately 38 million.[1] (See Figure 1.) Automobile sales declined 2.3 percent, to 37 million, but pushed the world car fleet up 2.1 percent, to 508 million.[2] (See Figure 2.) The ratio of people to cars stayed flat, at 11.7.[3] (See Figure 3.)

Europe, the world's leading car producer, accounts for 33 percent of global output and 37 percent of its fleet.[4] In Western Europe, carmakers produced 30 percent more than they sold, and increased output 6 percent, with rises of 12 and 10 percent in Germany and France, the region's top producers.[5] In Eastern Europe and the former Soviet Union, carmaking grew 8 percent, increasing 20 and 24 percent in Poland and the Czech Republic, but plummeting 15 percent in Russia.[6]

Asia produced 31 percent of the world's cars and has 17 percent of the global fleet.[7] Asia's automotive overcapacity reached 35 percent prior to the 1998 recession, contributing to an 11-percent production drop in 1998, with output by the two largest producers—Japan and South Korea—falling 9 and 26 percent.[8] China, the region's third-leading carmaker, saw only a 4-percent rise, while output declined 55 percent in Thailand—where sales have fallen 63 percent since 1996.[9]

North America is responsible for 30 percent of global carmaking and 29 percent of the world's autos.[10] Output dropped 1 percent in 1998, with a 5-percent fall in the United States, the world's leading producer, accompanied by gains of 5 and 19 percent in Canada and Mexico.[11] The U.S. carmaking decline masks, however, a growing output of sport-utility vehicles, minivans, and trucks—all of which are classified as light trucks and now account for half of new family vehicle sales.[12]

In Latin America, with 5 percent of global car production and 8 percent of the world car fleet, output declined 17 percent.[13] This was largely due to a 28-percent decline in Brazil, the region's top manufacturer.[14] In Argentina, the second leading carmaker, output increased by only a tenth of 1 percent.[15]

Overcapacity, the desire to minimize production costs, and an increasingly global market continued to push large automakers toward mergers.[16] Daimler-Benz and Chrysler completed a $40-billion consolidation that resulted in DaimlerChrysler, the world's fifth largest carmaker.[17] This led to the dissolution of the American Automobile Manufacturers Association, the main lobbying arm of General Motors, Ford, and Chrysler.[18]

Several industrial nations renewed efforts to improve fuel economy in 1998. The Japanese government announced it would submit in 1999 plans to require improved fuel efficiency.[19] European officials and carmakers, meanwhile, agreed to cut carbon emissions 25 percent by 2008.[20] While European operations of Ford and General Motors supported this plan, their North American branches have resisted attempts to increase the far worse automotive efficiency on that continent. This reflects the higher gasoline prices, greater awareness of global warming, and preference for small cars in Europe, as well as the heavy profits enjoyed by U.S. carmakers selling inefficient sport-utility vehicles, minivans, and pickup trucks.[21] In November, however, Californian regulators voted to require that these vehicles meet the more stringent emissions standards of cars.[22]

Scientific developments added to the accelerating push to move beyond the internal combustion engine. One U.S. government study found that catalytic converters, which are designed to cut smog, also increase emissions of nitrous oxide—a greenhouse gas 300 times as potent as carbon dioxide.[23] Two others revealed that diesel engines, while more efficient than gasoline ones, release more particulates—aggravating asthma and possibly contributing to cancer.[24]

The race to market hybrid-electric cars—which combine a gasoline engine and an electric motor—continued to speed up. Toyota announced that its model—which is twice as efficient as the average U.S. car—will be offered in North America and Europe by 2000.[25] Honda revealed plans to launch its version—with two-and-a-half times the average U.S. fuel economy—nationwide in the United States in late 1999.[26]

WORLD AUTOMOBILE PRODUCTION AND FLEET, 1950–98

YEAR	PRODUCTION (million)	FLEET
1950	8	53
1955	11	73
1960	13	98
1965	19	140
1966	19	148
1967	19	158
1968	22	170
1969	23	181
1970	23	194
1971	26	207
1972	28	220
1973	30	236
1974	26	249
1975	25	260
1976	29	269
1977	31	285
1978	31	297
1979	31	308
1980	29	320
1981	28	331
1982	27	340
1983	30	352
1984	31	365
1985	32	374
1986	33	386
1987	33	394
1988	34	413
1989	36	424
1990	36	445
1991	35	456
1992	35	470
1993	34	469
1994	36	480
1995	36	477
1996	37	486
1997	38	498
1998 (prel)	38	508

SOURCES: American Automobile Manufacturers Association; Standard & Poor's DRI.

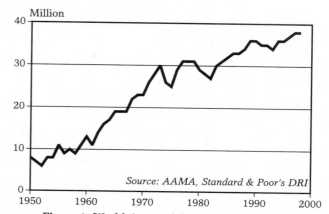

Figure 1: World Automobile Production, 1950–98

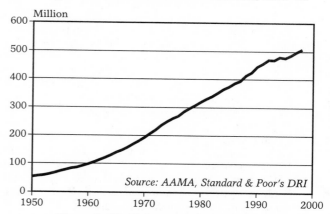

Figure 2: World Automobile Fleet, 1950–98

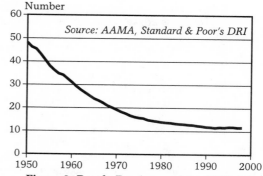

Figure 3: People Per Automobile, 1950–98

Bicycle Production Down Again
Gary Gardner

Global bicycle output dropped to 94 million units in 1997, the last year for which global data are available.[1] (See Figure 1.) The 5-percent decrease came on top of a 7-percent decline in 1996, when excess inventories stalled production.[2] The sagging output of recent years is attributed to increased protectionist measures in some countries and to growing interest in motorized transportation in others.

China saw output drop by 21 percent in 1997 because of its shift away from state-owned factories, the ongoing replacement of bicycles with motorbikes, and protectionist tariffs against Chinese exports.[3] Yet China remains the world leader, with 30 million bicycles produced in 1997, well ahead of Taiwan, which built 11.9 million. Just behind Taiwan is India, with 11.5 million units, making Asia home to well over half of world production. The European Union, the United States, and Japan claimed the next 23 percent of global production, with the balance split among dozens of others. Of the major producers, only Taiwan saw substantial increase in output in 1997; production there surged some 61 percent.[4]

On a brighter note, production of electric bicycles, a relatively new technology, jumped 16 percent in 1998—reaching 328,000 units globally.[5] (See Figure 2.) Japan is the leading producer, with more than a quarter of global sales, but interest is growing rapidly in Europe as well. Electric bikes use a small rechargeable motor to help riders pedal, thereby reducing rider effort and increasing the bicycle's attractiveness as a commuter vehicle. The biggest drawback is price: at $500–2,000 per bike, the market is limited.[6] Improvements in battery technology, however, could lower prices and expand the role of the bicycle in city transport substantially.[7]

Asia leads the world in bicycle use as well as production, with cycling in some cities accounting for more than half of all trips.[8] But in many Asian cities bicycle use has diminished with increased use of motorbikes and cars and in response to official catering to autos. Several cities in Asia, including Jakarta, Shanghai, and Ho Chi Minh City, have restricted bicycle use in an effort to reduce congestion resulting from an influx of private automobiles.[9] In 1998, Beijing also introduced some restrictions on cycling in a busy shopping district.[10]

Many European cities have long made room for bicycles in urban transportation, which is partly why bikes account for a respectable 20–30 percent of trips in some North European cities.[11] Copenhagen's City Bike program, which provides bicycles for cross-town use for a refundable fee, has more than doubled the fleet size, to 2,300 bikes, between 1995 and 1997.[12] In the Netherlands, some companies reduce parking and health care expenses by encouraging employees to cycle to work. For each kilometer cycled, companies contribute to a fund that underwrites climate-friendly investments in developing countries.[13] And in France, several cities banned cars for a day in September 1998 to promote alternative transport modes.

In the United States, cycling accounts for less than 1 percent of all trips, in part because of the low-density, sprawling development.[14] But public commitment to bicycle use has recently risen sharply. Federal transportation funding in 1991 added greatly to funding for cycling, resulting in a large increase in bikeways and in other measures designed to facilitate cycling.[15] The result has been a 29-percent rise in the tiny share of urban trips made by bicycle between 1991 and 1997, from 0.7 to 0.9 percent.[16] Yet funding for automobile infrastructure was far more generous, and the car's share of trips climbed from 87 to 89 percent.[17]

The growing interest in the automobile, often at the expense of bicycles, is not sustainable in much of the world. If every nation had cars at the U.S. rate, the world fleet would be 5 billion—10 times larger than today. With many cities already reeling from the pollution and congestion created by cars, such a figure is incomprehensible. As this reality dawns on urban planners, alternative forms of transportation are likely to get a more favorable review.

WORLD BICYCLE PRODUCTION, 1950–97

YEAR	PRODUCTION (million)
1950	11
1955	15
1960	20
1965	21
1966	22
1967	23
1968	24
1969	25
1970	36
1971	39
1972	46
1973	52
1974	52
1975	43
1976	47
1977	49
1978	51
1979	54
1980	62
1981	65
1982	69
1983	74
1984	76
1985	79
1986	84
1987	98
1988	105
1989	95
1990	94
1991	100
1992	103
1993	109
1994	107
1995	107
1996	99
1997 (prel)	94

SOURCES: United Nations, *The Growth of World Industry 1969 Edition*, Vol. I, *Yearbooks of Industrial Statistics 1979* and *1989 Editions,* and *Industrial Commodity Statistics Yearbook 1996; Interbike Directory,* various years.

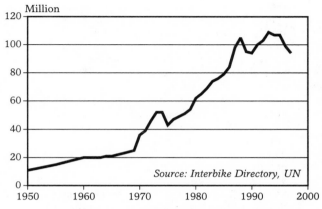

Source: Interbike Directory, UN

Figure 1: World Bicycle Production, 1950–97

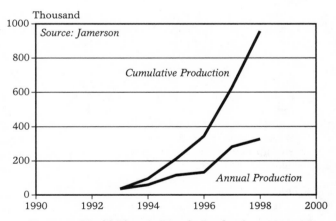

Source: Jamerson

Cumulative Production

Annual Production

Figure 2: World Electric Bicycle Production, 1993–98

World Air Traffic Soaring
Lisa Mastny

World air travel increased 2 percent in 1998, reaching an all-time high of 2.6 trillion passenger-kilometers (a measure of passenger traffic that takes into account distance flown).[1] (See Figure 1.) This was a slowdown from the 6-percent growth of the previous year, and can be traced largely to a decline in the traffic of Asian carriers.[2] For similar reasons, air cargo transport fell slightly in 1998, to 99 billion ton-kilometers.[3] (See Figure 2.)

But as the global economy picks up, the worldwide demand for aviation services is expected to take off again. Air travel has grown nearly 100-fold since 1950, at an average annual rate of some 9 percent. This trend will continue well into the next century, with world air traffic expected to increase another 10-fold by 2050—mostly in developing countries.[4]

To accommodate this growth, aircraft manufacturers predict delivery of some 600 new planes a year for the next 15 years.[5] By 2016, the world air fleet is expected to consist of some 23,000 planes, twice as many as in 1996.[6]

The International Air Transport Association attributes the continued growth in air traffic to low inflation and strong economic conditions in regions where the demand for air travel is highest, including North America and Europe.[7] Moreover, the cost of flying has fallen significantly in recent years, increasing the demand for air travel. In the past two decades alone, the number of passengers flying worldwide has more than doubled—from 679 million in 1978 to almost 1.5 billion in 1998.[8]

The rising demand for air travel comes at an increasingly high cost, however—particularly to the natural environment. Aviation accounts for at least 5 percent of annual world oil consumption and about 12 percent of the refined petroleum products used by the entire transport industry.[9] It is the most polluting form of transport per kilometer traveled, especially for short distances.[10]

Aircraft emissions play a significant—and growing—role in global climate change. They release carbon dioxide (CO_2) and nitrous oxides (NO_x), and they create vaporous jet plumes—all of which contribute to climate change.[11] On average, a single DC 10-30 flight from Los Angeles to Tokyo emits 266 tons of CO_2—or 1.8 tons per passenger if 150 people are on board.[12] In total, worldwide civilian air transport consumed 176 million tons of kerosene in 1990, releasing 550 million tons of CO_2 and more than 3 million tons of NO_x.[13]

At present, aviation accounts for only about 3 percent of human-caused CO_2 emissions and 2 percent of global NO_x emissions, but these could rise to as high as 11 percent and 6 percent respectively by 2050.[14] By then, aircraft emissions as a whole could be responsible for as much as 17 percent of total climate change, up from only 4 percent in 1990.[15]

Concerns about aviation's environmental impact, and the desire to cut costs, have led manufacturers such as Boeing/McDonnell Douglas and General Electric to invest in more fuel-efficient, low-emissions aircraft engines in recent decades.[16] Aircraft energy efficiency has improved at an average annual rate of 3–4 percent, and the world's airlines now use only about half as much fuel to carry a passenger a set distance as they did in the mid-1970s.[17]

Air travel is growing so rapidly, however, that overall emissions output is still likely to double by 2010—suggesting the need for other means of lessening the environmental impact.[18] One solution at Swiss airports has been to levy an extra tax of as high as 40 percent of the usual landing fees on aircraft that do not meet set NO_x emissions standards.[19] And in 1997 Denmark introduced an environmental charge of about $15 per trip on domestic flights, which has encouraged heavier rail travel and led to a 12–57 percent decline in air passengers, depending on the route.[20]

Somehow avoiding delays at airports—during which planes remain idle on the ground or circle in the air longer than necessary—could further reduce aviation's environmental impact, cutting emissions by as much as 12 percent.[21] Finally, the promotion of high-speed rail as an alternative for the inefficient, short-haul air routes of less than 500 miles could lead to significant reductions in the demand for air travel.[22]

WORLD AIR TRAVEL AND FREIGHT, 1950–98

YEAR	PEOPLE (bill. passenger-kilometers)	FREIGHT (bill. ton-kilometers)
1950	28	0.7
1955	61	1.2
1960	109	2.0
1965	198	4.8
1966	229	5.7
1967	273	6.5
1968	309	8.2
1969	351	9.8
1970	460	12.0
1971	494	13.2
1972	560	15.0
1973	618	17.5
1974	656	19.0
1975	697	19.4
1976	764	21.5
1977	818	23.6
1978	936	25.9
1979	1,060	28.0
1980	1,089	29.4
1981	1,119	30.9
1982	1,142	31.5
1983	1,190	35.1
1984	1,278	39.7
1985	1,367	39.8
1986	1,452	43.2
1987	1,589	48.3
1988	1,705	53.3
1989	1,774	57.1
1990	1,894	58.8
1991	1,845	58.6
1992	1,929	62.6
1993	1,949	68.4
1994	2,100	77.2
1995	2,248	83.1
1996	2,426	89.2
1997	2,570	99.8
1998 (prel)	2,621	99.0

SOURCE: International Civil Aviation Organization, Montreal.

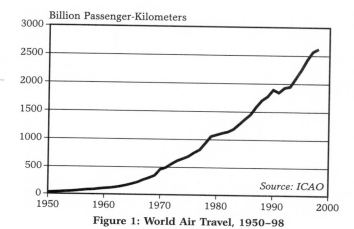

Billion Passenger-Kilometers

Source: ICAO

Figure 1: World Air Travel, 1950–98

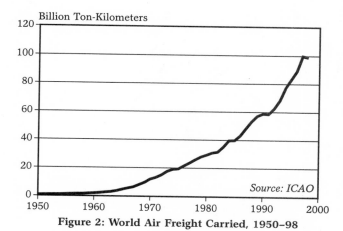

Billion Ton-Kilometers

Source: ICAO

Figure 2: World Air Freight Carried, 1950–98

Communications
Trends

Satellite Launches Get a Boost   Molly O'Meara

A total of 140 satellites were launched in 1998, up from 133 in 1997.[1] (See Figure 1.) This figure includes satellites for communications, Earth observation, science research, navigation, and military surveillance.[2]

Rivalry between the Soviet Union and the United States spurred the first satellite launches in the late 1950s.[3] Europe and Japan joined the space race in the 1960s, followed by China, India, and Indonesia in the 1970s.[4] Yet Soviet launches continued to dominate the world total through the 1980s until they plummeted at the end of the cold war.[5] (See Figure 2.)

Today, satellite launches are booming again, led by private companies.[6] Until the 1990s, commercial satellites accounted for no more than 10 percent of annual launches.[7] But between 1994 and 1998, this figure rocketed from 20 percent to more than 70 percent as commercial communications satellites eclipsed government satellites used for military and other purposes.[8] (See Figure 3.)

Historically, communications satellites have been "geostationary"—that is, they orbit some 36,000 kilometers above the equator, where their velocity matches that of the Earth so that the satellite always "sees" the same one fourth of the planet.[9] When a telephone call is routed through one of these satellites, conversation is delayed by a fraction of a second as the signals travel to and from the satellite. These satellites are better suited to radio, television, or data transmission. In 1998, a private venture, WorldSpace, launched the first of three such satellites intended to provide digital radio service to underserved populations in Africa, Asia, and Latin America.[10]

A new generation of communications satellites that travels closer to the Earth's surface to eliminate the time lag in transmission has the potential to expand telephone and Internet access.[11] Iridium, a constellation of 66 such satellites completed in 1998, is the first global satellite phone network.[12] At $3,000 per handset and $1–3 per minute, its use is limited to wealthy business travelers.[13] But more modest 1-satellite systems, which allow Internet links for just two hours a day, are already being used to transmit medical information in Africa.[14]

Another class of satellites, for Earth observation, is also finding new uses and commercial interest. While these satellites accounted for just 4 percent of total launches in 1998, their data are being used for a growing number of scientific endeavors.[15] In July 1998, the European Union, Russia, and three private companies announced plans for a global service that would provide data and maps for nature preservation, regional planning, forestry, agriculture, and emergency management.[16] The first Earth Observing System satellite, to be launched in 1999, will detect and track on a global scale humans' changes to the land, ocean, and atmosphere.[17] The resulting long-term data set is expected to revolutionize global climate models.[18]

Earth observation satellites are particularly well suited to aid in disaster alerts. Satellite surveillance of the oceans helps scientists predict El Niño weather patterns.[19] The U.N. Food and Agriculture Organization uses satellite images to assess crops and provide early warning of famine conditions in Africa.[20] University of Hawaii researchers have used satellite data to detect impending volcanic eruptions and monitor forest fires.[21] And satellite images of the Great Barrier Reef obtained from U.S. satellites will be sent over the Internet to Australian authorities to provide early warning of coral bleaching.[22]

The latest satellite boom brings both opportunities and dangers. For instance, as an industry once dominated by a few governments opens up to private enterprise, satellite data may increasingly be used to irresponsibly exploit forests, mineral reserves, and other natural resources. Also, several incidents in 1998 underscored the high-risk nature of the space business. Among the high-profile launch failures that year was the loss of 12 communications satellites on a single rocket.[23]

SATELLITE LAUNCHES
WORLDWIDE, 1957–98

YEAR	TOTAL (number)
1957	2
1960	16
1965	143
1966	121
1967	140
1968	123
1969	109
1970	121
1971	136
1972	120
1973	116
1974	113
1975	141
1976	149
1977	129
1978	146
1979	113
1980	119
1981	148
1982	131
1983	147
1984	150
1985	151
1986	129
1987	126
1988	128
1989	123
1990	150
1991	128
1992	114
1993	95
1994	107
1995	92
1996	82
1997	133
1998 (prel)	140

SOURCES: Jos Heyman, *Spacecraft Tables 1957–1997* (Riverton, Australia: Tiros Space Information, 1998); Jos Heyman, e-mail to author, 4 January 1999.

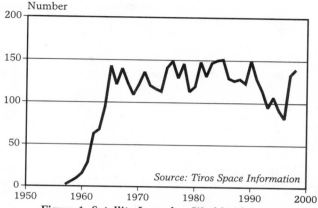

Figure 1: Satellite Launches Worldwide, 1957–98

Figure 2: Satellite Launches in the United States, Russia, and Rest of World, 1957–98

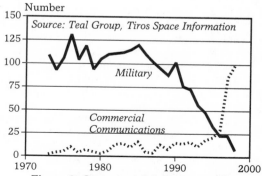

Figure 3: Commercial Communication and Military Satellite Launches, 1972–98

The number of lines that link telephones directly to the global phone network increased 5 percent, to 781 million, in 1997, the latest year for which data are available.[1] (This figure does not include cellular telephones.) (See Figure 1.) The fixed-line network has expanded steadily at 4–7 percent a year for the past four decades.[2]

Most people in industrial nations take the benefits of telephone access for granted. Phones connect far-flung family members, link businesses to customers, and help save lives in emergencies.[3] In 1997, the growing importance of information technology to human development led the United Nations to commit countries to the goal of access to basic communication services for all.[4]

Yet disparities in telephone access remain stark. Just 23 industrial countries account for 62 percent of all phone lines, even though they are home to less than 15 percent of the world's people.[5] Only 16 percent of homes in the developing world have a phone, whereas the household average is more than 90 percent in high-income nations, yielding a ratio of 40–70 phones per 100 people.[6] Variations within countries are often just as great, with urbanites better connected than rural people. For example, the region around Johannesburg and Pretoria has 22 phone lines per 100 people, more than 10 times the number in South Africa's most rural province.[7]

In the last decade, the pace of phone penetration has picked up. The number of phone connections per 100 people in developing countries rose from one to two between 1975 and 1985, but jumped to six by 1997.[8] Most of the gains have occurred in parts of Latin America and East Asia, however, and the gap between telephone-poor countries and telephone-rich ones has actually widened.[9]

Policy changes now under way may narrow this gap. From Asia to Africa, governments in the 1990s have been dismantling state-run phone monopolies and opening their markets to competition.[10] Since 1996, Côte d'Ivoire, Ghana, and South Africa have sold parts of their phone networks to private companies, which must expand service substan-

tially to fulfill their contracts.[11] Similar policies have succeeded in Mexico and Argentina, which were among the first Latin American countries to privatize in the 1990s.[12]

Technological change is also expanding the network.[13] As the Internet explodes in size, transmission of data is expected to surpass voice calls within the next few years.[14] The systems that are being built to meet this demand allow phone service to be provided in new ways—for instance, bundled together with cable television.[15] The cost of installing a new line can be defrayed by payments for both telephone and another service.[16]

Cellular phones, which use radio waves rather than an installed line, are another boost to the network.[17] Subscribers increased 48 percent in 1997, to 214 million.[18] (See Figure 2.) The distribution of cell phones is even more skewed than that of the fixed-line network: some 84 percent are in industrial countries.[19] But while these are a supplemental means of communication in well-wired nations, they are often substitutes for a conventional line in developing countries.

Wireless technology is particularly well suited to remote locales, as it is usually quicker and cheaper to set up radio antennae for cellular systems than to string wire from poles or bury it underground. Yak caravans in the mountains of Laos and Burma now use cell phones to find the best route to market during the rainy season.[20] In Bangladesh, the world's largest wireless pay phone project allows villagers to purchase cellular phones on a lease program and then sell calls to their neighbors.[21] Farmers use the phone to check on the price of crops in Dhaka to avoid being cheated by intermediaries.[22]

Elsewhere, cell phones have aided activists. Native Americans have used them to enlist the support of widely scattered tribes in demonstrations against nuclear disposal on tribal land.[23] And when students and businessmen wielding cellular phones flooded the streets of Bangkok to protest Thailand's military government in May 1993, the local press called it *mob mue thue*, "the cellular phone revolution."[24]

TELEPHONE LINES AND CELLULAR PHONE SUBSCRIBERS WORLDWIDE, 1960–97

YEAR	TELEPHONE LINES	CELLULAR PHONE SUBSCRIBERS
		(million)
1960	89	–
1965	115	–
1970	156	–
1975	229	–
1976	244	–
1977	259	–
1978	276	–
1979	294	–
1980	311	–
1981	339	–
1982	354	–
1983	370	–
1984	388	–
1985	407	0.7
1986	426	1.4
1987	446	2.5
1988	469	4.3
1989	493	7.3
1990	519	11.2
1991	545	16.2
1992	573	23.2
1993	606	34.2
1994	646	55.3
1995	692	88.8
1996	741	144.2
1997 (prel)	781	213.8

SOURCES: ITU, *World Telecommunication Indicators on Diskette* (1996); ITU, *Challenges to the Network* (September 1997); ITU "Telecommunications Industry at a Glance," December 1998.

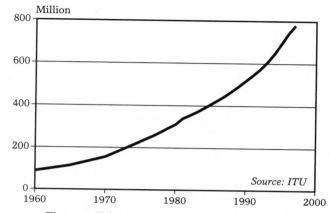

Figure 1: Telephone Lines Worldwide, 1960–97

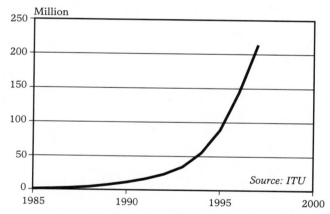

Figure 2: Cellular Mobile Telephone Subscribers Worldwide, 1985–97

Internet Continues Rapid Expansion   Payal Sampat

In 1998, some 43 million host computers wired an estimated 147 million people to the Internet.[1] (See Figure 1.) Since 1995, the Internet has grown roughly 50 percent each year, after 15 years of more than doubling in size annually.[2] Today 1 in every 40 people on the planet has access to this global electronic network.[3]

The United States, where the military first developed the Internet in the late 1960s, still leads the overall tally.[4] It is home to more than half of all Internet users—some 76 million people—although its share has fallen from 61 percent in 1997.[5] Japan, with almost 10 million users, comes a distant second, followed by the United Kingdom and Germany, with 8 million and 7 million people online.[6]

The Internet has primarily been used in wealthy nations for most of its decade-long public existence (see Figure 2), and even today, 9 out of 10 users live in the industrial world.[7] On a per capita basis, this disparity is even more stark—whereas 1 in 4 Australians or Swedes is online, India has just 1 Internet user per 2,070 people; the ratio in Africa (excluding South Africa) is 1 to 4,000.[8]

Yet the Internet has made rapid inroads in some parts of the developing world in recent years. China has the largest online population in this group, with 1.6 million users—twice as many as in 1997.[9] Analysts predict this figure will multiply severalfold in the next few years as China expands its Internet capacity and lowers access fees.[10] By 2002, China may have more Internet users than car owners.[11]

Latin America wired itself faster than any other region in 1998, almost doubling its per capita host count.[12] (See Figure 3.) Much of this growth was driven by Mexico and Argentina, where the host computer counts tripled.[13] Brazil, home to almost one fourth of Latin America's 4.5 million Internet users, is still the regional leader.[14]

Africa's online population inched past 1 million in 1998; nearly 85 percent of users there live in South Africa.[15] A few nations outstripped the continent's sluggish 20-percent growth rate in 1998: Namibia, for instance, quadrupled its host computer count,

while Nigeria's grew almost eightfold.[16] Reportedly 47 of 54 African capital cities now have some Internet access, but most have a user base of fewer than 2,000 people.[17]

In recent years, the Internet has become far more multilingual: an estimated 71 million people use the World Wide Web in languages other than English.[18] Spanish and German are the most popular, with 14 million users each.[19]

Why are so many people going online? The Internet is a fast and cost-effective way to communicate: it costs 35 times less to send the same data from Accra, Ghana, to Amsterdam by e-mail than by fax.[20] It is also a vast information store, although the quality of the contents is often questionable. At 12.5 trillion bytes, the Web's holdings are comparable to those of the U.S. Library of Congress—which houses some 20 trillion bytes of print records—while occupying a tiny fraction of the physical space.[21] And every day, 1.5 million new pages are added to the Web's existing collection, estimated at 829 million pages in August 1998.[22]

The Internet increasingly serves as a global marketplace. In 1998, almost $33 billion was spent online, nearly three times as much as in 1997.[23] Analysts predict Internet commerce will expand another 13-fold by 2002.[24]

When harnessed for sustainable development, the Internet has proved a potent tool. Environmental activists in the United States, Australia, and Canada, for instance, use it to get information about toxic emissions from local industries.[25] Similar online databases are being put together in Mexico, South Africa, and the Czech Republic.[26]

Medical students and doctors in Bangladesh, where up-to-date medical information is scarce, now receive the latest international health journals online through the efforts of a local nonprofit called Medinet.[27] In remote Niger, Touareg tribesfolk sell their crafts worldwide in a Canadian-funded "cyber-mall."[28] And some 6,000 students in various parts of Africa get reading materials, join discussion groups, and submit assignments over the Internet, as part of the University of South Africa's "Students On-line" program.[29]

INTERNET HOST COMPUTERS, 1981–98

YEAR	HOST COMPUTERS (number)
1981	213
1982	235
1983	562
1984	1,024
1985	2,308
1986	5,089
1987	28,174
1988	80,000
1989	159,000
1990	376,000
1991	727,000
1992	1,313,000
1993	2,217,000
1994	5,846,000
1995	14,352,000
1996	21,819,000
1997	29,670,000
1998	43,230,000

SOURCE: Network Wizards, "Internet Domain Surveys, 1981–1999," < http://www.nw.com >, updated January 1999.

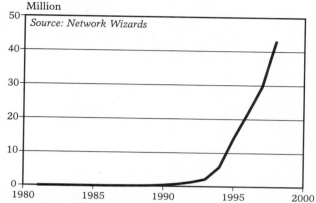

Figure 1: Internet Host Computers, 1981–98

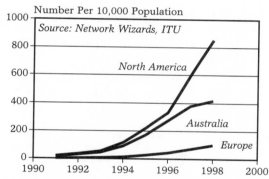

Figure 2: Internet Host Computers in North America, Australia, and Europe, 1991–98

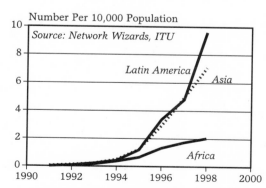

Figure 3: Internet Host Computers in Latin America, Asia, and Africa, 1991–98

Social
Trends

World Population Swells   Brian Halweil

The world's population swelled to 5.92 billion in 1998, adding 78 million people—slightly fewer than the previous year, but still the equivalent of another Germany.[1] (See Figures 1 and 2.) Nearly all these people were added in developing nations, already home to 4.85 billion people—more than 80 percent of the world.[2]

As human numbers soar toward 6 billion, population growth is slowing. Worldwide, the annual growth rate peaked at 2.2 percent in 1963, and has since slowed to 1.4 percent—the lowest level since a great famine in China sharply dropped the rate in 1960.[3] (See Figure 3.) Nevertheless, although the annual addition is less than the peak of 87 million reached in 1989, it is still more than twice as many people as were added annually at mid-century.[4]

Global data obscure wide regional discrepancies. In Europe and Japan, population is stable or declining, as the number of children each woman bears has fallen well below 2.1—the "replacement fertility" level necessary to offset deaths.[5] In dozens of African nations, in contrast, the average woman bears more than 6 children, leading to annual grow rates of 3 percent and a population doubling time of just over two decades.[6]

Worldwide, two out of five people live in nations where fertility has dropped to replacement level.[7] These nations will grow for some time before stabilizing, however, due to the disproportionately large share of the population entering their childbearing years—the result of past high fertility levels.[8] Included in this group are China and the United States, the first and third largest nations, home to a combined 26 percent of the world.[9]

The latest U.N. projections put world population in 2050 at 8.9 billion, a substantial reduction from the previous estimate of 9.4 billion, due to increased estimates of the lives AIDS will take in Africa and lowered estimates of birth rates in Nigeria.[10] According to these latest projections, the global population will hit 6 billion on 12 October 1999.[11]

Population growth accelerated following World War II, when public health measures, such as child vaccination programs, and improved nutrition reduced mortality levels throughout the world.[12] Since a concurrent reduction in fertility did not accompany these health gains, the population growth rate—the result of birth rate minus death rate—surged to unprecedented levels.[13]

In the 1960s and 1970s, however, birth rates began to decline almost everywhere as urbanization, increased female literacy, and contraception prevailed.[14] In South Korea, for example, fertility levels dropped from 7 children per woman in 1970 to 1.7 children today.[15] And in Bangladesh, the average woman today bears 3.3 children—compared with 7 children as recently as 1975.[16] Africa has seen less substantial decreases.[17]

Decreases in fertility can result from a variety of factors, especially educational and economic opportunities for women, which alter values and aspirations while expanding lifestyle options. In every nation where data are available, the more schooling a woman has, the fewer children she chooses to bear.[18]

Family planning programs—which provide contraception and reproductive health services—afford couples increased control over their reproductive destinies. In Egypt, the decline of children per woman from 5.2 in 1980 to 3.3 in 1997 coincided with a doubling of contraceptive use by married couples.[19]

To mark the fifth anniversary of the 1994 International Conference on Population and Development in Cairo, the U.N. General Assembly will meet in 1999 to evaluate progress on the plan of action agreed to there, which established—among other things—the goal of closing the gender gap in educational, economic, and other spheres.[20] Cairo also called for universal access to family planning by 2015, with industrial nations committing to bear one third of the cost.[21]

Unfortunately, support for international family planning programs has slumped in recent years as industrial nations have reneged on their promises.[22] Most recently, the U.S. Congress cut all U.S. funding for the U.N. Population Fund—the principal provider of global population assistance.[23]

WORLD POPULATION, TOTAL AND
ANNUAL ADDITION, 1950–98

YEAR	TOTAL (billion)	ANNUAL ADDITION (million)
1950	2.556	38
1955	2.780	53
1960	3.039	41
1965	3.345	70
1966	3.416	70
1967	3.485	72
1968	3.557	75
1969	3.631	75
1970	3.707	77
1971	3.784	77
1972	3.861	76
1973	3.937	76
1974	4.013	73
1975	4.086	72
1976	4.158	72
1977	4.231	72
1978	4.303	75
1979	4.378	76
1980	4.454	76
1981	4.530	80
1982	4.610	80
1983	4.690	79
1984	4.770	81
1985	4.851	82
1986	4.933	86
1987	5.018	86
1988	5.105	86
1989	5.190	87
1990	5.277	82
1991	5.359	82
1992	5.442	81
1993	5.523	80
1994	5.603	80
1995	5.682	79
1996	5.761	80
1997	5.840	78
1998 (prel)	5.919	78

SOURCE: U.S. Bureau of the Census, *International Data Base*, electronic database, Suitland, MD, updated 30 November 1998.

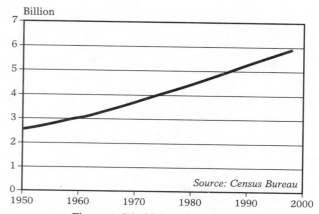

Figure 1: World Population, 1950–98

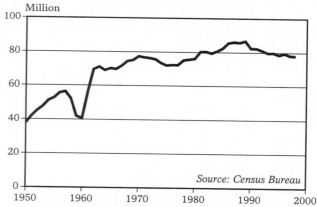

Figure 2: Annual Addition to World Population, 1950–98

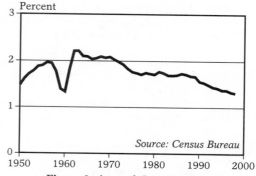

Figure 3: Annual Growth Rate of World Population, 1950–98

Life Expectancy Extends to New High Brian Halweil

Global life expectancy crept to a new high of 66.0 years in 1998, meaning that the average person born then will die in the year 2064.[1] (See Figure 1.) Each year since mid-century, global average life expectancy at birth has increased. A person born today will live 20 years—43 percent—longer than a person born in 1950.[2] Nonetheless, the increase of just 0.2 years over 1997 continues the recent slowdown in gains, as humans approach possible biological limits to life extension.[3]

Though this upward trend prevails for most nations, global data mask wide regional disparities. Also, there is evidence that as national life spans are beginning to converge, internal disparities among population groups are widening.[4]

While life spans in industrial nations have extended nine years since 1950, developing nations have added 24 years (nearly 60 percent)—demonstrating the rapid pace of early gains in life expectancy. Life expectancy in the industrial world stands at 75 years, compared with 64 years in poorer nations.[5] (See Figure 2.)

Growth in the world's poorer regions has been unequal as well. Since 1950—when the average person born in both Asia and Africa lived roughly 40 years—Asians have added some 25 years to their lives, while Africans have added just over 10.[6] And in many African nations raked by hunger, disease, and social turmoil, people on average can expect to live only 45 years.[7]

The average life expectancy in Asia is 65 years, though life spans in this massive region range from 80 in Japan—the world leader for longevity—to 61 in India and just over 40 in Afghanistan.[8]

In general, life expectancy correlates with income level, though some poorer nations—such as Cuba, where life span tops that of the United States—defy this pattern.[9] Moreover, life expectancy does not always correlate with health. Those with long life spans may simultaneously suffer from chronic conditions that reduce the quality of life, as in North America, where life span averages 75 years while half the populace is clinically overweight.[10]

Worldwide, women outlive men by nearly 5 years.[11] This phenomenon holds across nations, and explanations range from the anti-aging properties of estrogens to the evolutionary importance of female longevity for raising offspring.[12]

The extension of life span is largely attributed to improvements in water quality, diet, and sanitation services, as well as in access to health care and education.[13] Modern public health measures, such as immunization, have drastically reduced infant and child mortality, which can greatly distort life expectancy.[14] For instance, the phenomenal 30-year gain in Chinese life span since 1950 was largely due to a slashing of infant mortality from 195 deaths per 1,000 births to 38 deaths.[15] Beyond these factors, medical advances, such as disease-fighting drugs and treatments, have reduced the burden of infectious diseases and postponed the fatality of chronic illness.

Nevertheless, several nations have bucked the historic trend in reduced mortality. The collapse of health care systems following the 1990 breakup of the Soviet Union has driven life expectancy in Russia below 1950 levels.[16] AIDS has trimmed two decades from life spans in the hardest hit African nations.[17] (See Figure 3). Resistance to antibiotics, the emergence of new diseases, and numerous unexpected crises—such as lethal arsenic levels found recently in large portions of Bangladesh's groundwater—threaten to stall future gains worldwide.[18]

As life spans extend, the human population is aging. The share of the world's population over the age of 60 will more than double—from 9 percent to 21 percent—by 2050, with this share reaching 40 percent in several industrial nations.[19] The changing age structure may strain resources in many of the world's poorer nations confronted with growing elderly populations even as they struggle with massive populations of youth, while in industrial nations, a declining work force relative to a swelling retired population may precipitate a pension crisis.[20]

WORLD AVERAGE LIFE EXPECTANCY, 1950–98

YEAR	LIFE EXPECTANCY (years)
1950	46.5
1955	49.6
1960	52.4
1965	56.0
1966	56.4
1967	56.8
1968	57.2
1969	57.6
1970	58.0
1971	58.3
1972	58.7
1973	59.0
1974	59.4
1975	59.8
1976	60.1
1977	60.4
1978	60.7
1979	61.0
1980	61.4
1981	61.7
1982	62.0
1983	62.4
1984	62.7
1985	63.1
1986	63.3
1987	63.5
1988	63.7
1989	63.9
1990	64.1
1991	64.4
1992	64.6
1993	64.9
1994	65.1
1995	65.4
1996	65.6
1997	65.8
1998 (prel)	66.0

SOURCE: United Nations, *World Population Prospects: The 1998 Revision* (New York: December 1998).

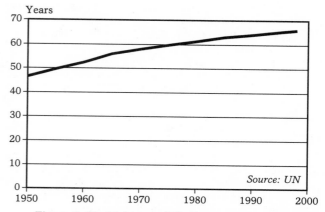

Figure 1: World Average Life Expectancy, 1950–98

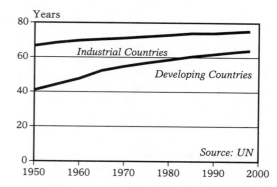

Figure 2: Life Expectancy in Industrial and Developing Countries, 1950–98

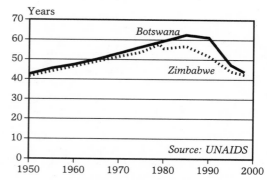

Figure 3: Life Expectancy in Zimbabwe and Botswana, 1950–98

Since the beginning of the AIDS epidemic in the early 1980s, the number of people infected with HIV—the virus that causes AIDS—has climbed to nearly 50 million.[1] (See Figure 1.) Nearly 6 million people were infected in 1998, and 2.5 million people died from AIDS.[2] (Each year since 1980, there has been a record number of new infections and AIDS deaths.)[3] Cumulative AIDS deaths stand at over 14 million (see Figure 2), and given that 34 million people currently have HIV, the number is expected to keep climbing.[4]

Spurred by poverty and lack of widespread prevention efforts, the virus continues to rake across sub-Saharan Africa—where 7 of 10 global HIV infections and 9 of 10 global AIDS deaths occur.[5] In a dozen African nations, at least 10 percent of the adult population carries the virus.[6] And in the hardest hit nations, such as Zimbabwe and Botswana, one of four adults is infected and average life expectancy has been cut to pre-1950 levels.[7] Barring a medical miracle, future AIDS deaths in these nations will bring population growth to a halt.[8]

Though infection rates in Asia remain low, the total number of people infected expands rapidly.[9] Thriving commercial sex industries and growing drug use fuel the epidemics in many nations, including Myanmar, Viet Nam, and Cambodia—Asia's most infected country, where 2.4 percent of adults test positive.[10]

In India and China, the virus continues to spread beyond high-risk urban populations, such as prostitutes and intravenous drug users, to the general population, where it is more difficult and costlier to contain.[11] India is home to an estimated 4 million infected individuals—more than any other nation.[12] And in early 1998, the Chinese Ministry of Health noted that HIV has now been reported in every province.[13]

Since 1994, the number living with HIV in Eastern Europe has surged nearly sevenfold.[14] General collapse of economic and health care systems—on top of soaring drug use—fuels the epidemic in the former Soviet bloc.[15]

With the help of antiviral drugs that prolong the onset of the disease, AIDS deaths have declined in the United States and Western Europe, though new HIV infections rise steadily as risky behaviors persist.[16] In the United States, 64 percent of new infections occur in blacks and Hispanics, who account for just 24 percent of the population.[17]

In contrast to other epidemics in human history, which predominantly affected the young and the elderly, AIDS strikes hardest at the economically active population—the cornerstone of a nation's development.[18] At the household level, as wage-earners die off, families struggle to find alternate sources of income.[19] The millions of children orphaned by AIDS attest to the profound effects on those not directly infected.[20]

Health care systems—along with national budgets—are being overwhelmed by the epidemic.[21] The cost of providing antiviral treatment to all infected individuals in Malawi, Mozambique, Uganda, and Tanzania dwarfs those countries' gross national products.[22]

The 12th Annual World AIDS Conference in July 1998 shone the spotlight on "the have-nots of the epidemic": the vast majority of those infected who are unable to enjoy the benefits of pharmaceutical treatment.[23] Participants cast HIV spread as a symptom of socioeconomic discrimination—stemming from inadequate access to health care and education—and urged a renewed response to the pandemic as a development issue.[24] For example, in Latin America—as in other regions—infection rates and spread are most severe in impoverished nations, such as Bolivia and Honduras.[25]

At the same time, infection rates have slowed or declined in several nations that adopted strong prevention programs, including Senegal, Tanzania, Thailand, and Uganda.[26] Successful efforts have included free distribution of condoms, needle exchange programs, sex education at all levels of schooling, and support from religious and civil leaders.[27]

And in roughly half of the developing world, the epidemic still has not spread widely in the general population or even high-risk groups, providing an opportunity for governments that realize that prevention now costs a fraction of treatment later.[28]

CUMULATIVE HIV INFECTIONS AND AIDS DEATHS WORLDWIDE, 1980–98

YEAR	HIV INFECTIONS (million)
1980	0.1
1981	0.3
1982	0.6
1983	1.1
1984	1.9
1985	2.8
1986	3.9
1987	5.3
1988	6.9
1989	8.9
1990	11.5
1991	14.4
1992	17.8
1993	21.6
1994	25.9
1995	30.6
1996	35.8
1997	41.4
1998 (prel)	47.2

YEAR	AIDS DEATHS (million)
1980	0.0
1981	0.0
1982	0.0
1983	0.0
1984	0.1
1985	0.2
1986	0.3
1987	0.5
1988	0.8
1989	1.3
1990	1.8
1991	2.5
1992	3.4
1993	4.6
1994	5.9
1995	7.6
1996	9.5
1997	11.8
1998 (prel)	14.3

SOURCE: Neff Walker, UNAIDS, Geneva, e-mail to author, 11 December 1998.

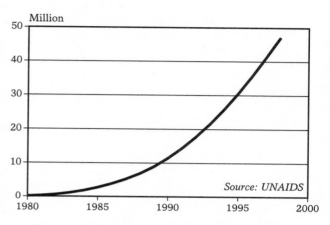

Figure 1: Estimates of Cumulative HIV Infections Worldwide, 1980–98

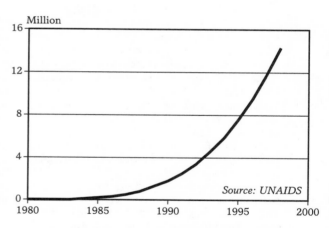

Figure 2: Estimates of Cumulative AIDS Deaths Worldwide, 1980–98

Polio Nearly Eradicated   Lisa Mastny

Reported polio cases worldwide dropped to just over 3,600 in 1998—the lowest case-count on record, according to the World Health Organization (WHO).[1] (See Figure 1.) Overall, reported polio cases have declined a remarkable 90 percent since 1988, when WHO launched its global vaccination campaign to eradicate wild polio virus by 2000.[2] The actual number of polio cases worldwide is thought to be about 10 times the figure reported.[3]

For much of this century, and particularly prior to discovery of the polio vaccine in the 1950s, poliomyelitis was considered one of the most deadly and crippling diseases of our time. Today some 10–20 million people worldwide—including many children in the developing world—remain paralyzed from the virus, unable to walk or breathe without the help of leg braces or devices such as the "iron lung."[4]

Polio is one of very few diseases that can actually be wiped out because the virus is transmitted only through person-to-person contact. Moreover, there exists a highly effective and cheap (about $1 per dose, or $3 per child) oral vaccine, which usually provides lifelong immunity to polio.[5]

The disappearance of polio is the result of strong social and political commitment by national governments and the international community. By 1998, 118 countries had conducted at least one round of National Immunization Days, during which all children under five are given two doses of oral polio vaccine one month apart—compared with only 21 countries a decade earlier.[6] (See Figure 2.) In 1997 alone, 450 million children—about two thirds of the world's under-five population—were immunized during campaigns in 80 countries.[7]

Widespread child immunization has significantly altered the geography of polio transmission. Whereas 10 years ago polio circulated freely on all continents except Australia, in 1998 a record 188 countries reported zero cases—up from only 94 a decade earlier.[8] (See Figure 3.) The only region with official "polio-free" status is the Americas, but the Western Pacific, Eastern and Western Europe, and parts of Northern and Southern Africa are also now considered polio-free following eradication efforts.[9]

Despite the worldwide decline, 27 countries—primarily in South Asia and Africa—were still reporting polio transmission as of late 1998.[10] Obstacles to eradication include a lack of basic health infrastructure for vaccine distribution and the crippling effects of civil war. In countries such as Angola and Somalia, internal conflict has meant the suspension of immunization programs, severance of vaccine supply lines, and destruction of health services.[11] In some war-torn countries, however—including Sudan and Sri Lanka—immunization efforts have actually led to momentary cease-fires, as weapons are laid down to allow health workers to reach and vaccinate young children.[12]

As the target year for polio eradication nears, WHO and its partners in the global effort are worried that support for the project may wane before the biggest hurdles are overcome. Funds are still lacking for the Initiative's challenging final phase—door-to-door "mopping-up" campaigns to immunize children in high-risk districts. Although 50–80 percent of the costs are covered by the countries themselves, WHO estimates that an extra $370 million in international support will be needed before 2001.[13]

If all goes well, the world will achieve official "polio-free" status at the earliest by 2005, and global child immunization will end after another five years.[14] From that point on, countries will begin to realize the tremendous benefits of no longer having to immunize infants or to treat or rehabilitate people affected by polio, saving an estimated $1.5 billion per year.[15] Western Europe alone will save about $200 million annually, and the United States will save about $230 million.[16]

In addition to financial savings, successful polio eradication will leave behind a legacy of effective international health cooperation, as well as a global disease prevention network that can be used to combat other common childhood killers—including measles, tetanus, tuberculosis, whooping cough, and diphtheria.

REPORTED POLIO CASES WORLDWIDE, 1975–98

YEAR	TOTAL
1975	49,293
1976	44,390
1977	40,832
1978	47,950
1979	48,107
1980	52,552
1981	66,052
1982	51,900
1983	40,219
1984	35,345
1985	38,637
1986	33,038
1987	39,866
1988	35,251
1989	26,207
1990	23,484
1991	13,508
1992	14,777
1993	10,487
1994	8,641
1995	7,035
1996	4,074
1997 (prel)	5,186
1998 (prel)	3,624

SOURCE: World Health Organization, February 1999.

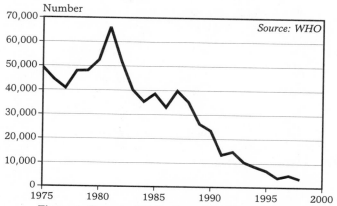

Figure 1: Reported Polio Cases Worldwide, 1975–98

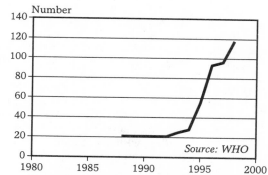

Figure 2: Countries That Have Conducted National Immunization Days, 1988–98

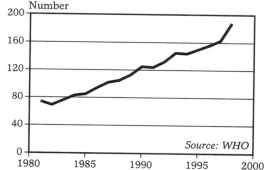

Figure 3: Countries Reporting Zero Polio Cases, 1981–98

Refugee Numbers Drop Again — Michael Renner

As of January 1998, 22.4 million people qualified for and received refugee assistance, according to the U.N. High Commissioner for Refugees (UNHCR).[1] (See Figure 1.) This is the third consecutive year in which the official refugee numbers declined. They fell by less than 2 percent between January 1997 and January 1998, but are now down 19 percent from the January 1995 peak of 27.4 million.[2]

Out of the 22.4 million total population "of concern" to UNHCR, just under 12 million people were recognized refugees, about 1 million asylum seekers, 3.5 million recent returnees who continue to need assistance, and about 6 million internally displaced persons and "others of concern."[3]

In 1997, Afghanistan continued to be by far the most important country of origin: more than 2.6 million Afghans have found asylum in Iran, Pakistan, India, and Western Europe.[4] Iraq, Somalia, Burundi, and Bosnia-Herzegovina each have generated refugee populations of more than a half-million people.[5]

Asian countries provided asylum to the largest number of refugees receiving UNHCR assistance—7.5 million.[6] (See Figure 2.) Africa was a close second with 7.4 million, followed by Europe (6.1 million).[7] Iran carried the heaviest burden, with about 2 million refugees in its territory, followed by Rwanda (1.6 million), Bosnia-Herzegovina (1.3 million), and Pakistan (1.2 million).[8] The far richer United States and Germany hosted 1.2 million and 1.1 million refugees.[9]

The UNHCR figures do not cover everyone uprooted and in need of assistance. First of all, they do not include an estimated 3.2 million Palestinians who are cared for by the U.N. Relief and Works Agency for Palestine Refugees in the Near East (UNRWA).[10]

In addition, there are perhaps as many as 30 million internally displaced persons, their plight distinguished from that of international refugees only by the fact that they did not (and often were not able to) cross a border.[11] Thus they are not protected under international refugee law and may receive assistance only with the consent of their own governments. Although UNHCR's involvement with the internally displaced has increased substantially in recent years, its assistance extends only to about 4.5 million of them.[12]

Finally, there are people in "refugee-like situations." Typically, they live in conditions similar to those of refugees, but do not meet the narrow official definition. Estimates of their numbers are rough, but the U.S. Committee for Refugees believes there were at least 3.9 million at the end of 1997.[13]

All in all, there may be some 56 million refugees and internally displaced persons.[14]

During 1997, an estimated 900,000 refugees—less than half as many as in 1996—repatriated either with UNHCR's help or on their own.[15] The largest repatriations took place in Rwanda (220,000), Bosnia-Herzegovina (109,000), and Burundi (89,000).[16] Other significant return flows occurred in Afghanistan, Sudan, Angola, Somalia, and Congo, but ongoing or renewed armed conflict in these countries makes it unclear whether returnees will remain safe.[17]

Many richer nations have tightened their legal provisions in recent years, leading to concern by refugee assistance groups that the principle of asylum is being eroded.[18] From 1988 to 1997, 6 million asylum applications were submitted in 22 western countries and 4 East European nations.[19] During the same period, only 605,000 asylum-seekers were recognized under the 1951 U.N. Refugee Convention; another 413,000 were granted humanitarian status.[20] Several tens of thousands of people worldwide were returned forcibly or expelled during 1997.[21]

Although they close the doors on asylum seekers with increasing frequency, industrial countries still account for 18 of the top 20 donors that provided $1.1 billion in 1997 to UNHCR, UNRWA, and the International Organization for Migration.[22] In absolute terms, the United States provided the most aid ($353 million), but in per capita terms Norway was dominant.[23] Overall, however, donor governments have chronically failed to provide adequate support for refugees. UNHCR, UNRWA, the Red Cross, and others face ongoing funding shortfalls.

REFUGEES RECEIVING U.N. ASSISTANCE, 1961–98[1]

YEAR	TOTAL (million)
1961	1.4
1962	1.3
1963	1.3
1964	1.3
1965	1.5
1966	1.6
1967	1.8
1968	2.0
1969	2.2
1970	2.3
1971	2.5
1972	2.5
1973	2.4
1974	2.4
1975	2.4
1976	2.6
1977	2.8
1978	3.3
1979	4.6
1980	5.7
1981	8.2
1982	9.8
1983	10.4
1984	10.9
1985	10.5
1986	11.6
1987	12.4
1988	13.3
1989	14.8
1990	14.9
1991	17.2
1992	17.0
1993	19.0
1994	23.0
1995	27.4
1996	26.1
1997	22.7
1998 (prel)	22.4

[1]All data are as of January 1 of the year indicated.
SOURCE: United Nations High Commissioner for Refugees, various data series.

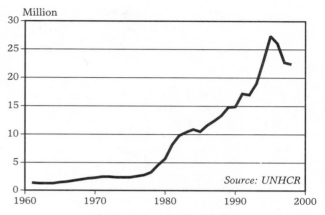

Figure 1: Refugees Receiving U.N. Assistance, 1961–98

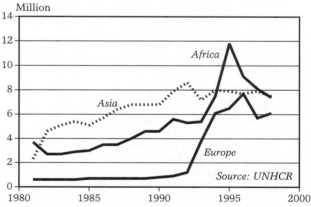

Figure 2: Refugees Receiving U.N. Assistance in Asia, Africa, and Europe, 1981–98

Cigarette Production Falls

Lester R. Brown

The world produced 5.61 trillion cigarettes in 1998, down from 5.64 trillion in 1997.[1] (See Figure 1.) This second straight annual decline dropped production by more than 1 percent from the historical high of 5.68 trillion cigarettes in 1996.[2]

Cigarette production per person in 1998 fell 2 percent from the preceding year, continuing a decade-long trend.[3] (See Figure 2.) After peaking in 1990 at 1,027 cigarettes per person, production has fallen to 948 per person, a drop of nearly 8 percent or 1 percent annually.[4]

Total production has fallen in the last few years in both China and the United States, the two biggest manufacturers. In China, overproduction and the buildup of cigarette stocks led to a government reduction of production quotas. Since peaking in 1995 at 1.74 trillion cigarettes, production there has dropped to 1.68 trillion, a decline of more than 3 percent.[5]

In the United States, where both smoking and cigarette exports are falling, production dropped from 758 million in 1996 to 716 million in 1998, a decline of nearly 6 percent.[6] The number of cigarettes smoked per person has fallen from 2,940 in 1981 to 1,739 in 1998—a drop of 41 percent.[7] (See Figure 3.)

In Japan, the third largest consumer, cigarette smoking is also declining. It dropped by 2 percent in 1998 in response to greater awareness of the links between cigarette smoking and health and to a tax increase imposed in 1997.[8] Future tax hikes are expected to reinforce the declining consumption trend.

The fall in U.S. consumption is expected to continue as cigarette prices rise in response to an agreement by the tobacco industry to reimburse state governments for Medicare costs of treating smoking-related illnesses in recent decades. The industry agreed in 1998 to pay state governments $251 billion—nearly $1,000 for every American.[9] This payment, to be spread out over the next 25 years, is forcing cigarette prices upward. Between January 1998 and January 1999, the cost of a pack of cigarettes went up by roughly half.[10] Further price hikes will be needed to cover the reimbursement to the states.

In addition to state lawsuits to cover costs, the Department of Justice has assembled a task force to file a lawsuit to recover federal Medicare costs associated with smoking. Early indications are that it will seek from $250–500 billion in compensation from the industry.[11]

Six other national governments—those of Bolivia, Guatemala, the Marshall Islands, Nicaragua, Panama, and Venezuela—have now filed lawsuits against the U.S. tobacco industry in U.S. courts that are also designed to recover the costs of treating smoking-related illnesses.[12] And Brazil has announced plans to file suit to recover $51 billion in health care expenditures.[13]

Awareness of the disease and death toll of cigarette smoking is rising. Smoking has been identified as the known or probable cause of at least two dozen diseases or groups of diseases. Prominent among these are cardiovascular disease, including both heart attacks and strokes; several forms of cancer, most notably lung cancer; and various respiratory illnesses, including emphysema, bronchitis, and pneumonia.[14]

An estimated 400,000 Americans die each year from smoking-related causes—more than eight times as many as die in automobile accidents.[15] Worldwide, the World Health Organization (WHO) projects that the number of smoking-related deaths will increase from an estimated 3 million to 10 million over the next generation as smoking spreads in developing countries.[16] Smoking fatalities of 3 million rival those from AIDS, at 2.5 million and growing.[17]

Some 35 years have passed since the first U.S. Surgeon General's *Report on Smoking and Health* was published, which put the issue of smoking firmly on the public agenda.[18] With the United States leading the way, the world appears to be crossing a threshold on smoking. In early 1999, WHO announced that it would seek a worldwide ban on tobacco advertising and was considering seeking a similar prohibition on smoking in public.[19]

WORLD CIGARETTE PRODUCTION, 1950–98

YEAR	TOTAL (billion)	PER PERSON (number)
1950	1,686	660
1955	1,921	691
1960	2,150	707
1965	2,564	766
1966	2,678	784
1967	2,689	772
1968	2,790	785
1969	2,924	805
1970	3,112	840
1971	3,165	836
1972	3,295	853
1973	3,481	884
1974	3,590	895
1975	3,742	916
1976	3,852	926
1977	4,019	950
1978	4,072	946
1979	4,214	962
1980	4,388	985
1981	4,541	1002
1982	4,550	987
1983	4,547	969
1984	4,689	983
1985	4,855	1,001
1986	4,987	1,011
1987	5,128	1,022
1988	5,250	1,026
1989	5,258	1,013
1990	5,419	1,027
1991	5,351	998
1992	5,363	985
1993	5,300	960
1994	5,478	978
1995	5,599	985
1996	5,681	986
1997	5,643	966
1998 (prel)	5,609	948

SOURCE: USDA, FAS, *World Cigarette Database*, electronic Database, February 1999; data for 1950–58 are estimates based on U.S. data.

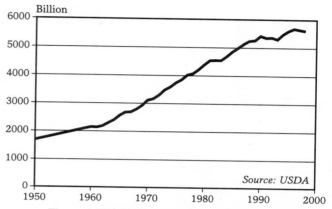

Figure 1: World Cigarette Production, 1950–98

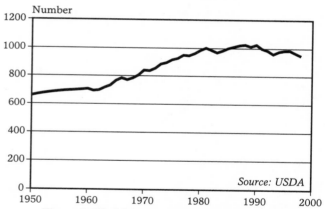

Figure 2: World Cigarette Production Per Person, 1950–98

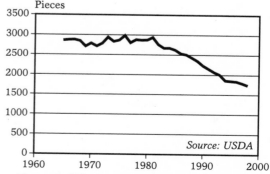

Figure 2: U.S. Cigarette Consumption, 1965–98

Military Trends

Wars Increase Once Again

Michael Renner

The number of wars worldwide rose to 31 in 1998, up from 25 in 1997, according to AKUF, a study group at the University of Hamburg.[1] (See Figure 1.) This was an increase of 24 percent—the first since 1992.[2] In addition, 18 armed conflicts took place during 1998 that were below the definitional threshold of war, compared with 21 such conflicts in 1997.[3]

Due to definitional and methodological reasons, other analysts report somewhat different numbers. The Conflict Data Project at the University of Uppsala, Sweden, puts the number of armed conflicts for 1997 (the most recent year they report) at 33—of which 21 were "major armed conflicts" and 12 "minor."[4] (See Figure 2.) And Project Ploughshares in Waterloo, Canada, reports 37 armed conflicts for 1997.[5]

Of the total of 49 wars and armed conflicts active in 1998, as identified by AKUF, 26 had their origin during the 1990s, and another 8 during the 1980s. But some conflicts are far more protracted: 8 started during the 1970s, 5 during the 1960s, and 1 goes back to the late 1940s.[6]

With just one exception—the fighting in Serbia's Kosovo province—all armed conflicts are now taking place in developing countries.[7] According to the Uppsala Conflict Data Project, Africa and Asia have by far the highest number—14 each in 1997. Africa is the only region where armed conflicts have been on the upswing in recent years.[8] (See Figure 3.)

The Uppsala team reports 103 armed conflicts in 69 different locations during 1989–97. Of these, 45 percent were minor conflicts and 55 percent major ones.[9] The vast majority—97 of the 103—took place exclusively within the boundaries of a single country. The remaining 6 involved wars between opposing states; of these, just one—between India and Pakistan—remained active in 1997.[10]

The fact that almost all contemporary violent conflicts are being waged on the territory of a single state does not mean that there is no international dimension. The Uppsala team identified 9 cases of intrastate conflict in which foreign interventions occurred.[11] Moreover, in many cases there are a variety of connections among internal wars within a region. For example, the civil wars in Rwanda and Burundi mutually influenced each other to some degree, and the Rwandan genocide of 1994 had a powerful spillover effect on the former Zaire, including the overthrow of the Mobutu dictatorship and a new insurrection against the Kabila regime that has drawn six neighboring countries into the fray.[12]

Among the costliest ongoing wars, in terms of human lives lost, are those in Afghanistan, Algeria, Sri Lanka, and Sudan.[13]

The analysts at the Universities of Hamburg and Uppsala and those at Project Ploughshares include in their tallies only conflicts that involve government forces among the protagonists, at least on one side. Increasingly, however, fighting involves opposing warlords, ethnic militias, criminal organizations, and others that do not have the trappings of sovereignty and whose fighters do not wear a state's uniforms and badges.

Researchers with the PIOOM Foundation in Leiden, Netherlands, use far broader criteria in order to capture these nonstate conflicts in their statistics.[14] It is not surprising, then, that they report far higher numbers. PIOOM data suggest that while high-intensity conflicts—major wars—have indeed declined in recent years, low-intensity conflicts and violent political conflicts have sharply increased in number—from 84 in 1993 to 144 in 1997.[15]

At least part of this increase is explained by improved monitoring and data gathering, as well as by greater disaggregation—counting conflicts rather than conflict locations. (In some countries, such as India, several local conflicts are going on at the same time and PIOOM now counts these separately instead of simply recording India as a single conflict location.)[16]

Although the PIOOM data are far from definitive—as the project itself acknowledges—they point to the need to devote greater resources to monitoring the many cases of low-intensity conflicts and near-conflict situations. Without such early conflict warning, it will be exceedingly difficult to make conflict prevention more successful.

ARMED CONFLICTS, 1950–98

YEAR	CONFLICTS (number)
1950	12
1955	14
1960	10
1965	27
1966	28
1967	26
1968	26
1969	30
1970	30
1971	30
1972	29
1973	29
1974	29
1975	34
1976	33
1977	35
1978	36
1979	37
1980	36
1981	37
1982	39
1983	39
1984	40
1985	40
1986	42
1987	43
1988	44
1989	42
1990	48
1991	50
1992	51
1993	45
1994	41
1995	37
1996	28
1997	25
1998	31

SOURCE: Arbeitsgemeinschaft Kriegsurachenforschung, Institute for Political Science, University of Hamburg.

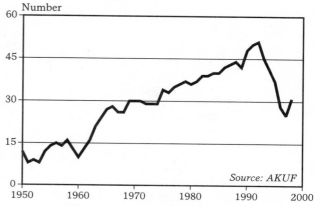

Figure 1: Armed Conflicts, 1950–98

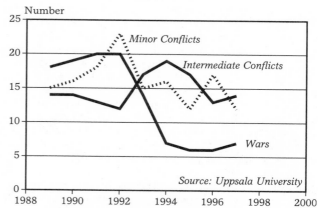

Figure 2: Armed Conflict Trends, 1989–97

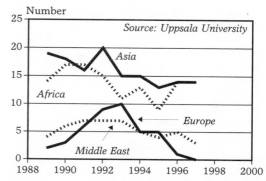

Figure 3: Armed Conflict Trends by Region, 1989–97

U.N. Peacekeeping Expenditures Drop More Michael Renner

Projected expenditures for U.N. peacekeeping stood at $852 million for the period July 1998 to June 1999, down from $992 million a year earlier.[1] (See Figure 1.) This is a 14-percent reduction, and a decline of 76 percent from the peak in 1995 (after inflation). The number of soldiers, military observers, and civilian police in the service of peacekeeping missions stood at 14,398 at the end of October 1998, down from almost 80,000 in 1994.[2] (See Figure 2.)

Last year marked the fiftieth anniversary of U.N. peacekeeping. Only 13 operations were established during the first 40 years, compared with 36 in the past decade alone.[3] More than 750,000 persons from 110 countries have served in all U.N. peacekeeping missions.[4] Of the 49 missions to date, 17 were dispatched to countries in Africa, 9 each to Europe and the Middle East, 8 to Central America and the Caribbean, and 7 to Asia.[5]

During 1998, a total of 17 missions were active; 12 of them came into existence during the 1990s, 2 in the 1970s, 1 in the 1960s, and 2 date back to the very origins of peacekeeping in 1948 and 1949—one in the Mideast; the other in Kashmir.[6] The U.N. Security Council approved two new missions during 1998, one in the Central African Republic (taking over from a regional peacekeeping force) and a small observer mission in Sierra Leone.[7] In the last few years, however, Council members (and the United States in particular) have on the whole shown a strong aversion to getting involved in several conflicts, preferring inaction or contracting the task out to ad hoc "coalitions of the willing."[8]

A number of existing missions have been reduced in size during the last few years—primarily because the Security Council is reluctant to commit resources and personnel.[9] In 1999, the presence in Angola was terminated, amid indications that full-scale war will return, and a mission in Macedonia ended when China vetoed its extension.[10]

Most of the remaining missions now resemble more closely the limited peacekeeping model of the cold war years (focused on monitoring ceasefires and troop withdrawals, and creating buffer zones) than the more complex and ambitious operations of the early 1990s (that involved such tasks as the disarmament and demobilization of former combatants, electoral assistance, and monitoring of human rights compliance).[11]

At the end of 1998, the largest missions were those in Lebanon (with about 4,500 personnel) and Bosnia (close to 2,000); five other missions (in Cyprus, on the Golan Heights, at the Iraq-Kuwait border, in Angola, and in the Central African Republic) each deployed about 1,000 peacekeepers.[12]

As of 31 December 1998, U.N. member states owed a total of $1.6 billion for peacekeeping operations, or roughly two years' worth of operations.[13] (See Figure 3.) The United States remained by far the largest debtor, with $976 million in unpaid dues—61 percent of the total.[14]

In some conflicts, U.N. operations have been deployed alongside non-U.N. forces, and in others the "coalitions of the willing"—dispatched by regional organizations or composed of ad hoc coalitions of states—have entirely replaced the United Nations.[15] This has raised questions about in whose interest these forces are acting and whether they can be held accountable.

By far the largest non-U.N. operation remains SFOR, the NATO-led force in Bosnia. It deploys about 33,000 soldiers and cost an estimated $4 billion in 1998.[16] Others include the Multinational Force and Observers (MFO) in the Sinai (started in 1982; annual cost $51 million), the Peace Monitoring Group BELISI in Bougainville (1998; $24 million), and the Military Observer Mission MOMEP at the Ecuador-Peru border (1995; $15 million).[17] Russia runs four peacekeeping operations in conflict-ridden former Soviet republics, and the Organization for Security and Co-operation in Europe maintains 12 observer missions, primarily in Eastern Europe.[18] Altogether, at least 29 non-U.N. observer, peacekeeping, and peace enforcement missions were active in 1997.[19]

U.N. PEACEKEEPING EXPENDITURES, 1986–98

YEAR	EXPENDITURE (mill. 1997 dollars)
1986	335
1987	323
1988	345
1989	789
1990	552
1991	561
1992	1,971
1993	3,324
1994	3,547
1995	3,490
1996 (Jan.–June)	754
1996*	1,324
1997*	992
1998*	852

*July to June of following year.
SOURCES: U.N. Department of Peacekeeping Operations; Office of the Spokesman for the U.N. Secretary-General.

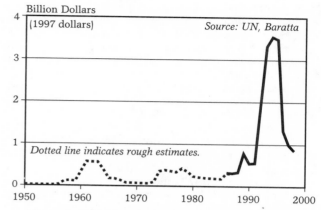

Figure 1: U.N. Peacekeeping Expenditures, 1950–98

Figure 2: U.N. Peacekeeping Personnel, 1950–98

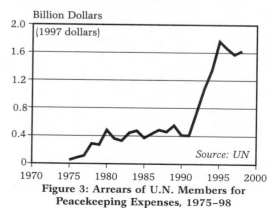

Figure 3: Arrears of U.N. Members for Peacekeeping Expenses, 1975–98

Nuclear Arsenals Shrink Michael Renner

The number of nuclear warheads worldwide declined from 39,807 in 1996 to 36,110 in 1997, a drop of 9 percent.[1] (See Figure 1.) Of these, about 20,000 are actively deployed, about 14,000 await eventual dismantlement, and the remainder are held in reserve.[2] Since its 1986 peak, the size of the global nuclear arsenal (strategic and tactical warheads) has declined by 48 percent.[3]

The United States retains 12,000 warheads, while Russia has 23,000.[4] The other three long-standing nuclear powers—France, China, and the United Kingdom—have a little more than 1,000 warheads combined.[5]

During the 1970s and 1980s, the Soviet Union and the United States deployed as many as 4,500 strategic "launchers" (bombers, land-based missile silos, and submarine missile tubes) to fire off these warheads. Now, the number of launchers on both sides has fallen to about 2,500.[6]

The United States is now the only nation with nuclear weapons outside its borders, but the number has shrunk from a peak of about 10,000 in 1975 to some 150.[7]

The START treaties between Russia and the United States require cutting the numbers of missiles, submarines, and bombers, but they do not mandate the destruction of warheads removed from the launchers. Still, both have dismantled a significant number of warheads: the United States took apart 10,482 warheads in 1990–97.[8]

All the same, the nuclear era is far from over. U.S. warhead production stopped in 1990, but new design work continues. U.S. explosive testing stopped in 1992 (and in 1990 in Russia), but new "subcritical" tests and computer simulations may yield much of the same information. And sizable arsenals will be retained. Of 85 tons of U.S. weapons-grade plutonium, 47 tons are to be kept for weapons purposes.[9] Russia is the only country still producing new warheads, but the age of its arsenals and its lack of financial resources may nevertheless translate into a sharp decline of its nuclear stockpile in coming years.[10]

Since 1945, seven countries have conducted a total of 2,051 tests in 24 different locations.[11] (See Figure 2.) Of these, 26 percent took place in the atmosphere, with the remainder underground. The United States carried out more than half the total (1,030), the Soviet Union 715, France 210, and China and the United Kingdom 45 each.[12]

In 1997, it seemed as though nuclear tests had finally been banished for good worldwide when, for the first time since 1959, not a single bomb was exploded. And the 1996 Comprehensive Nuclear Test Ban Treaty has attracted growing numbers of signatures (151 so far, though not of all the countries required to bring the treaty into force).[13] But in May 1998, India and Pakistan conducted several tests. India claimed to have detonated five devices and Pakistan claimed a total of six, though analysts suspect that these are both exaggerations.[14]

From the beginning of the atomic age to 1996, the United States has spent a conservatively estimated $5.6 trillion (in 1997 dollars) on nuclear weapons and weapons-related programs.[15] Producing the warheads—a total of 70,299 from 1945 to 1990—claimed $417 billion of this sum, while producing and deploying the weapons systems that carry the warheads cost about $3.3 trillion. The United States manufactured 6,135 intercontinental missiles, more than 18,000 shorter-range ballistic missiles, and more than 50,000 nuclear-capable nonballistic missiles, as well as 4,680 nuclear-capable bombers and 191 nuclear-powered submarines.[16] Targeting and controlling the weapons absorbed another $845 billion, and a variety of programs to defend against Soviet nuclear weapons took $954 billion. Some $33 billion went to dismantling warheads. Waste management and environmental cleanup efforts have received $67 billion so far, but will require at least $300 billion more during the next 75 years, according to official estimates.[17]

There are no corresponding figures for the other nuclear powers. One rough estimate, though extremely conservative, suggests an expenditure of $8 trillion worldwide.[18]

WORLD NUCLEAR ARSENALS, 1945–97

YEAR	NUCLEAR WARHEADS (number)
1945	6
1950	374
1955	33,267
1960	32,069
1965	37,741
1966	38,738
1967	39,186
1968	38,257
1969	37,465
1970	37,776
1971	39,445
1972	41,817
1973	44,414
1974	45,818
1975	46,841
1976	47,536
1977	48,544
1978	50,064
1979	52,485
1980	54,329
1981	55,658
1982	57,507
1983	59,686
1984	61,447
1985	63,223
1986	69,075
1987	67,302
1988	65,932
1989	63,450
1990	60,642
1991	57,017
1992	53,136
1993	49,612
1994	46,247
1995	42,976
1996	39,807
1997	36,110

SOURCE: Robert S. Norris and William M. Arkin, *Bulletin of the Atomic Scientists,* November/December 1997.

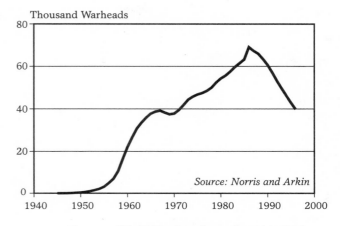

Figure 1: World Nuclear Arsenal, 1945–1997

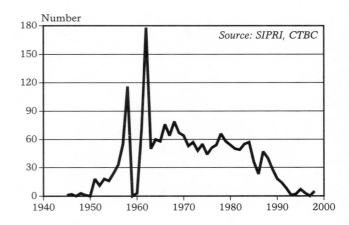

Figure 2: Nuclear Warhead Tests, 1945–98

Part TWO

Special Features

Environmental Features

Transgenic Crops Proliferate
Brian Halweil

The global area planted to transgenic crops shot up to 28 million hectares in 1998—nearly three times the area in the preceding year, and more than 15 times as much as in 1996.[1] (See Table 1.) By comparison, 225 million hectares around the world are planted in wheat—the most widely cultivated crop.[2]

Also known as genetically modified or genetically engineered crops, transgenic crops have been altered by inserting genes to express a desired trait, such as herbicide tolerance or increased oil content.[3] Unlike crop varieties developed through traditional plant breeding, transgenics often contain genes from unrelated species—of plant, animal, bacteria, or other origin—with which the crop could not reproduce naturally.[4]

Though several European governments have called for a moratorium on commercial planting of these crops pending further assessment of possible health and ecological risks, the global area planted to transgenics stands to soar in the near future.

Since a 1986 field trial of tobacco engineered to resist viruses, more than 60 transgenic crops—ranging from corn to strawberries, from apples to potatoes—have been tested in at least 45 countries.[5] In 1992, China became the first nation to grow transgenics for commercial use, though industrial nations have dominated the harvest ever since.[6]

Farmers in the United States sowed their first transgenic crop in 1994, followed by farmers in Argentina, Australia, Canada, and Mexico in 1996.[7] By 1998, 9 nations were growing transgenics, and that number is expected to reach 20–25 by 2000.[8]

The United States has dominated the explosive growth in genetically modified crops, with 74 percent of global acreage.[9] Argentina and Canada trail a distant second and third.[10] Only in these three nations do transgenics constitute a substantial share of any crop harvest. In 1998, more than a third of the American soybean crop was transgenic, as was nearly one quarter of the corn and 20 percent of the cotton.[11] Roughly 55 percent of the Argentine soybean crop was transgenic, as well as 45 percent of the Canadian crop of rapeseed, which is crushed to produce canola oil.[12]

Since the Flavr-Savr tomato—engineered for delayed ripening—appeared in American supermarkets in 1994, genetically modified foods have infiltrated the global food supply.[13] In the United States, where transgenic corn and soybeans show up as high fructose corn syrup or soybean oil in processed foods, an estimated 70 percent of such foods already contain some genetically modified ingredients—though it is not labeled as such.[14] Transgenic foods are likely on the shelves in many nations that do not even grow modified crops, as the United States is the source of roughly half of global corn and soybean exports as well as a large

Table 1: Global Area of Transgenic Crops, 1996–98[1]

COUNTRY	1996	1997	1998	SHARE OF GLOBAL ACREAGE, 1998
		(million hectares)		(percent)
United States	1.5	8.1	20.5	74
Argentina	0.1	1.4	4.3	15
Canada	0.1	1.3	2.8	10
Australia	<0.1	0.1	0.1	1
Mexico	<0.1	<0.1	0.1	1
Spain	–	–	<0.1	<1
France	–	–	<0.1	<1
South Africa	–	–	<0.1	<1
Total	1.7	11	27.8	100

[1]China is not included because the accuracy of acreage data has been questioned. SOURCE: Clive James, *Global Review of Commercialized Transgenic Crops: 1998* (Ithaca, NY: International Service for the Acquisition of Agri-biotech Applications, 1998).

share of processed food exports.[15]

While an array of transgenic crops are now grown commercially, 52 percent of the global area of transgenics is planted in soybeans and 30 percent in corn.[16] Cotton—almost entirely on U.S. soil—and rapeseed in Canada account for most of the remaining hectares.[17]

The most prevalent traits in the global transgenic harvest are "input" traits, which facilitate or replace the use of agrochemical inputs such as pesticides and fertilizers.[18] For example, 7 out of 10 transgenic hectares worldwide are planted in crops that tolerate a specific herbicide—allowing farmers to eradicate weeds without killing the crop.[19] And Bt-crops—corn, cotton, and potatoes endowed with genes to churn out the pest-killing *Bacillus thuringiensis* toxin and therefore require fewer pesticide applications—account for nearly all the remaining transgenic area.[20]

In contrast, the future harvest will likely emphasize "output" traits tailored to post-harvest uses, such as high-oil corn designed for fattening livestock.[21] Other modifications will fuel the production of designer foods with altered flavor, color, or nutrient content.[22] Moreover, the growing number of transgenic varieties engineered with more than one desired trait—for example, high-oil, Bt-corn that also tolerates herbicides—reflects the dominant trend toward "trait stacking."[23]

The swift acceptance of transgenics in North America stands as the exception to the global rule. From England to India, farmers and activists have destroyed transgenic test plots in protest. Many governments have exercised caution over possible risks to ecological and human health.

The range of novel substances in transgenics—including pesticides, viral proteins, and compounds never before part of the human diet—raises the fear of widespread food allergies, for instance.[24] Indeed, in 1996 test-marketing, a soybean modified with a Brazil nut gene provoked an unexpected allergic response in those with nut allergies.[25]

Pesticide-producing crops have been shown to harm nontarget insects, and may harm other organisms as pesticide-laden residues persist in the soil.[26] Weeds that acquire pesticide-producing abilities through cross-pollination with neighboring transgenics may upset insect and animal populations.[27]

Last year, Canadian farmers reported weeds that had acquired herbicide tolerance from neighboring transgenic crops, confounding weed control efforts and confirming fears of genetic pollution just two years after commercialization.[28] And weeds with newly acquired traits that outcompete surrounding plants may threaten biodiversity—a special concern in global centers of crop diversity.

Moreover, the debut of transgenic crops has unleashed a stampede of gene patenting by companies craving control over potentially lucrative crop traits, with related concerns that a once-common resource is being ceded to exclusive corporate control.[29] Further, the integration of genetic traits that demand the use of specific agrochemicals—such as Monsanto's Round-Up Ready soybeans that tolerate Monsanto's Round-Up herbicide—allows agribusiness corporations substantial control over farming practices.

Proprietary agreements attached to transgenic seeds often restrict farmers from trading, selling, or replanting seed.[30] And a recently conceived seed sterilization technology—billed as a patent protection system by its developers, but dubbed the Terminator gene by its critics—that prevents replanted seed from germinating will transform proprietary agreements into a biological reality.[31]

Signatories to the United Nations Convention on Biological Diversity met in February 1999 to finalize the Biosafety Protocol—an international accord governing the safe transfer, handling, and use of genetically modified organisms, including transgenic crops.[32] The talks broke down when food exporters—primarily industrial nations—refused to agree to labeling requirements and to responsibility and redress clauses for possible ecological or health damage caused by transgenics, which were favored by most developing countries.[33]

Pesticide-Resistant Species Flourish   Brian Halweil

Insects, plant diseases, and weeds continue to dodge farmers' best efforts to kill them by evolving resistance to pesticides. Today nearly 1,000 major agricultural pests—including some 550 insect and mite species, 230 plant diseases, and 220 weeds—are immune to pesticides, a development almost unheard of at mid-century.[1] (See Figure 1.) As modern agriculture leans heavily on pesticides, spreading resistance threatens to increase pest-induced crop losses and weaken food security.

Pesticide resistance is a textbook example of life adapting under the pressures of natural selection. In a genetically diverse pest population, a few individuals will likely be able to survive exposure to a given pesticide. Repeated pesticide use kills the vast majority of the population, giving the resistant few a survival advantage by exposing so much new terrain to their offspring. Resistance, however, is largely the result of pesticide overuse. Attempts to eradicate every last pest rather than just control the population accelerates the resistance process by allowing the resistant few to dominate.[2]

The incidence of pesticide-resistant organisms began to rise after World War II when farmers throughout the industrial world started using synthetic pesticides to eliminate agricultural pests.[3] It accelerated in the 1960s with the development and dissemination of Green Revolution crop varieties heavily dependent on chemical fertilizers and pesticides.[4]

The first modern pesticides—organochlorine insecticides, such as DDT—were introduced in the 1940s, and initially helped farmers cut crop losses dramatically.[5] But the first DDT-resistant insects were reported shortly thereafter, in 1947, and since then insects and mites have acquired resistance to each successive generation of insecticides with remarkable speed and persistence.[6] In fact, reports are beginning to trickle in of resistance to nicotine-analogue insecticides introduced only a few years ago to deal with insects resistant to all previous classes of pesticides.[7]

By 1990, the rate at which resistance was spreading to new insect species had begun to decrease, largely due to a drop in the number of insecticides coming to market as environmental concerns and regulations boosted the cost of developing new chemicals. And the latest highly species-specific insecticides do not provoke the same widespread resistance problems as earlier insecticides. In addition, after a half-century of heavy pesticide use, industrial nations have in effect exhausted their stock of nonresistant species—resistance has already been reported in nearly all major agricultural pests.[8]

Many pests are now resistant to several pesticides—a trend for which data are still spotty, though multiple resistance is known to be soaring. Major pests of pesticide-intensive crops, like cotton and certain vegetables, are resistant to a dozen different classes of insecticides. And today some insects, such as the diamondback moth and palm thrips, resist all insecticides that farmers can legally spray on them.[9] In the former Soviet Union, Colorado potato beetles resistant to all available chemicals decimate the region's staple food.[10]

Herbicides and chemicals used to control plant diseases—introduced later than insecticides—have fared no better. Weeds resistant to all available herbicides, such as annual ryegrass and canary grass, choke fields from Australia to India.[11] The global apple harvest depends on just a few fungicides still effective against the fungi causing the devastating apple scab.[12] And antibiotics used against bacterial plant diseases have been losing effectiveness since the late 1950s—mirroring the struggle to control human bacterial infections.[13]

Once pests become resistant, farmers often throw even more pesticides—or more toxic compounds—on their crops, which in turn may encourage subsequent resistance, the beginnings of a cycle known as the "pesticide treadmill."[14] The long-term results include higher costs of production, as well as yield declines from pest-induced crop losses.[15]

Resistance transforms minor crop pests into major headaches. In recent years, whiteflies—a once-negligible group of pests that acquired resistance in the 1980s—have inflicted tens of millions of dollars of crop damage in California and forced the abandonment of over 1 million hectares of South American cropland.[16]

Resistance costs the United States an estimated $1.5 billion each year in increased pesticide expenses and reduced crop yields.[17] And in cotton-growing areas around the Aral Sea in Russia, resistance led to increased pesticide use, drops in yield, soaring production costs, and the near collapse of ecological and human health in the region.[18]

In these ways, pesticide resistance drives the paradox of modern pest control: despite enormous increases in pesticide use since mid-century, the share of crops lost to pests has not changed substantially, and has even increased in some regions.[19] In the United States, for example, while pesticide use jumped 10-fold from the 1940s to the 1990s, the share of crop lost to pests actually rose from 30 to 37 percent.[20]

Most resistance problems have occurred in the industrial world—where roughly 80 percent of pesticides are used—though as developing nations mimic the chemical-intensive model of pest control, resistance problems will likely follow there too. In China, cotton yields already fell by one third between 1991 and 1993, largely due to cotton bollworm resistance.[21] And in India, resistance in a bug that preys on chickpeas and pigeonpeas—two essential food crops—has surfaced in recent years.[22]

The rapid commercialization of genetically modified crops also threatens to exacerbate resistance trends.[23] Bt-crops—engineered to churn out large quantities of the pesticidal Bt toxin throughout the growing season—will likely encourage resistance, endangering use of this relatively safe and highly effective pesticide.[24] And varieties engineered to tolerate

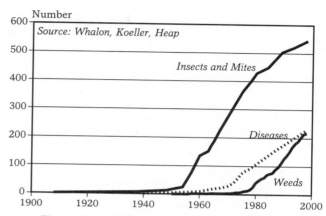

Figure 1: Pesticide-Resistant Species, 1908–98

glyphosate herbicide have already spread this trait via pollen to nearby weeds, rendering them immune to glyphosate.[25]

Fortunately, pesticides are not the only option for pest control. Farmers can often prevent pest outbreaks through such practices as crop rotations, intercropping, and release of beneficial insects.[26] And integrated pest management (IPM)—which combines a diversity of nonpesticidal tactics with sparing pesticide use—can slow the spread of resistance by reducing selection pressures.[27]

In 1986, with rice fields plagued by pesticide-resistant brown plant hoppers, the Indonesian government withdrew $100 million in annual pesticide subsidies, banned 57 pesticides, and launched a national IPM program.[28] Since then, pesticide use has fallen by 60 percent, while the rice harvest has increased some 25 percent.[29] And in Sinaloa, Mexico, an IPM program for tomatoes—emphasizing release of natural enemies and better timing of pesticide applications—boosted yields and grower income, though pesticide use dropped by half.[30]

Still, in most nations, pesticide subsidies, the political clout of agrochemical interests, and other institutional mechanisms continue to encourage excessive pesticide use and to deter safer, more effective alternatives.[31]

Harmful Algae Blooming Worldwide

Anne Platt McGinn

In coastal ecosystems worldwide, algae carrying biological toxins are working their way into previously unharmed waters. Although they are a naturally occurring phenomenon, the frequency and severity of harmful algal blooms (HABs) has increased in the past couple of decades, as has the appearance of novel toxic species.[1]

Since 1986, China's State Oceanographic Administration has reported five major "red tide" episodes (with two in 1998), each affecting more than 500 square kilometers.[2] Hong Kong harbor experienced its first red tide in 1977. Within a decade, the area averaged 35 episodes a year.[3]

One reason for the upswing is an ever-growing wash of nutrients from land, combined with degraded habitat areas, which offer prime staging grounds for HABs.

The vast majority of algae are beneficial, even necessary to life on the planet. Technically known as phytoplankton, algae form the base of the marine food chain and help regulate climate.[4] Through photosynthesis, they take carbon dioxide from the atmosphere and convert it into simple sugars to be consumed by marine animals and oxygen that maintains a livable atmosphere.[5]

Of the roughly 4,100 phytoplankton, about 300 produce characteristic "red tides," which actually range from green to brown or red in color, depending on the species.[6] Of this group, only 60–80 are known to contain biotoxins that can poison marine species and sometimes people. The problem is that once algae take hold, they are very difficult to contain.

Some algae become harmful by virtue of their biomass—golden-brown algae, for example, produce 1–2 million cells per milliliter of seawater.[7] Growing over vast areas of surface water, blooms block sunlight and air exchange. When the algae die, they sink to bottom waters where bacteria digest them, consuming more oxygen in the process. Eventually, the bacteria-laden waters become so depleted of oxygen (hypoxia) that they suffocate fish, forcing them to either flee or die.[8]

During the past 30 years, the number of oxygen-depleted coastal water bodies has tripled worldwide.[9] In the Gulf of Mexico, this process rendered 16,000 square kilometers of water biologically dead in 1997.[10] Large portions of the Adriatic, Baltic, and Black Seas also suffer from seasonal hypoxic events, prompting beach closures, loss of tourism revenue, and massive fish kills.[11]

Most experts link HAB outbreaks to increasing quantities of nitrogen and phosphorus in coastal areas, largely from nutrient-rich wastewater and agricultural runoff.[12] These two nutrients are necessary for life, and in proper quantities they help plants grow faster. But in areas with limited water flows, the waters can suffer from overenrichment (eutrophication), which triggers the oxygen depletion that is conducive to blooms.[13] Between 1976 and 1986, for example, the population of Tolo harbor, Hong Kong, increased sixfold, while nutrients tripled and the incidence of HABs rose eightfold.[14]

Biotoxins associated with HABs are often consumed by zooplankton, larvae, and small fish, and then work their way up the food chain to fish, marine mammals, and people who eat them.[15] Among the human diseases connected with HABs are paralytic, diarrhetic, and neurotoxic shellfish poisoning and ciguatera fish poisoning. The latter afflicts 10,000–50,000 people each year.[16]

As the harmful blooms spread, so do the associated costs. (See Table 1.)[17] Since 1991, economic losses from fish kills, public health problems, and losses in tourism revenues from harmful algae have totaled an estimated $280 million in the United States.[18] In spring 1998, a red tide wiped out more than $10 million worth of high-value fish in Hong Kong's mariculture industry.[19]

More than 100 endangered Mediterranean monk seals—one third of the world's population—were found dead along the West African coast in late spring 1997, a die-off researchers have linked to algal toxins.[20]

Between 1970 and 1990, the number of areas recording cases of paralytic shellfish poisoning (PSP) doubled worldwide.[21] Until 1970, cases of the PSP were limited to North America, Europe, and Japan.[22] Twenty years later, blooms of PSP-producing algae appeared in communities across the southern hemisphere, including Australia and South Africa, where they are thought to have been released from ships' ballast water tanks.[23] In September 1997, a PSP outbreak in Kerala, India, forced authorities to shut down shellfish beds and ban sales, leaving nearly 1,000 families without work.[24]

Habitat alteration and changes in ocean temperatures are also responsible for the spread of HABs.[25] Ciguatera poisoning, for example, tends to flare up in the wake of careless tourists, hurricanes, and El Niño, all of which can disturb coral reefs and allow dangerous algae to expand their range, thus increasing the chances that fish will eat them.[26] Cases of PSP in Borneo, Papua New Guinea, and the Philippines rise during El Niño years, as the warmer waters favor growth of algae and their toxins.[27]

Not only are HABs occurring in new places, they are also becoming more dangerous. Officially recognized as a public health problem in California in 1927, scientists recorded a threefold increase in the average toxin concentration of PSP between 1964–75 and 1980–1991.[28]

Some HABs are new to science. More than 60 harmful algal toxins are identified today, compared with just

22 in 1984.[29] Many of them exhibit unique traits. In 1991, for example, thousands of menhaden suddenly died in the Pamlico-Albemarle Sound of North Carolina, the second largest nursery area for marine fish on the U.S. Atlantic seaboard. A toxic phytoplankton, *Pfiesteria piscicida,* was identified as the cause.[30] Its human health effects range from respiratory distress to memory loss and learning impairment.[31] *Pfiesteria* has since spread to other estuaries, including the Chesapeake Bay.[32]

Several new technologies are used in the fight to control HABs, including satellite monitoring, which can detect the emergence and movement of blooms, and weather-tracking systems that predict the conditions favorable to blooms.[33] Reducing the inputs of pollution may help, but perhaps the best insurance against the spread of HABs is the protection and rehabilitation of coastal habitat areas that act as nature's filter zone.[34]

TABLE 1: ECONOMIC LOSSES FROM RED TIDES IN FISHERIES AND AQUACULTURE FACILITIES, 1972–98

DATE	LOCATION	SPECIES	LOSS (mill. dollars)
1972	Japan	Yellowtail	~47
1977	Japan	Yellowtail	~20
1978	Japan	Yellowtail	~22
1978	Korea	Oyster	4.6
1979	Maine	Many species	2.8
1980	New England	Many species	7
1981	Korea	Oyster	>60
1985	Long Island, NY	Scallops	2
1986	Chile	Red salmon	21
1987	Japan	Yellowtail	15
1988	Norway and Sweden	Salmon	5
1989	Norway	Salmon, rainbow trout	4.5
1989–90	Puget Sound, WA	Salmon	4–5
1991	Washington state	Oysters	15–20
1991–92	Korea	Farmed fish	133
1996	Texas	Oysters	24
1998	Hong Kong	Farmed fish	32

SOURCE: See endnote 17.

Urban Air Taking Lives   Molly O'Meara

Air pollution continues to exceed health guidelines in many cities, particularly in the developing world, according to recent data compiled by the World Resources Institute and earlier numbers submitted from national and local authorities to the Global Environment Monitoring System (GEMS/AIR).[1] This joint project of the World Health Organization (WHO) and the U.N. Environment Programme ran from 1975 through 1996; it introduced pollution monitoring technology to developing countries and served as an information clearinghouse.[2]

Sulfur dioxide and particulate matter are the most commonly recorded pollutants. A corrosive gas, sulfur dioxide is released mainly by burning coal and fuel oil, as well as by industrial activities such as metal smelting, oil refining, and paper manufacturing.[3] Fossil fuel combustion is also the principal human source of particulates, which include dust, soot, and other particles that become suspended in the atmosphere.[4]

Sulfur dioxide and particulates present a widespread threat to human health. Alone or in combination, these pollutants cause coughing and lung damage and aggravate existing respiratory problems.[5] Daily particulate levels closely track hospital admissions and death rates.[6] Long-term exposure to fine particulates, which transport toxic substances deep into the lungs, may increase the risk of cancer.[7] In addition, particulate matter reduces local visibility, while acidic sulfur compounds corrode buildings and monuments, and drift beyond cities to damage forests, lakes, and crops.[8] Both sulfur dioxide and particulate matter remain above safe levels in a number of major cities.[9] (See Figures 1 and 2, which illustrate trends in selected cities for which long-term records exist.)

At one time or another, more than 80 cities in 50 countries contributed to the GEMS/AIR network.[10] Many were sporadic or short-term participants, however, so data from 1985 to 1995 only exist for a few urban areas.[11] In 1980, 40 countries were reporting data, but by 1995 that number had dropped to 2, although

in 1996 it rose again to 25.[12] Moreover, the recorded data may be flawed, and differences in monitoring methods make city-to-city comparisons difficult.[13] A new program run by WHO, the Air Management Information System, aims to overcome these problems.

Over the past several decades, clean air laws have prompted declines in sulfur and particulate levels in most industrial nations. Building on a 1979 treaty to combat transboundary air pollution, a number of European countries and Canada forged progressively stricter agreements on sulfur emissions, the most recent of which went into force in 1998.[14] Although the United States dropped out of that international process, pressure from environmentalists and Canada resulted in domestic legislation that spurred a 35-percent drop in sulfur emissions between 1970 and 1998.[15]

Sulfur dioxide and particulate levels alone, however, do not give a complete picture of urban air pollution. Expanding vehicle fleets are keeping nitrogen oxides, hydrocarbons, and carbon monoxide at high levels in many cities.[16] In sunlight, nitrogen oxides and hydrocarbons react to form ozone, which harms human health and constitutes the main ingredient in smog.[17] According to a survey in the early 1990s, more than 80 percent of people in 105 European cities were exposed to unhealthy ozone levels at least once a year.[18] In 1997, the United States strengthened rules on ozone and smaller particulates; in part because of the tougher guidelines, 129 metropolitan areas—home to 107 million Americans—did not meet national standards that year.[19]

The whole suite of air pollutants plagues cities in the developing world.[20] Coal burning for industry, electricity generation, and household use contributes to dramatically high levels of sulfur and particulates in urban China and India.[21] Among the world's most polluted cities in the mid-1990s were Chonqing, China, which exceeded the WHO standard for sulfur dioxide by nearly seven times, and Kanpur, India, with particulates at five times the health standard.[22] Cooking or heating with coal,

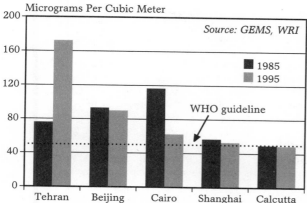

Micrograms Per Cubic Meter

Source: GEMS, WRI

■ 1985
■ 1995

WHO guideline

Figure 1: Average Annual Sulfur Dioxide Concentration,
Selected Cities, 1985 and 1995

wood, or other biomass can make air even dirtier indoors. These traditional home fuels are used in some cities but are more common in rural areas, where indoor air pollution may take 1.8–2.8 million lives each year.[23]

In addition to high levels of sulfur and particulates, traffic pollution is blanketing developing cities, particularly in Asia and Latin America. Vehicles contribute an estimated 60–70 percent of key urban air pollutants in Central America and 50–60 percent in India.[24] In 1995, ozone levels in Mexico City exceeded the national standard on 324 days; during the same year, the hourly standard in Santiago, Chile, was surpassed 404 times.[25]

Another pollutant that often comes from vehicles is lead. Some 90 percent of atmospheric lead comes from leaded gasoline.[26] This toxic metal impairs the kidneys, liver, reproductive system, and blood-forming organs, and causes irreversible brain damage at high levels.[27] Recent studies suggest that 64 percent of children in Delhi and 65–100 percent of children in Shanghai have unhealthy blood levels of lead.[28] In Cairo in early 1999, worsening traffic contributed to atmospheric lead levels in the city's

industrial areas that exceeded WHO guidelines by a factor of 11.[29]

As more people live in polluted cities, dirty urban air takes more lives. Cities in developing countries hosted nearly 60 percent of the 1.3 billion people added to the world population between 1980 and 1995.[30] Researchers estimate that air pollution in 36 large Indian cities killed some 52,000 people in 1995, a 28-percent increase from the early 1990s.[31] China reported at least 3 million deaths from urban air pollution between 1994 and 1996.[32] The World Bank calculates that 178,000 lives would have been saved in 1995 if China's 30 largest cities had met national "Class 2" air quality standards, which are a bit less stringent than WHO guidelines.[33]

Children, whose developing lungs are especially vulnerable, are increasingly at risk. A recent examination of 207 cities ranked Mexico City, Beijing, Shanghai, Tehran, and Calcutta as the five worst in terms of exposing children to air pollution.[34] These cities are home to the largest population of young children choking on the worst combination of sulfur dioxide, particulates, and nitrogen oxides. Just by breathing, these children inhale the equivalent of two packs of cigarettes each day.[35]

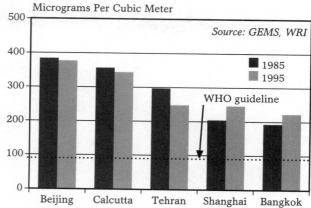

Micrograms Per Cubic Meter

Source: GEMS, WRI

■ 1985
■ 1995

WHO guideline

Figure 2: Average Annual Particulate Concentration,
Selected Cities, 1985 and 1995

Biomass Energy Use Growing Slowly

Seth Dunn

In 1995, according to the International Energy Agency (IEA), the world's use of biomass energy—fuelwood, agricultural residues, animal waste, charcoal, and other chemical fuels derived from the sun through photosynthesis and stored in organic plant matter—stood at the equivalent of 930 million tons of oil, accounting for approximately 14 percent of final energy use.[1] (See Table 1.) Widely relied upon for millennia by preindustrial societies, biomass energy was a dominant source among most industrial nations until the late nineteenth century.[2] Although its global share of final energy use has since declined, more energy is derived from biomass than from coal and about as much as from natural gas.[3]

Recent growth in the use of biomass for energy is attributed primarily to population growth in developing countries and increased use in industrial countries. Other trends include a stable global per capita rate; a gradual shift away from more primitive forms, such as use of dung and straw for cooking, toward more modern applications, including for heat and power generation; increased energy efficiency through, for example, improved cooking stoves; and a renewed interest among policymakers in both traditional and modern biomass energy due to growing population needs, technological advances, and environmental concerns.[4]

The relative importance of biomass energy varies considerably between rich and poor nations. In industrial countries, former Eastern Bloc nations, and the Middle East, it provides just 2–3 percent of total energy.[5] In Africa, Asia, and Latin America, however, biomass accounts for a full third of overall energy use.[6]

Indeed, 90 percent of biomass energy use is in the developing world.[7] Several of the poorest countries—Angola, Bangladesh, the Congo, Ethiopia, Mozambique, Myanmar, Nepal, and Tanzania—rely on this source for 80–90 percent of their energy.[8] For an estimated 2 billion people—one third of the world—biomass provides the main source of household energy.[9] Some 80 percent of the rural population and 20 percent of city dwellers in developing countries depend on it—mostly in the form of woodfuel—for their cooking and heating needs.[10] Biomass energy also serves as a major fuel input for many traditional and agricultural industries such as baking, brewing, textile manufacturing, tobacco and tea-curing, fish-smoking, and brick-making.[11]

The remaining 10 percent of biomass energy use, in the industrial world, accounts for 3

TABLE 1: BIOMASS ENERGY USE, WORLD AND BY REGION, 1995

REGION/COUNTRY	BIOMASS ENERGY USE (mill. tons of oil equivalent)	SHARE OF TOTAL ENERGY (percent)
Africa	205	60
South Asia	235	56
East Asia	106	25
China	206	24
Latin America	73	18
Industrial countries	81	3
Other developing countries	24	1
World	930	14

SOURCE: International Energy Agency (IEA), *World Energy Outlook 1998* (Paris: Organisation for Economic Co-operation and Development (OECD)/IEA, 1998); IEA, *Biomass Energy: Data, Analysis, and Trends* (Paris: OECD/IEA, 1998).

percent of that region's overall energy, mainly from household wood burning, district heating, and combined use of heat and power in industry.[12] The United States, the largest industrial country user, relies on biomass for 4 percent of its energy; in Austria, Sweden, and Finland, the figures are 12, 18, and 23 percent.[13] In Western Europe, biomass accounts for about 3 percent of total energy, a figure the European Union aims to increase to 8.5 percent by 2010.[14]

In developing countries, reliance on traditional biomass traps people in poverty by saddling women and children with burdensome time commitments for fuelwood gathering.[15] Cooking with biomass also releases suspended particulates, carbon monoxide, methane, and organic compounds; extended exposure to these can result in respiratory infections, lung cancer, and blindness, and can endanger pregnancies.[16] These hazards can be lessened by improving ventilation, introducing more-efficient stoves, using cleaner fuels, increasing awareness of the health effects of biomass burning, and centralizing conversion facilities.[17]

Interest in "modernizing" biomass energy is evident in developing-country efforts to increase biomass conversion for liquid and gaseous transport fuels and the cogeneration of heat and electric power. Examples include the use of ethanol fuel from sugarcane residues in Brazil, the use of solid waste and animal manure in biogas digesters in India and China, and sugarcane bagasse–derived cogeneration in Brazil, India, Thailand, and Mauritius.[18]

Recent concerns have centered on potential ecological impacts of energy crops and forest plantations, including loss of biodiversity, soil nutrient loss and erosion, and water pollution. Guidelines for less destructive use of biomass have been spelled out in Austria, Sweden, the United Kingdom, and the United States, and are under development for Europe.[19]

Despite these concerns, it is generally recognized that biomass energy's environmental impacts are less than those from fossil fuels, and that biomass energy crops can be man-aged in ways that are less ecologically damaging than intensive agriculture.[20] Experts point to the potential role of bioenergy in providing a "carbon dioxide–neutral" form of energy, sequestering carbon in forest "sinks," and substituting directly for fossil fuels.[21] And interest in the economic benefits of modern biomass—rural employment, energy self-sufficiency, lower pollution—is transforming the traditional view of biomass as a noncommercial, "poor man's" transition to fossil fuels into one of a potentially important twenty-first century energy source.[22]

Projections of the future role of biomass in world energy supply range widely. The Shell International Petroleum Company projects a biomass share of 14–22 percent by 2060; the Intergovernmental Panel on Climate Change projects a 25–46 percent share by 2100.[23] These scenarios assume greater recognition of biomass's environmental and economic benefits, modern technological improvements—such as biomass gasification and the use of fuel cells—that raise efficiency from 20 to as much as 60 percent, and extensive use of degraded forestland in developing countries and idled cropland in industrial nations.[24] The IEA, however, assumes more limited technological change and an income-driven switch to conventional fuels, projecting an average annual growth rate for biomass of 1 percent between 1995 and 2020.[25]

While its overall use is likely to increase in coming years, biomass energy still faces two major ecological constraints: high water requirements and low photosynthetic efficiency.[26] These limit biomass production to regions where rainfall is sufficient to support crop yields and force it to compete with other potential land uses, including food production, carbon sequestration, and habitat protection.[27] A 1997 study in BioScience argues that land, labor, and water requirements make large-scale biomass use unlikely, concluding that as major improvements are made in energy efficiency and the use of other alternative energy sources, biomass will be needed to support humans by stabilizing the biosphere's natural ecosystems.[28]

Economic Features

Transportation Shapes Cities Molly O'Meara

Just as a human body relies on its network of vessels to circulate blood to its organs, a city depends on its transportation system to move people and goods to jobs, schools, and stores. Researchers Peter Newman and Jeff Kenworthy have examined transportation trends between 1970 and 1990 in 47 major metropolitan areas to reveal differences in the "health" of urban transportation in Asia, Australia, Europe, and North America.[1]

One measure of a robust transportation system is the diversity of travel modes. U.S. cities are dominated by a single mode: the private car. On average, each person in the U.S. cities sampled in 1990 logged 10,870 kilometers (6,750 miles) of city driving—more than a round trip across North America.[2] Growth in car use in the U.S. cities between 1980 and 1990 was 2,000 kilometers per person, nearly double the increase in the Canadian cities, which have the next highest driving level.[3] (See Figure 1.)

In industrial countries, urban car use has tended to rise as population density has declined.[4] U.S. cities have led the trend toward dispersed, low-density development.[5]

Between 1983 and 1990, the average roundtrip commute to work in the United States grew 25 percent, to 17 kilometers (11 miles).[6] As cities sprawl, cars become essential while transit, bicycling, and walking become less practical. Compact Asian and European cities thus have the highest levels of nonmotorized transport.[7]

As car use rises, car-related problems mount. Fatal crashes, for example, increase.[8] The exception is cities in developing countries, where low car use is offset by poor signals and safety regulations.[9] Nonetheless, highly car-reliant U.S. cities exceed even developing Asian cities in per capita traffic fatalities.[10] (See Table 1.) Worldwide, traffic accidents kill some 885,000 people each year—equivalent to 10 fatal jumbo jet crashes per day—and injure many times more.[11]

Car-choked cities also lose time and money in traffic jams.[12] Wasted fuel and lost productivity cost $74 billion annually in U.S. metro areas.[13] But new roads attract more cars, so regions that have invested heavily in road construction have fared no better at easing congestion than those that have invested less.[14]

Building more roads also worsens environmental damage. Cars burn more fossil fuels per person than any other type of urban transport. Toxic ingredients in car fumes—carbon monoxide, sulfur dioxide, nitrogen oxides, fine particles, and sometimes lead—are a major source of urban air pollution.[15] Nitrogen and sulfur that travel beyond the city acidify lakes, forests, and farms, while carbon contributes to global climate change.[16] And cars devour not just energy, but land. Each car needs as much road as 4–8 bicycles and as much parking as 20 bikes.[17] Roads and parking may pave over as much as one third of car-reliant cities.[18] A city's water quality and quanti-

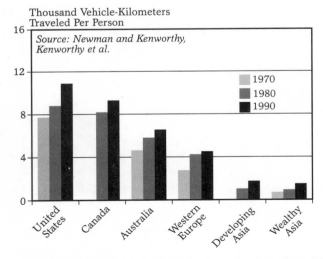

Thousand Vehicle-Kilometers Traveled Per Person

Source: Newman and Kenworthy, Kenworthy et al.

1970
1980
1990

Figure 1: Annual Per Capita Car Use in Selected World Cities, by Regional Average, 1970–90

ty suffer in proportion to the amount of paved roads and parking that cover its watershed.[19]

A recent World Bank study suggests that the high costs of automobile dependence outweigh the benefits of car transportation, eroding economic development.[20] In the United States, a 1998 survey of leading real estate investors and analysts came to a similar conclusion: denser cities that boast alternatives to the car are better investment bets than sprawling suburban agglomerations.[21]

Coordinated transportation and land use policies, both local and national, can lessen the need for travel and boost transportation options. In the Netherlands, for instance, cities follow a national "ABC" policy to steer new development to easily accessible "A" locations, which are the best served by public transit and bicycle paths.[22]

Local and national governments can also adjust road and parking fees to reflect the high cost of car use and limit unnecessary trips.[23] For more than 20 years, downtown-bound drivers in Singapore have paid a fee that rises during rush hours; since 1998, the fee has been automatically deducted from an electronic card.[24] In the United States, state and national policies are beginning to target parking subsidies, worth $31.5 billion a year.[25] A 1992 California law requires employers who offer free parking to also provide a cash alternative; this spurred a 17-percent drop in solo driving at several firms.[26] In 1998, a national transportation act changed the tax code to support these "cash-outs."[27]

Decoupling car ownership from car use removes incentives to drive. Once a person pays for a car, he may want to use it as much as possible to get his money's worth.[28] New car-sharing networks eliminate that desire by providing easy access to a car, without the costs of owning or the hassles of renting.[29] More than 100,000 people participate in car sharing in Germany, Austria, Switzerland, and the Netherlands.[30] Italy is set to join the club in 1999 with national incentives for cities to organize electric car-sharing services.[31]

Such innovations are becoming more important as we approach the point, sometime during the next decade, when more than half the world will live in urban areas.[32] Nearly 90 percent of the 2.7 billion people due to be added to world population between 1995 and 2030 will live in cities of the developing world.[33] Car-reliant U.S. cities have the greatest potential to diversify. At present, they offer a poor model for the many cities that will be building and expanding their transportation systems in the years to come.

TABLE 1: TRANSPORTATION INDICATORS IN SELECTED CITIES, BY REGIONAL AVERAGE, 1990

REGION	DRIVING	COMMUTE TO WORK		TRANSPORT DEATHS
		PUBLIC TRANSPORT	WALKING/CYCLING	
		(percent)		(per hundred thousand)
United States	86.4	9.0	4.6	14.6
Australia	80.4	14.5	5.1	12.0[2]
Canada	74.1	19.7	6.2	6.5[3]
Western Europe	42.8	38.8	18.4	8.8
Developing Asia[1]	38.4	35.7	25.8	13.7
Wealthy Asia	20.1	59.6	20.3	6.6

[1]Does not add to 100 due to rounding.   [2]Excludes Canberra.   [3]Toronto only.
SOURCES: Peter Newman and Jeff Kenworthy, *Sustainability and Cities: Overcoming Automobile Dependence* (Washington, DC: Island Press, 1999); Jeff Kenworthy et al., *An International Sourcebook of Automobile Dependence in Cities 1960–1990* (Boulder, CO: University Press of Colorado, in press).

Corporations Driving Globalization
Michael Renner

Large corporations are powerful actors in many national economies, and they are strong moving forces behind the growing trend toward global economic integration. By dint of their size and global reach, they play an important role in worldwide production and consumption trends. Their power and influence rivals or surpasses that of many national governments. Not all transnational corporations (TNCs) are large, and not all large companies are necessarily transnational in their operations, but the overlap between both categories is substantial.

A growing number of companies are operating in more than one country, and some have a globe-spanning presence. In 1970, there were some 7,000 TNCs.[1] Today, by the count of the United Nations Conference on Trade and Development (UNCTAD), there are at least 53,607, with at least 448,917 foreign subsidiaries.[2] (Because of incomplete data, the actual numbers may be even higher.) Some 81 percent of the parent companies are based in industrial countries.[3] Among the 100 largest firms, just two—Daewoo of South Korea and Petróleos de Venezuela—are from developing countries.

The leading companies clearly pack a powerful economic punch in terms of assets and sales. *Fortune* magazine reports that the 500 largest corporations had assets worth $34 trillion in 1997, brought in $452 billion of profits on $11.5 trillion of revenues, and employed 36.8 million people.[4] *The Economist* calculated in 1993 that the world's 300 largest corporations controlled about 25 percent of the world's productive assets.[5]

In order to analyze the international reach of major companies, UNCTAD compiles data on the foreign subsidiaries of the leading 100 TNCs. (These figures exclude the parent companies and hence understate the extent of corporate economic power.) Their combined capital assets grew fourfold between 1982 and 1997 (in constant 1997 dollar terms); their sales doubled.[6] The subsidiaries' net contribution to the world economy—their value added—amounts to 7 percent of the gross

world product.[7]

The role of TNCs as job creators is comparatively anemic. TNCs worldwide were estimated by UNCTAD in 1994 to employ some 73 million people, of which 60 percent were at parent companies and the remainder at subsidiaries.[8] As UNCTAD explains, these workers "belong to the core workforce in modern, technologically advanced activities." Nevertheless, they account for only 3 percent of the global work force.[9] And social activist David Korten notes that the Fortune 500 firms shed nearly 4.4 million jobs from 1980 to 1993,or more than a quarter of their total work force.[10] During the same period, sales of these companies grew 1.4 times and their assets, 2.3 times.[11]

Transnational corporations rely not only on exports to serve markets in foreign countries but also, with the help of foreign direct investment (FDI), on production within those countries. The subsidiaries' share of world exports has ranged from one quarter to one third during the 1980s and 1990s.[12] But TNCs' sales outside their home countries are growing 20–30 percent faster than their exports, and sales of goods and services by foreign subsidiaries—valued at $9.5 trillion in 1997—surpass worldwide exports of goods and services by about 50 percent.[13]

During the past two decades, through foreign investments, many companies have rapidly increased the degree to which they are international in their operations. As barriers to international capital movements have been abolished or reduced in many countries, the annual flow of foreign direct investment has surged upward, causing FDI stock to grow 3.7-fold between 1980 and 1997, to $3.5 trillion or about 9 percent of gross world product.[14] Not even the Asian economic crisis interrupted this trend. Capital formation due to foreign investment is growing two to three times faster than capital formation as a whole, indicating, as UNCTAD puts it, "an increasing internationalization of national production systems."[15]

Out of the world's top 100 TNCs, 31 operated in 50 or more countries in 1996 (and 9 in at least 75 countries); in 49 companies, foreign assets account for 50 percent or more of the total corporate assets; in 65 firms, the foreign sales constitute at least 50 percent of the total sales. In 53 TNCs, at least half their employees are based in foreign countries.[16]

Even as companies increasingly internationalize, they also grow bigger through takeovers. Indeed, the corporate world is undergoing swift change as mergers and acquisitions are exploding both in number and in monetary value. Between 1980 and 1998, a total of 217,948 merger and acquisition deals were announced worldwide, for a combined value of $11.9 trillion.[17]

The value of worldwide mergers rose from about $33 billion in 1980 to $2.5 trillion in 1998 (in 1997 dollars).[18] (See Figure 1.) Most deals in 1998 took place among U.S. companies (worth $1.7 trillion, the equivalent of 20 percent of U.S. gross national product), although the merger wave is expected to sweep over Europe during 1999.[19] The biggest takeover deal was announced in December 1998, combining the oil giants Exxon and Mobil for about $80 billion.[20] Other huge combinations were announced in the telecommunications, auto, and financial industries.[21] Roughly one quarter of all mergers involve takeovers across international borders, growing from $6 billion worth in 1980 to $680 billion in 1998 (in 1997 dollars).[22]

After the record mergers in 1998, most industry analysts believe that "the sky is the limit" in coming years. Even large-scale business operations are increasingly seen as insufficiently large in a globalizing world. And company executives may regard a rival's acquisitions as an incentive or a warning signal to pursue their own takeovers.

One result of combining corporate giants into even larger organizations is a shrinkage in the number of major manufacturers in some industries. For example, the number of major automobile producers may fall from the current 15 worldwide to perhaps 5–10 by 2010. The pharmaceutical industry is already highly concentrated, with just seven dominant firms.[23] The oil industry is also undergoing a major consolidation. But mergers are not just transforming extractive and manufacturing industries; in fact, the dollar value of cross-border mergers and acquisitions in the services sector (banking, finance and insurance, and telecommunications) has been larger than in the manufacturing sector every year since 1995.[24]

Putting together corporate giants of unprecedented size may or may not make business sense.[25] But the larger implications—for employment, environmental impact, technological change, corporate political influence, and corporate accountability—are worth pondering for governments and societies at large.[26]

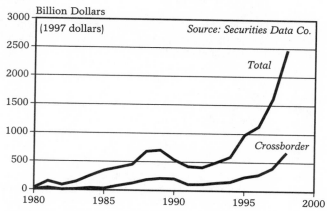

Figure 1. Worldwide Mergers and Acquisitions, 1980–98

Government Corruption Widespread

David Malin Roodman

Government corruption—the abuse of public office for private gain—is widespread, according to surveys and polls collected by the Berlin-based group Transparency International (TI).[1] These surveys, conducted by organizations ranging from the World Bank to Gallup International, ask in-country business people or randomly chosen citizens to gauge a nation according to criteria such as perceived prevalence of bribe-taking among legislators. TI collates the surveys each year and reports average scores for 85 nations.[2] (See Table 1.)

The term "corruption" encompasses embezzlement, kickback schemes in the assignment of government contracts, and bribery of officials ranging from parliamentarians to bureaucrats.[3] TI's efforts to document an ancient problem have heightened awareness of corruption as a major barrier to economic development.[4]

Notably, at the World Bank's annual meeting in 1996, Bank President James Wolfensohn declared war on the "cancer of corruption."[5] In 1996 and 1997, the Bank and the International Monetary Fund set precedents in delaying loans to Afghanistan, Cambodia, Congo, Kenya, Nigeria, Papua New Guinea, and Sudan over concerns that corruption was diverting funds and subverting the purposes of the loans.[6]

Data from the surveys have also aided statistical analysis of links between corruption and development. Some researchers have suggested that "low-level" corruption among bureaucrats who have the power to block business projects might make doing business easier in some countries, aiding development.[7] But the first systematic, international comparative study, by economist Paulo Mauro, found a negative correlation between the level of reported corruption in a country and its economic rate of growth.[8]

Another study found that prevalence of corruption appears to deter foreign investment: an increase in corruption from the level of Singapore to that of Mexico had the same dampening effect as raising taxes on foreign investment 21–24 percentage points over the long run.[9] That result, released in May 1997,

may have seemed an aberration when booming but relatively bribe-ridden nations were the darlings of investors—but within weeks, the Thai baht entered a free fall, casting a new light on the matter. Corruption alone should not be blamed for the global economic crisis; nevertheless, nations scoring low on TI's list, including Brazil, Russia, Thailand, and Indonesia, have generally fared worse than those scoring higher, including Chile, Hong Kong, Malaysia, and Taiwan.[10]

Corruption contributes to other ills. Another study by Mauro found that more-corrupt governments spend less on education.[11] They may divert funds toward projects such as roads, which harbor more opportunities for kickbacks. Yet cutting education hinders economic growth and increases inequities by blocking an escape route from poverty.

Corruption is also implicated in government moves that harm the environment and violate human rights. Payoffs to factory inspectors, for example, undermine enforcement of pollution regulations.[12] In Malaysia, Indonesia, and other Asia-Pacific nations, top officials have granted domestic or foreign businesses rights to log tropical forest land occupied by indigenous hunter-gatherers or pastoralists.[13] This has led to the displacement and impoverishment of thousands of people even as it has channeled billions of dollars in profits into private bank accounts of both the officials and the loggers.[14]

One technique for fighting corruption is to make sure that government officials are paid well, in order to reduce the appeal of bribes.[15] In the Philippines' Department of Environment and Natural Resources, for example, low pay has contributed to rampant corruption among logging concession administrators.[16]

Adoption and enforcement of strong anti-corruption laws, periodic auditing of officials, and an independent judiciary are also essential; enforcement will never stamp out corruption completely, but it will increase the risks for bribe-takers.[17] Reducing the discretion of bureaucrats and making their actions public—say, by instituting public, competitive bidding for government contracts—will help too.[18] Perhaps the most effective tool to that end is passing "freedom of information laws" that give citizens access to most government documents. Eight of the 10 highest-scoring countries on TI's list have such laws.[19]

One danger in focusing on nations where bribe-taking is common is that it can overshadow similar problems in more-developed nations. Japanese timber importers, for example, ought not be blind to the logging-related corruption that they indirectly finance.[20] In the United States, campaign donations equaled $2.4 billion in the 1996 federal election cycle.[21] That money, most of it from large corporations, inevitably influenced government actions to favor special over public interests.

In addition, many bribes taken by officials in developing countries are given by compa-nies based in industrial ones. One analysis has pinpointed the major trading partners of the most corrupt countries—partners that are therefore probably home to major bribe-givers.[22] (See Table 2.) The prominence of nations such as France and Italy on this list is not surprising: in most industrial countries, bribes to foreign officials are legal and tax-deductible.[23]

In a promising move, the world's industrial democracies have signed a "soft law" treaty to outlaw bribes to foreign officials.[24] It went into force in early 1999, but is less binding than most international accords, and enforcing it will be hard since companies often disguise bribes as consulting fees.[25] Few governments have yet passed the domestic laws needed to implement the treaty; the United States, however, has effectively done so with a law enacted in 1977.[26] But if enough governments implement the treaty aggressively, it could become a useful step toward reducing corruption worldwide.

TABLE 1: PERCEIVED LEVEL OF CORRUPTION IN SELECTED COUNTRIES, 1998

COUNTRY	AVERAGE SCORE FROM SURVEYS AND POLLS[1] (lower score = more reported bribe-taking)
Nigeria	1.9
Indonesia	2.0
Colombia	2.2
Russia	2.4
Kenya	2.5
India	2.9
Thailand	3.0
Mexico	3.3
China	3.5
Brazil	4.0
South Korea	4.2
Italy	4.6
Hungary	5.0
Malaysia	5.3
Taiwan	5.3
Japan	5.8
Chile	6.8
United States	7.5
Hong Kong	7.8
Germany	7.9
Singapore	9.1
Canada	9.2
Denmark	10.0

[1]A lower score indicates more bribe-taking, but a score of 10.0 does not imply complete lack of corruption. SOURCE: Transparency International, "1998 Corruption Perceptions Index" (Berlin: 22 September 1998).

TABLE 2: APPARENT TENDENCY OF SELECTED MAJOR EXPORTING COUNTRIES TO BRIBE, EARLY 1990S

COUNTRY	RELIANCE ON EXPORTS TO NATIONS WHERE BRIBERY IS COMMON[1] (lower score = more apparent bribe-giving)
Belgium & Luxembourg[2]	−8.0
France	−7.2
Italy	−6.8
South Korea	−5.7
United Kingdom	−5.3
China & Hong Kong[2]	−4.5
Germany	−2.6
Singapore	−2.5
Japan	−1.7
United States	0.7
Sweden	6.5
Malaysia	6.7

[1]Scores—not on a simple 0-to-10 scale—result from a statistical analysis of trade data and the previous edition of the data referenced in Table 1. The analysis controls for distance between importer and exporter, composition of exports, and other factors. [2]Treated as one country statistically. SOURCE: Johann Graf Lambsdorff, "An Empirical Investigation of Bribery in International Trade," *European Journal of Development Research*, June 1998.

Social
Features

Unemployment Plagues Many Nations   Michael Renner

In modern economies, wage employment is the main source of income for the vast majority of people. Quantitative and qualitative trends in employment are thus important determinants of economic equality and well-being and, in a larger sense, social stability.

Worldwide, at least 150 million people were unemployed at the end of 1998—some for so long that they are considered "unemployable."[1] In addition, as many as 900 million people are "underemployed"—involuntarily working substantially less than full-time, or earning less than a living wage.[2] Altogether, about 35 percent of the world's labor force is affected.[3]

Furthermore, considerable numbers of "discouraged" workers have given up hope of finding work and are usually not even counted as unemployed.[4] In Germany, for instance, in addition to the 4.4 million unemployed in 1997, another 1.9 million workers were "discouraged" and 700,000 more were in various "make work" schemes camouflaging unemployment, for a total of 7.0 million.[5]

The world's labor force—the part of the population working or available for work—has grown from 1.2 billion people in 1950 to an estimated 2.9 billion in 1998, outstripping the growth in job creation.[6] During the next half-century, the world will need to create more than 1.9 billion jobs, as some 40 million people will enter the labor force each year.[7]

Rapid technological change and globalization have contributed to a growing gap in job security and pay between skilled workers—professionals and technicians in particular—and those lacking skills or possessing outdated ones. For example, manufacturing employment in western industrial countries stayed roughly even for skilled workers between 1970 and 1994, but declined 20 percent for unskilled workers.[8]

Technological development and increased capital mobility have allowed growing numbers of companies to embrace measures such as temporary or part-time hiring, parceling out components of the work process ("outsourcing"), and replacing domestic work forces with a large pool of cheap labor in developing countries. Particularly for lower-skilled workers, job tenure and income security are more tenuous as a result.[9]

Among the advanced industrial countries, Japan has managed to keep joblessness relatively low. But the unemployment rate has been climbing there too, rising above 4 percent in 1998 for the first time since the end of World War II.[10] In most other industrial countries, the figure has been considerably higher. This is particularly true in the European Union, where about 10 percent of the work force—some 18 million people—are unemployed.[11] (See Table 1.)

By contrast, the United States has managed to reduce its unemployment rate. But higher job creation has come at a cost: U.S. manufacturing workers are the only ones among advanced industrial countries to suffer real wage losses. Between 1978 and 1997, real wages for production or nonsupervisory workers (excluding agriculture) declined by 9 percent.[12] In the first half of the 1990s, 80 percent

TABLE 1: UNEMPLOYMENT RATES BY REGION AND SELECTED COUNTRIES, 1987 AND 1997

REGION OR COUNTRY	1987	1997
	(percent)	
Western Europe	10.4	10.5[1]
Japan	2.8	3.4
United States	6.2	4.9
Latin America and Caribbean	5.7[2]	7.4
China	2.0	3.0[3]
India	3.4	2.3[4]
Other Asian Countries	4.3[2]	4.2[3]
Central and Eastern Europe	7.2[4]	9.6[3]

[1]10 percent in late 1998. [2]1990. [3]1996. [4]1993.
SOURCES: International Labour Office, *World Employment Report 1998–99* (Geneva: 1998); "The Main EU Statistical Indicators On-Line," EUROSTAT Web site, < http://europa.eu.int/en/eurostat/indic/indic14.htm >, viewed 23 December 1998. No comprehensive data are available for Africa.

of male workers and 60 percent of female workers saw their wages decline.[13] Almost 29 percent of all U.S. workers now have jobs that pay wages at or below the poverty level.[14]

Since the end of the cold war, Eastern Europe and the states of the former Soviet Union have seen a rapid rise in unemployment, from about zero to an average of close to 10 percent.[15] The United Nations reported an unemployment rate of 11.5 percent in Russia as of mid-1998.[16] Only the Czech Republic, Belarus, Azerbaijan, and Uzbekistan have fared somewhat better. Joblessness has been accompanied by lower real wages and dramatic increases in income inequality.

The East Asian economic crisis has so far added at least 10 million people to the world's unemployment rolls.[17] It is estimated that the unemployment rate in Indonesia could hit 15 percent, and an additional 20 percent of the population—some 40 million people—are expected to fall into poverty.[18] In South Korea, unemployment rose from 2 percent in 1996 to 7 percent in 1998, and is expected to reach 8–9 percent or higher.[19] In Thailand, unemployment may rise to 6 percent, up from 2 percent in 1996, increasing the poverty rate from 16 percent to 28 percent.[20] Unemployment benefits and other protective measures are sparse in most Asian countries.[21]

Other Asian countries—those in transition to a market economy (Cambodia, China, Laos, Mongolia, and Viet Nam)—all face serious labor market problems resulting from their vast amount of excess labor in state and collective enterprises.[22]

In China, perhaps as many as 30 million workers will lose jobs as the pruning of state industries continues.[23] It is estimated that layoffs in 1998 alone affected 3.5 million workers, bringing the official unemployment rate to 5–6 percent.[24] The government announced that 400,000 coal mining jobs will be lost in 1999 as small mines are closed.[25] Laid-off urban workers increasingly compete with a "floating" population of some 100 million people migrating to cities from rural areas.[26] In 1997, women accounted for 39 percent of China's work force but 61 percent of its laid-

off workers.[27] Three quarters of all laid-off women are still unemployed after one year.[28]

Latin American countries have seen little improvement in their employment situation despite an upturn in their macroeconomic performance. The restructuring of the public sector that has taken place in many countries has been accompanied by massive layoffs. Real wages have deteriorated.[29] The International Labour Organization (ILO) notes that demand for unskilled labor in the formal sector has fallen considerably, pushing workers into the informal sector. This is the underbelly of the economy—where working conditions are typically unregulated and poor, social security is mostly nonexistent, and wages are mostly very low.[30]

In sub-Saharan Africa, the labor force is growing at 2.9 percent a year.[31] Since job creation in the formal sector is limited, most employment necessarily takes place in the informal sector.[32] According to the ILO, in sub-Saharan Africa the informal sector employed more than 60 percent of the urban work force in 1990, mostly at wages below the official minimum wage.[33] Each year, some 8.7 million persons enter the labor market.[34]

One of the most unsettling aspects of the jobs crisis is large-scale youth unemployment, which virtually everywhere is substantially higher than for the labor force as a whole. The ILO estimates there are about 60 million people between the ages of 15 and 24 who are in search of work but cannot find it.[35] Of these, 11 million are in western industrial countries.[36]

High rates of population growth in many developing countries translate into massive pressure on job markets there. In China, 26 percent of the population is age 15 or younger; in Latin America, the figure is 34 percent; in South and Southeast Asia, 36 percent; and in Africa, 44 percent.[37] The economically active population in developing countries is set to grow by about 685 million people between 1995 and 2010—96 percent of the growth in the world labor force.[38] People's well-being, the social fabric of many nations, and peace within societies will depend on most of these new job seekers finding gainful employment.

NGOs Proliferate Worldwide   Curtis Runyan

In the past four decades, NGOs have experienced a dramatic surge in number, diversity, and influence worldwide.[1] These not-for-profit, nongovernmental organizations are now influencing decisions and helping to set agendas that were once determined solely by governments and corporations—from policies on international trade and investment to initiatives on literacy, international aid, and human rights. Perhaps the most striking example of the growing efficacy of NGOs was the Nobel Prize–winning campaign by more than 350 NGOs in 1997 that pushed through an international treaty banning landmines despite opposition from the United States.[2]

NGOs espouse an incongruous set of ideologies, agendas, and causes—from promoting women's rights, organizing labor, and providing humanitarian aid to setting up neighborhood watch groups, advocating public safety and health measures, and organizing educational, recreational, or cultural events.[3] As such, creating a broad definition for this "wild assortment" of organizations—in different contexts referred to as private voluntary organizations, civil society, and the nonprofit sector—is no simple task.[4] Compiling accurate data on NGOs is further complicated by the varying roles and legal definitions of nonprofit organizations in different countries.

The *Yearbook of International Organizations* documented 985 active "international NGOs" (groups operating in at least three countries) in 1956.[5] By 1996 that number had increased to more than 20,000.[6] (See Figure 1.) The number of NGOs operating within countries has grown even more quickly. Half of all NGOs in Europe have been founded in the past decade.[7] The number of NGOs in the United States is now estimated at 2 million.[8]

This growth has been more dramatic in the developing world. In India, which has a tradition of community voluntarism inspired by Mahatma Gandhi, more than a million independent groups now take part in grassroots development efforts.[9] NGOs have traditionally proliferated in countries with less-centralized governments and larger middle classes, and they are now making striking inroads in former Eastern bloc countries, where more than 100,000 nonprofit groups were set up between 1988 and 1995.[10] These groups have even begun to take hold in China, despite the country's restrictive state control.[11]

In 22 industrial and developing countries studied by Johns Hopkins University's Center for Civil Society Studies, the nonprofit sector in 1995 spent in excess of $1.1 trillion (equal to the gross domestic product (GDP) of the United Kingdom), employed 19 million workers, and used 10 million volunteers.[12] On average, the sector accounted for 5.7 percent of GDP and employed 5 percent of the work force (not including agriculture).[13]

In most countries the majority of NGOs provide education, health, and social services. (See Table 1.) Two thirds of all nonprofit employment is devoted to efforts to facilitate such services as primary and secondary education, hospital and health care, income support, and emergency aid and relief.[14]

Political scientists attribute the rise in prominence of NGOs in part to a shifting economic and political architecture.[15]

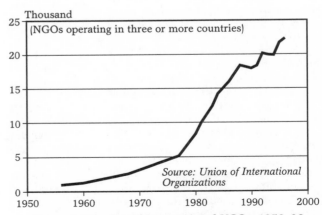

Figure 1: Number of International NGOs, 1956–96

TABLE 1: NGO EMPLOYMENT, BY SECTOR, MID-1990s[1]

SECTOR	SHARE (percent)
Education and research	23.1
Social services	20.6
Culture, sports, and recreation	18.9
Health care	15.7
Business and professional associations, unions	6.3
Development and housing	6.1
Other	3.5
Law, advocacy, and politics	3.0
Environmental protection and education	2.5
Philanthropic foundations	1.2
International (human rights, relief, and aid groups)	1.0

[1]NGOs have 29 million people on staff (10 million of whom are volunteers) in the 22 countries surveyed. SOURCE: Lester M. Salamon and Helmut K. Anheier, *The Emerging Sector Revisited: A Summary of Initial Estimates* (Baltimore, MD: The Johns Hopkins University Center for Civil Society Studies, 1998).

Globalization—including the liberalization of capital and trade flows as well as the spread of new technologies—has significantly altered the role of governments and economic markets.[16] Political shifts such as the collapse of state socialism, chronically slow development in impoverished nations, and a rethinking of social welfare policies in industrial countries have forced nations to redirect their energies.[17] Traditional priorities of national security, such as military protection, are becoming less compelling in light of social and environmental problems threatening "human security," including a lack of access to food, shelter, employment, education, and health services.[18]

In many cases, NGOs have proved more adept than both governments and the free market at responding to these human security needs.[19] In Bangladesh, where 5,000 NGOs are involved with literacy programs, a child is more likely to learn to read with the assistance of an NGO than through a state organization.[20] Worldwide, NGOs now deliver more development assistance than the entire U.N. system.[21]

The proliferation of inexpensive information technologies has also boosted the power and presence of NGOs, allowing people to mobilize and organize cheaply and effectively. Human rights activists prevented what could have been a violent crackdown at the start of the Chiapas rebellion in 1994 by using the Internet and worldwide media attention to monitor and limit the Mexican government's response.[22] In 1995, Greenpeace garnered worldwide support in its campaign to halt Shell Oil's ocean dumping of the Brent Spar oil rig by using a satellite uplink to show footage of its activists on board the rig.[23]

NGOs have used their flexibility, small scale, technical expertise, and connections to the grassroots to spark something of an "organizational revolution"—forging an effective middle ground between the state and the free market.[24] However, these groups serve a huge range of interests, and whether they promote the interests of one person, an industry, or an entire country, they are subject to relatively little scrutiny.[25] A growing number of nonprofit organizations are funded and controlled by corporate interests.[26] Indeed, nonprofit industry and trade groups employ four times as many people as environmental groups do.[27]

Due to the free-form nature of NGOs, there is increasing concern within the nonprofit sector over the potential for abuse. There are no laws or international conventions requiring NGOs to disclose their funding sources. Many NGOs now operate as little more than industry front groups, such as the Global Climate Coalition (which was set up by the fossil-fuel industry to stifle climate-change negotiations).[28] And even well-intentioned NGOs are not immune: in the recent Rwandan genocide, warring factions forced aid workers supplying and operating refugee camps to assist soldiers.[29]

Surprisingly little NGO funding comes from foundations and organized philanthropy—an average of 11 percent in the 22 countries surveyed by the Center for Civil Society Studies.[30] On average, NGOs receive 47 percent of their income from fees for services rendered, and 42 percent from public support.[31]

Malnutrition Still Prevalent Brian Halweil

Nearly 1 billion people worldwide do not get enough to eat each day, and several billion get enough calories but their poor diets fall short in providing basic nutrients.[1] At the same time, an estimated 600 million people worldwide—mostly in North America and Europe—are overnourished and overweight.[2] Accordingly, the World Health Organization estimates that nearly half of the population in just about every country suffers from some form of malnutrition—whether it is undernutrition or overnutrition.[3]

Malnutrition is a pathological condition in which the intake of calories, protein, or other essential micronutrients does not balance with needs.[4] When intake falls below a person's needs on a chronic basis, the result is an underweight person; excessive intake results in overweight. Regardless of the form it takes, malnutrition levies a heavy toll on human health, leading to increased susceptibility to disease, reduced levels of energy and productivity, and increased morbidity and mortality.[5]

Roughly one out of five people in the developing world—an estimated 828 million, primarily women and children—goes hungry every day, lacking enough calories and protein to satisfy basic body requirements.[6] The greatest concentration of these less fortunate people is in South Asia and sub-Saharan Africa.[7] More than 20 percent of South Asia's population is starving, with rates as high as 30 percent in Bangladesh and 70 percent in impoverished and war-torn Afghanistan.[8] Some 200 million—over one out of five people—go hungry in India alone.[9] South Asia is home to about half of the world's starving children.[10]

In sub-Saharan Africa, widespread poverty and conflict combine to deny nearly 40 percent of the population—more than 200 million people—adequate food.[11] East African nations, such as Somalia, Ethiopia, and Mozambique, are hit hardest, with over 60 percent of their populations going hungry.[12]

Weather-related crop failure or food shortages related to violent conflict significantly exacerbate hunger, but overall starvation most often stems from poverty.[13] The world's undernourished are concentrated in the poorest regions and poorest nations, since the poor lack the purchasing power to obtain food.[14] For instance, while just over 10 percent of the people in Chile and Costa Rica go hungry, in poorer Western Hemisphere nations like Bolivia and Haiti, the figures are 30 and 70 percent, respectively.[15]

In addition, billions of poor people get enough total calories, but lack essential micronutrients, such as iron or Vitamin A.[16] Stemming from overly monotonous diets, these deficiencies represent the most widespread form of malnutrition worldwide—though less recognizable than hunger or obesity.[17] Iron deficiency affects nearly 3.6 billion worldwide (leading to energy-sapping anemia in 2 billion people); nearly 840 million lack sufficient iodine, and Vitamin A deficiency affects over 40 percent of children worldwide.[18]

Undernourished children are at a higher risk for most infectious diseases—including pediatric killers like diarrhea and pneumonia.[19] About half the deaths in children worldwide are associated with malnutrition—more than 6 million deaths each year.[20] Since inadequate food intake in childhood leads to permanent mental and physical stunting, underweight children today represent a potent barrier to a nation's social and economic progress.[21] (See Table 1.)

A different situation prevails in wealthy, industrial nations, where sedentary lifestyles combine with excessive consumption of high-fat and high-sugar foods to create overweight populations.[22] (See Table 2.) In the United States, 55 percent of adults—nearly 100 million people—are overweight, with a slightly smaller share in Canada, Scandinavia, and West European nations.[23] In Eastern Europe and the former Soviet bloc, the incidence of being overweight has long been above 50 percent, although the recent economic downturn in Russia has plunged tens of millions into poverty and boosted rates of hunger.[24]

Despite a surge in weight-loss programs and diet book sales, industrial-world diets continue to deteriorate along with exercise regimens,

TABLE 1: SHARE OF CHILDREN UNDER
FIVE YEARS OF AGE WHO ARE
UNDERWEIGHT, SELECTED COUNTRIES,
MID-1990S

COUNTRY	SHARE (percent)
Bangladesh	56
India	53
Ethiopia	48
Viet Nam	45
Nigeria	35
Indonesia	34

SOURCE: M. de Onis et al., "The Worldwide Magnitude of
Protein-Energy Malnutrition: An Overview from the WHO
Global Database on Child Growth" (Geneva: WHO, January
1998).

boosting the prevalence of overweightness and
obesity dramatically in recent decades.[25] The
share of the U.S. population that is overweight
has doubled since the 1960s, while the percentage of obese people—those most severely
overweight—in England and Canada doubled
in the last 10 years alone.[26]

In the developing world, too, the widespread decline of physical activity as nations
urbanize, combined with rising intake of
high-fat livestock products and convenience
foods, promotes soaring levels of lifestyle
malnutrition.[27] Cities throughout the developing world host an ironic coexistence of underweight and overweight people.[28] In several
Latin American nations, such as Brazil and
Colombia, the prevalence of overweight people—at 30 and 40 percent—approaches that in
some European nations.[29]

Being overweight or obese is a significant
risk factor for most chronic noncommunicable diseases, including diabetes, cardiovascular disease, stroke, and various cancers.[30] A
recent survey indicated that roughly 70 percent of diabetes cases could be averted if
patients were not overweight.[31] And debilitat-
ing conditions—like asthma, arthritis, osteo-
porosis, and back pain—disproportionately
afflict the overweight.[32]

Despite excessive food intake, the overweight also suffer from diet-related deficien-

cies. Sugar- and fat-rich foods—high in calories
but low in fiber, calcium, iron, Vitamin C, and
other essential nutrients—squeeze out more
nutritious food items, leading to nutrient starvation masked by weight gain.[33] And diets
high in processed foods often provide some
micronutrients, such as sodium, in amounts
far greater than is healthy.[34]

Illnesses related to being overweight consume a growing share of health care costs in
industrial nations.[35] A 1990 estimate put the
costs of obesity in the United States at $69
billion—7 percent of national health care
expenses.[36] The soaring incidence of overweight children in the industrial world suggests a dismal nutritional future.[37]

Likewise, the nutrition transition under
way in developing nations ushers in a costly
epidemiological transition, as these nations
become home to more victims of heart
attacks, stroke, and other diseases of affluence.[38] In China, the incidences of coronary
illness and diabetes have surged in step with
decreasing intake of dietary fibers and a doubling of meat consumption following rapid
income growth in recent decades.[39] Even as
the developing world struggles to control
waterborne infections and other diseases of
poverty, these countries face soaring health
care costs related to affluent malnutrition.[40]

TABLE 2: SHARE OF ADULTS WHO
ARE OVERWEIGHT, SELECTED
COUNTRIES, MID-1990S

COUNTRY	SHARE (percent)
United States	55
Russian Federation	54
United Kingdom	51
Germany	50
Colombia	43
Brazil	31

SOURCE: WHO, "Obesity: Preventing and Managing the
Global Epidemic," Report of a WHO Consultation on
Obesity, Geneva, 3–5 June 1997; NHLBI, "Clinical
Guidelines on the Identification, Evaluation, and Treatment
of Overweight and Obesity in Adults" (Bethesda, MD:
National Institutes of Health, 17 June 1998).

Sperm Counts Dropping
Brian Halweil

The average sperm count—the number of individual sperm in a given volume of semen—of men in the United States and Europe has plummeted by over 50 percent since the late 1930s, according to a recent analysis.[1] The finding fuels ongoing concerns that male reproductive health may be deteriorating, and that environmental pollutants may be the cause.[2]

Based on 61 studies published since 1938—involving a total of nearly 15,000 subjects—average sperm counts among healthy American men dropped from 120 million sperm per milliliter of semen in 1938 to just under 50 million in 1988, a decline of 1.5 percent a year.[3] In Europe, sperm counts fell by roughly the same amount between 1971 and 1990, though twice as fast—by 3.1 percent each year.[4] (See Figure 1.)

Though only one sperm is required to fertilize an egg, once sperm count drops below a certain level, infertility becomes increasingly common.[5]

Concerns of declining human sperm counts were first voiced in the mid-1970s, and since then several studies have suggested a substantial drop since mid-century.[6] A study of 1,350 Parisian men showed sperm counts declining from 89 million per milliliter in 1973 to 60 million in 1992—a 2.1-percent drop per year—and studies from Canada, Sweden, Greece, Italy, Belgium, and other European nations found similar declines in recent decades.[7]

Though a scientific consensus is emerging that sperm counts have decreased in certain areas, controversy remains over the global extent of the problem.[8] Indeed, there appears to be considerable geographic variation in sperm counts.[9] While declines have been demonstrated in Danish men, for instance, Finnish sperm counts appear unchanged.[10] Studies from men in four U.S. cities show considerable variation in average sperm count.[11] And a recent study suggests that sperm counts may vary considerably even within the city of London.[12]

Nonetheless, other distressing signs of deteriorating male reproductive health have surfaced in the last half-century.[13] Since 1960, rates of testicular cancer have grown two- to fourfold in Great Britain, the Nordic and Baltic countries, Australia, New Zealand, and the United States, while the incidence of malformed sperm, undescended testicles, and other disorders of the male reproductive system has also soared in industrial nations.[14]

Considerable controversy revolves around the proposed causes of declining sperm counts, though the prevailing explanation—the endocrine disruption hypothesis—implicates environmental chemicals that masquerade as hormones.[15] Since hormones such as estrogen or androgen orchestrate the development and everyday function of organisms, exposure to hormone-mimicking chemicals can disrupt these development signals.

Specifically, synthetic chemicals that mimic the female sex hormone estrogen—known as "environmental estrogens"—may influence male organisms *in utero* or early in development, when hormone sensitivity is high and when proper function of the male

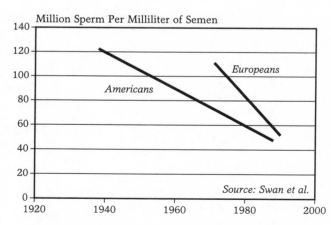

Million Sperm Per Milliliter of Semen

Americans

Europeans

Source: Swan et al.

Figure 1: Average Sperm Count of American and European Men, 1938–90

reproductive tract can be easily derailed.[16]

Abundant clinical evidence supports this hypothesis, indicating that lab animals exposed to even traces of estrogen-mimicking chemicals develop reproductive disorders, ranging from testicular cancer to infertility.[17] For example, exposing pregnant laboratory rats to dioxins—pervasive pollutants generated in paper production and waste incineration—resulted in testicular abnormalities, feminine sexual behavior, and reduced or no sperm production in male offspring.[18]

Similar results have been reported for phthalates, another group of ubiquitous environmental contaminants commonly used in products ranging from food and beverage containers to fabrics, and widely detected in drinking water and cows' milk.[19] Male mice exposed *in utero* to butyl benzyl phthalate, a component in many plastics, had substantially reduced testis size and up to 20 percent less sperm production in adulthood than mice whose mothers were not exposed.[20]

Information on the human health effects of environmental estrogens comes from accounts of maternal exposure to diethylstilbestrol—a synthetic estrogen routinely administered to pregnant women from the 1940s to the 1970s.[21] While the female offspring of these women suffer a high incidence of many rare genital diseases, the male offspring have an increased incidence of genital malformations, including small testes and penises and reduced sperm counts.[22]

Exposure to various pesticides with known estrogenic activity has been associated with reduced sperm production and infertility in agricultural workers.[23] And human studies have also demonstrated decreased sperm function with increased semen concentrations of two estrogenic pollutants: polychlorinated biphenyls and a metabolite of the pesticide DDT.[24]

Examples of similar reproductive havoc in wildlife populations have also been attributed to estrogen-mimicking chemicals.[25] In one of the best documented cases, alligators in Florida's Lake Apopka, contaminated with organochlorine insecticides with known estrogenic properties, were severely demasculinized—with greatly reduced fertility and without proper male sexual organs.[26]

From the United Kingdom to the United States, male fish living in waterways polluted with environmental estrogens are born with ovaries and eggs rather than sperm ducts.[27] Abnormal reproductive development and reduced fertility have coincided with exposure to estrogen-like compounds in mammals as diverse as otters, polar bears, and panthers.[28]

Currently, endocrine-disruptive activity has been demonstrated for roughly 60 chemicals, though only a tiny fraction of the estimated 80,000 manufactured chemicals in use today have been screened for endocrine-disrupting effects.[29] These common chemicals include certain pesticides, such as endosulfan, the most widely used insecticide in North America; the components in plastics, detergents, cosmetics, and fabrics; and other industrial products and by-products.[30]

Detection of these chemicals in our food and drinking water as well as in seemingly remote locales has led some to describe our environment as "a virtual sea of estrogens."[31] And while many of the chemicals now known to disrupt reproductive and hormone systems have been banned in the industrial world, their use grows in developing nations—though insufficient data prevent historical sperm count analyses for these nations.[32]

Pinning down the extent—and possible causes of—sperm count decline requires better data on sperm counts as well as on human exposure to endocrine disruptors. The International Study of Semen Quality in Partners of Pregnant Women—started in 1997, with study centers in four European cities, four U.S. cities, and one city in Japan—aims to identify geographic variation in sperm counts and possible environmental drivers.[33] In late 1998, Japan's Ministry of Health and Welfare initiated a major research project to examine trends in sperm counts of Japanese men.[34] And by congressional mandate, the U.S. Environmental Protection Agency is currently testing 15,000 chemicals for possible effects as endocrine disruptors.[35]

People Everywhere Eating More Fast Food   Gary Gardner

Fast-food restaurants are multiplying rapidly worldwide, the result of a confluence of social, economic, and cultural trends. Fast food now accounts for roughly half of restaurant revenues in the United States—triple its share in the early 1970s—and the industry continues to expand there and in other industrial countries.[1] But some of the most rapid growth is found in prospering developing countries, where demographic and sociological changes are altering the way people eat.

As used here, "fast-food restaurants" refers to chain outlets that primarily offer drive-through, carryout, counter, or delivery food service. The industry leader is McDonald's, which operates more than 23,000 restaurants in 113 countries; in 1997, McDonald's opened five new restaurants a day.[2] The company accounts for 45 percent of global brand name fast-food establishments and 60 percent of the sales.[3] But McDonald's faces stiff competition from a host of other chains. The next nine largest U.S.-based chains operate a total of more than 75,000 restaurants—three times as many as McDonald's.[4] The growth of these 10 companies over the last decade has been phenomenal. (See Figure 1.)[5]

Data for the U.S. chains' share of the global fast-food market are not available, but it is likely to be high: McDonald's alone reports having the highest market share in the "great majority" of the countries in which it operates.[6] The global reach of these restaurants is a relatively new phenomenon: overseas outlets owned by the top 50 U.S. restaurant chains grew from 900 in the early 1970s to more than 32,000 in 1997.[7] McDonald's and Kentucky Fried Chicken (KFC) now generate about half of their revenues from their non-U.S. operations, and 85 percent of McDonald's 1997 openings took place outside the United States.[8]

Fast-food outlets trace their roots to the drive-in restaurants—where "carhops" served people in their parked cars—that thrived in southern California in the 1940s and 1950s.[9] But the first true fast-food restaurant opened in 1948, when the McDonald brothers remodeled their hamburger drive-in restaurant in San Bernardino around the core characteristics of fast-food chains: self-service, disposable dinnerware, and quick service.[10] Once strategic franchising was added to the mix in 1955 and the keys to McDonald's success were copied by other restaurant chains, fast-food outlets of all kinds spread rapidly throughout the United States and, later, the world.[11]

The emphasis on speedy delivery of food is a response to changing societal conditions. The rise in single-person households and single-parent families and the increase in the ranks of working women in the postwar era have together reduced the time available for meal preparation and placed a premium on convenience.[12] By one estimate, most of the meals eaten in the United States today are prepared outside the home and are often eaten while on the go: the second most popular place for Americans to eat breakfast is in their car.[13] In addition to these changes in lifestyle, increases in disposable income in many countries and heavy advertising—McDonald's is the world's nineteenth largest advertiser—have helped boost fast-food sales.[14]

One reason these trends are worrisome is the health effects of fast food, which is often high in calories, sodium, fat, and cholesterol. At many fast-food restaurants, a single meal gives a disproportionate share—and sometimes more than 100 percent—of the recommended daily intake of these elements.[15] Excessive consumption of fast food produces a diet high in saturated fats and low in fruits and vegetables, which increases the risk of obesity, coronary heart disease, hypertension, diabetes, and several forms of cancer.[16] Fifty-five percent of Americans are considered overweight or obese, the result of poor eating habits (often including excessive consumption of fast food) and a sedentary lifestyle.[17] In developing countries, too, the prevalence of obesity, hypertension, and coronary heart disease are all much greater in urban areas—where fast food and street vendors are commonly found—than in rural areas.[18]

The global expansion of American fast food also has far-ranging cultural effects. Hamburgers, pizza, chicken, and cheese are a growing part of diets even in countries previously unfamiliar with them. Many chains alter their menus to some degree to cater to local tastes, but most companies strive for consistency of products and services across countries. Management strategies are also standardized to ensure consistency. McDonald's now offers its "Hamburger University" management training curriculum in 24 languages, and Tricon Global Restaurants disseminates a "brand toolkit" of marketing materials that help build a consistent image globally for its Pizza Hut, KFC, and Taco Bell restaurants.[19]

The cultural impact of fast-food outlets often extends beyond the restaurant industry. McDonald's and Burger King have both teamed with Walt Disney Productions for joint promotions of fast food and new movies, thereby pushing American entertainment as well as diet into markets worldwide.[20] In June 1998, McDonald's and Disney launched their first global promotion, offering McDonald's customers a toy—packaged for 38 different language markets—depicting a character from the new Disney movie *Mulan*.[21] McDonald's is now experimenting with "video walls" in a few of its restaurants to show Disney films.[22]

The huge volume of food purchased by fast-food restaurants also affects agriculture. Some 28 percent of U.S. potato production in 1997, for example, became french fries—the vast majority of which were used in fast-food restaurants.[23] Such a large market presence allows fast-food chains to bargain for the lowest potato prices. Those who can supply potatoes cheaply are large-scale farmers and processors, who can capture significant economies of scale. Partly as a result of these dynamics, potato farming in Idaho has become more concentrated over the past quarter-century: the area devoted to potato production has increased by a third, but the number of farmers has fallen by half.[24]

While growth in fast food is brisk, some consumers are looking for higher quality alternatives. Rushed American consumers are turning to supermarkets for prepared foods such as rotisserie chicken and selections from salad bars; sales of these "home meal replacements" surged 13 percent between 1996 and 1997, and are projected to more than triple between 1997 and 2005.[25] Those in less of a hurry are also finding alternatives. Fresh organic foods are increasingly popular in Europe, Japan, and the United States. And a "slow food" movement founded in 1986 in Italy to promote appreciation of food and the cultural experience of shared meals now claims 60,000 members in 400 clubs worldwide.[26] Whether these trends will dampen the rapid expansion of fast food remains to be seen.

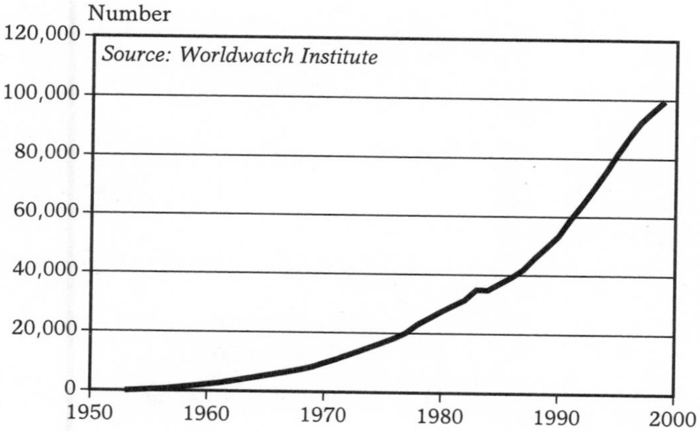

Figure 1: Estimated Number of Restaurants Worldwide of the Top 10 U.S. Fast-Food Chains with International Operations

Military Features

Small Arms Found in All Nations   Michael Renner

The devastating impact of so-called small arms and light weapons—weapons that can be carried by an individual or a pack animal—is attracting growing attention worldwide.[1] Some 500 million military-style small arms are believed to be in circulation.[2]

The domestic and international proliferation of small arms has encouraged an impulsive reliance on violence to settle unresolved disputes. These weapons are used both in wars that pit nations against one another and in the far greater number of "civil wars" involving ethnic militias, private armies, insurgent groups, and criminal organizations.

There is far more capacity in the world to produce small arms than to manufacture major weapons such as tanks or jet fighters. The United Nations Institute for Disarmament Research (UNIDIR) in Geneva has identified close to 300 companies in 52 countries that were manufacturing small arms and related equipment in 1994.[3] And the number of countries had increased by 25 percent since the mid-1980s.[4] A more recent count, based on the 1998–99 edition of *Jane's Infantry Weapons*, comes up with 377 companies in 49 countries.[5]

The United States, Russia, China, Germany, Belgium, Italy, Switzerland, Austria, the Czech Republic, Bulgaria, and Israel are among the most important producers and exporters of small arms.[6]

Small arms production is taking place under license in at least 24 developing countries, many of which are also exporting weapons.[7] Prominent among them are Brazil, Chile, Egypt, Iran, South Africa, Turkey, India, Indonesia, North and South Korea, Pakistan, and Singapore.[8]

The Soviet/Russian Kalashnikov assault rifle (AK-47) has been sold around the world in such enormous quantities that it has become the premier symbol of the small arms trade. At least 50 million and perhaps as many as 70 million copies have been produced to date.[9] They have been adopted by the national armed forces of some 78 countries.[10] (See Table 1.) But in addition, as *Jane's* explains, "practically all communist-influ-enced guerrilla and nationalist movements of recent decades seem to have obtained...stocks of AK-47s."[11] A dozen countries have produced Kalashnikov rifles. And weapons whose design is based on the Kalashnikov have been manufactured in Israel, South Africa, Croatia, Finland, and India.[12]

Adopted by the armies of 94 countries, the Belgian FN-FAL rifle is the most widely distributed military rifle.[13] Another weapon found in many arsenals around the world is the German G-3; it has been produced in 12 other countries in addition to Germany.[14] Many of these licensed producers have been granted marketing rights, so G-3 rifles may be found almost anywhere, according to *Jane's*.[15]

Assault rifles are among the most mass-produced weapons. Worldwide, it is estimated that at least 100 million are in circulation.[16] At least 79 companies in 50 countries produce assault and sniper rifles, or have done so recently.[17] Some 111 models of military rifles are currently in production.[18] Another 10 are classified as "available" (that is, production could be geared up in response to orders). And 37 models are no longer in production, though in same cases large stocks still exist.[19] Meanwhile, five new types are currently in development or nearing production.[20]

Other small arms, too, are available in bewildering variety. For instance, 64 different models of submachine guns are now produced, or were recently produced, by 45 companies in 29 countries; similarly, 91 models of machine guns have been manufactured by 46 companies in 30 countries.[21] And a total of 54 firms in 30 countries are identified as makers of pistols.[22]

Recent years have witnessed a growing number of initiatives to stop the proliferation of small arms. Most governmental efforts have emphasized cracking down on illegal production and transfers. The Organization of American States, for example, passed a convention toward that end in November 1997.[23] A growing list of organizations is joining the bandwagon: among them are the European Union, the Group of Eight industrial nations, the North Atlantic Treaty Organization, the

Organisation for Economic Co-operation and Development, and the World Customs Organization.[24] But it is rapidly becoming clear that legal transfers must attract greater scrutiny as well.[25]

Many different departments and agencies of the United Nations have become involved because small arms violence undermines their objectives—whether it be peacekeeping, humanitarian assistance, child welfare, or social development. In June 1998, the United Nations launched an effort to better coordinate these endeavors.[26]

Pursuing weapons collection efforts, the U.N. system kicked off a "weapons for development" program in Albania in early 1999.[27] It also provided support for arms collection in Mali and helped bring about a three-year moratorium on the import, export, and manufacture of small arms in West Africa endorsed by 16 states in the region.[28] Elsewhere on the continent, South Africa became a leader by pledging to destroy its 260,000 surplus small arms instead of selling them off cheaply, as is still standard practice.[29]

Nongovernmental organizations have played a critical role from the very start, and, along with like-minded governments, their prodding will continue to be indispensable. In early 1998, a Web-based organization called "Prep Com" was set up to facilitate exchange of information; by early 1999, it had 173 members from more than 60 countries.[30] In 1999, Prep Com will become the International Action Network on Small Arms, to coordinate the many small arms–related campaigns.[31]

TABLE 1: PRODUCTION AND DISTRIBUTION OF SELECTED SMALL ARMS

TYPE OF WEAPON	NUMBER PRODUCED (million)	COUNTRIES PRODUCING THE WEAPON (number)	COUNTRIES WITH WEAPON IN INVENTORY (number)
Assault Rifles			
AK-47[1], AK-74			
(Soviet Union/Russia)	50–70	12	78
M-16 (United States)	8	6	67
G-3 (Germany)	7+	13	64
FN-FAL (Belgium)	5–7	12	94
Galil (Israel)	n.a.	2	14
Submachine Guns			
Uzi (Israel)	10	4	47
HK MP5 (Germany)	n.a.	7	42
Sterling[1]			
(United Kingdom)	n.a.	3	40
Beretta M12[1] (Italy)	n.a.	n.a.	24
Machine Guns			
FN-MAG (Belgium)	0.2	6	81
RPD, RPK[2] (FSU/Russia)	n.a.	7	46
MG3[2] (Germany)	n.a.	7	13
Bren L4[2]			
(United Kingdom)	n.a.	4	22

[1]No longer in production. [2]No longer in production in country of origin, but still manufactured elsewhere under license.
SOURCES: Terry J. Gander, ed., *Jane's Infantry Weapons 1996–97* and *Jane's Infantry Weapons 1998–99* (Coulsdon, U.K.: Jane's Information Group Ltd., 1996 and 1998); U.N. General Assembly, "Report of the Panel of Governmental Experts on Small Arms" (New York: 27 August 1997).

NOTES

GRAIN HARVEST DROPS
(pages 30–31)

1. U.S. Department of Agriculture (USDA), Foreign Agricultural Service (FAS), *Grain: World Markets and Trade* (Washington, DC: February 1999).
2. Ibid.; U.S. Bureau of the Census, *International Data Base*, electronic database, Suitland, MD, updated 30 November 1998.
3. USDA, op. cit. note 1; USDA, *Production, Supply, and Distribution (PS&D)*, electronic database, Washington, DC, updated February 1999; 1950–59 grain data from USDA, "World Grain Database," unpublished printout, Washington, DC, 1991; Bureau of Census, op. cit. note 2.
4. USDA, op. cit. note 1; Michael R. Gordon, "Food Crisis Forces Russia to Swallow its Pride," *New York Times*, 7 November 1998.
5. USDA, op. cit. note 1.
6. Ibid.
7. Ibid.
8. Ibid.
9. Ibid.
10. Ibid.
11. Ibid.
12. Ibid.
13. Ibid.; John Pomfret, "Yangtze Flood Jolts China's Land Policies," *Washington Post*, 22 November 1998.
14. USDA, *PS&D*, op. cit. note 3.
15. USDA, op. cit. note 1.
16. Ibid.; USDA, "World Grain Database," op. cit. note 3; USDA, *PS&D*, op. cit. note 3.
17. USDA, op. cit. note 1; USDA, "World Grain Database," op. cit. note 3; USDA, *PS&D*, op. cit. note 3.
18. USDA, *PS&D*, op. cit. note 3.
19. "Bumper Crops in 1998, But Farmers Face Losses," *New York Times*, 13 January 1999.
20. Sam Howe Verhovek, "Northwest Farms and Industry Pinched by Asia's Fiscal Crisis," *New York Times*, 1 October 1998.
21. Keith B. Richburg, "Indonesian Collapse Less Severe Than Feared," *Washington Post*, 25 January 1999.
22. Ibid.; World Bank, "Indonesia: Rice Security During the Crisis," *World Bank Brief*, October 1998.
23. USDA, *PS&D*, op. cit. note 3; Bureau of Census, op. cit. note 2.
24. U.N. Food and Agriculture Organization, *The State of Food and Agriculture* (Rome: 1998).

SOYBEAN HARVEST DOWN
(pages 32–33)

1. U.S. Department of Agriculture (USDA), Foreign Agricultural Service (FAS), *Oilseeds: World Markets and Trade* (Washington, DC: February 1999); USDA, *Production, Supply, and Distribution (PS&D)*, electronic database, Washington, DC, updated February 1999.
2. USDA, *PS&D*, op. cit. note 1; U.S. Bureau of the Census, *International Data Base*, electronic database, Suitland, MD, updated 30 November 1998.
3. USDA, *Oilseeds*, op. cit. note 1.
4. USDA, *PS&D*, op. cit. note 1.
5. Ibid.; Bureau of Census, op. cit. note 2.
6. USDA, *Oilseeds*, op. cit. note 1.
7. USDA, *PS&D*, op. cit. note 1.
8. USDA, *Oilseeds*, op. cit. note 1.
9. Ibid.
10. USDA, *PS&D*, op. cit. note 1.
11. Ibid.
12. Ibid.
13. Ibid.
14. Preliminary 1997 estimate from Maurizio Perotti, fishery statistician, Fishery Information, Data, and Statistics Service, Fisheries Department, U.N. Food and Agriculture Organization, Rome, e-mail to Anne McGinn, 19 November 1998.

15. USDA, *PS&D*, op. cit. note 1.
16. Ibid.
17. USDA, *Oilseeds*, op. cit. note 1.
18. Ibid.
19. Ibid
20. Ibid
21. Ibid
22. Ibid.

MEAT PRODUCTION GROWTH SLOWS (pages 34–35)

1. U.S. Department of Agriculture (USDA), Foreign Agricultural Service (FAS), *Livestock and Poultry: World Markets and Trade* (Washington, DC: October 1998).
2. Ibid.; U.S. Bureau of the Census, *International Data Base*, electronic database, Suitland, MD, updated 30 November 1998.
3. USDA, op. cit. note 1.
4. Ibid.
5. U.N. Food and Agriculture Organization, *The State of Food and Agriculture* (Rome: 1998).
6. USDA, op. cit. note 1.
7. Ibid.
8. Ibid.
9. Ibid.; Eric J. Wailes et al., "China's Livestock Feed Use Relationships: Preliminary Results from a Survey in Seven Provinces," paper presented at Western Region Coordinating Committee Annual Meeting, Honolulu, HI, 12–13 January 1998.
10. USDA, op. cit. note 1.
11. Ibid.
12. Ibid.; Michael R. Gordon, "Food Crisis Forces Russia to Swallow its Pride," *New York Times*, 7 November 1998.
13. USDA, op. cit. note 1.
14. Ibid.
15. Ibid.
16. Ibid.; Wailes et al., op. cit. note 9.
17. Wailes et al., op. cit. note 9.
18. USDA, op. cit. note 1.
19. Ibid.
20. Ibid.
21. Ibid.
22. Ibid.
23. Ibid.
24. Ibid.
25. Ibid.
26. Ibid.

FISHERIES FALTER (pages 36–37)

1. Preliminary 1997 estimates from Maurizio Perotti, fishery statistician, Fishery Information, Data, and Statistics Service, Fisheries Department, U.N. Food and Agriculture Organization (FAO), Rome, e-mail to author, 19 November 1998.
2. Population data from U.S. Bureau of the Census, *International Data Base*, electronic database, Suitland, MD, updated 30 November 1998.
3. "Worst Fishing for 17 Years," Fish Information Service, < http://www.sea-world.com/fis/hot-news/article.asp?value = 7386 >, viewed 17 January 1999; ranking of fish species from FAO, *Fishery Statistics: Capture Production, 1996* (Rome: 1998).
4. FAO, op. cit. note 3.
5. Gary Mead, "El Niño Wreaks Havoc on Fish Meal Industry," *Financial Times*, 28 May 1998.
6. S.M. Garcia and C. Newton, "Current Situation, Trends, and Prospects in World Fisheries," in E.K. Pikitch, D.D. Huppert, and M.P. Sissenwine, *Global Trends: Fisheries Management*, American Fisheries Society (AFS) Symposium 20 (Bethesda, MD: AFS, 1997).
7. FAO, op. cit. note 3.
8. One fourth from Garcia and Newton, op. cit. note 6.
9. Daniel Pauly et al., "Fishing Down Marine Food Webs," *Science*, 6 February 1998.
10. Jill M. Casey and Ransom A. Myers, "Near Extinction of a Large, Widely Distributed Fish,"*Science*, 31 July 1998.
11. "New Limits on Pollock Fishing Sought," *Washington Post*, 5 December 1998.
12. Jocelyn Kaiser, "Sea Otter Declines Blamed on Hungry Killers," *Science*, 16 October 1998.
13. "New Limits on Pollock Fishing Sought," op. cit. note 11.
14. J.A. Estes et al., "Killer Whale Predation on Sea Otters Linking Oceanic and Nearshore Ecosystems," *Science,* 16 October 1998.
15. U.N. Secretary-General, *Oceans and the Law of the Sea: Report of the Secretary-General*, presented 8 October 1998 to U.N. General Assembly, available at < http://www.un.org/Depts/los/a53_456.htm >, viewed 19 January 1999.
16. Ibid.
17. Ben Spiess, "Ships Tangle in Battle Over Drift Nets," *USA Today*, 5 June 1998.
18. Gareth Porter, *Too Much Fishing Fleet, Too Few Fish: A Proposal for Eliminating Global Fishing*

Overcapacity (Washington, DC: World Wildlife Fund, 1998).

19. John Fitzpatrick and Chris Newton, *Assessment of the World's Fishing Fleet, 1991–1997* (Washington, DC: Greenpeace International, May 1998).

20. Shahid Hussain, "Overfishing Can Be Fatal," *The Dawn* (Karachi, Pakistan), 23 November 1998.

21. U.S. National Oceanic and Atmospheric Administration (NOAA), "U.S. Gains Agreement by World Fishing Nations at U.N. Meeting to Reduce Excess Capacity, Save Sharks and Seabirds," press release (Washington, DC: 22 February 1999).

22. NOAA, "U.S. Achieves Conservation Objectives at Recent International Meeting on Atlantic Salmon," press release (Washington, DC: 23 June 1998).

GRAIN STOCKS DOWN SLIGHTLY
(pages 38–39)

1. U.S. Department of Agriculture (USDA), Foreign Agricultural Service (FAS), *Grain: World Markets and Trade* (Washington, DC: February 1999); days of consumption are calculated by dividing annual global grain consumption by 365 and then dividing the result by world carryover stocks.

2. USDA, *Production, Supply, and Distribution,* electronic database, Washington, DC, updated Februrary 1999.

3. Ibid.

4. Ibid.

5. Ibid.

6. Michael R. Gordon, "Food Crisis Forces Russia to Swallow its Pride," *New York Times,* 7 November 1998.

7. Ibid.; USDA, op. cit. note 2.

8. USDA, op. cit. note 1.

9. USDA, op. cit. note 2.

10. Ibid.

11. Ibid.

12. USDA, op. cit. note 1.

13. Ibid.

14. USDA, op. cit. note 2.

15. Ibid.

16. Wheat prices from commodity time-series provided by Charles Van Lahr, agricultural statistician, National Agricultural Statistics Service, USDA, e-mail to author, 27 January 1999.

17. Idled land from USDA, Economic Research Service, "AREI Updates: Cropland Use in 1997," No. 5 (Washington, DC: 1997).

18. USDA, op. cit. note 1.

GRAIN AREA DECLINES
(pages 42–43)

1. U.S. Department of Agriculture (USDA), *Production, Supply, and Distribution,* electronic database, Washington, DC, updated February 1999.

2. Ibid.

3. Ibid.; U.S. Bureau of the Census, *International Data Base,* electronic database, Suitland, MD, updated 30 November 1998.

4. Tim Dyson, *Population and Food: Global Trends and Future Prospects* (London: Routledge, 1996).

5. U.N. Food and Agriculture Organization (FAO), *FAOSTAT Statistics Database,* < http://www. apps.fao.org >, viewed 16 November 1998; cropland here refers to land under temporary crops, temporary meadows for mowing or pasture, land under market and kitchen gardens, and land temporarily fallow (less than five years).

6. USDA, op. cit. note 1.

7. Ibid.

8. Ibid.

9. Ibid.; USDA, Economic Research Service (ERS), "AREI Updates: Cropland Use in 1997," No. 5 (Washington, DC: 1997).

10. USDA, ERS, International Agriculture and Trade Reports, "China: Situation and Outlook Series" (Washington, DC: July 1998).

11. Mark W. Rosegrant, Claudi Ringler, and Roberta Gerpacio, "Water and Land Resources and Global Food Supply," paper prepared for the 23rd International Conference of Agricultural Economists on Food Security, Diversification, and Resource Management: Refocusing the Role of Agriculture, Sacramento, CA., 10–16 August 1997 (Washington, DC: International Food Policy Research Institute (IFPRI), 1997); Daniel B. Wood, "Suburbia Consumes California's Fruit Basket to the World," *Christian Science Monitor,* 11 September 1997.

12. USDA, op. cit. note 1.

13. FAO, *World Agriculture: Towards 2010* (New York: John Wiley & Sons, 1995).

14. Sara J. Scherr, "Soil Degradation: A Threat to Developing-Country Food Security by 2020?"

Food, Agriculture, and the Environment Discussion Paper 27 (Washington: IFPRI, February 1999).

15. USDA, op. cit. note 1.

16. Ibid.; Bureau of Census, op. cit. note 3; United Nations, *World Population Prospects 1950–2050: The 1998 Revision* (New York: December 1998).

17. Mark W. Rosegrant and Claudia Ringler, "World Food Markets into the 21st Century: Environmental and Resource Constraints and Policies," revision of a paper presented at the RIRDC-sponsored plenary session of the 41st Annual Conference of the Australian Agricultural and Resource Economics Society, held in Queensland, Gold Coast, Australia, 22–25 January 1997.

18. FAO, op. cit. note 13.

19. Ibid.

20. USDA, op. cit. note 1.

21. Idled land from USDA, op. cit. note 9.

22. FAO, op. cit. note 13; Rosegrant, Ringler, and Gerpacio, op. cit. note 11.

IRRIGATED AREA UP (pages 44–45)

1. U.N. Food and Agriculture Organization (FAO), *FAOSTAT Statistics Database*, <http://www.fao.org>, Rome, viewed 30 December 1998; U.S. Department of Agriculture (USDA), *Agricultural Resources and Environmental Indicators, 1996–97* (Washington, DC: 1997); Bill Quinby, USDA, Economic Research Service, discussion with author, 25 January 1999.

2. FAO, op. cit. note 1.

3. Ibid.

4. Ibid.

5. Ibid.; population from United Nations, *World Population Prospects 1950–2050: The 1998 Revision* (New York: December 1998).

6. FAO, op. cit. note 1.

7. Ibid.

8. Ibid.

9. Ibid.

10. FAO, "Food Production: The Critical Role of Water," in *Technical Background Documents 6–11: Vol. 2* (Rome: 1996).

11. Pierre Crosson, "Future Supplies of Land and Water for World Agriculture," revision of a paper presented at a conference of the International Food Policy Research Institute in February 1994, Resources for the Future, Washington, DC, August 1994.

12. Sandra L. Postel, "Water for Food Production: Will There Be Enough in 2025?" *BioScience*, August 1998.

13. David Seckler, David Molden, and Randolph Barker, "Water Scarcity in the Twenty-First Century," International Water Management Institute (Colombo, Sri Lanka: unpublished, 27 July 1998).

14. Figure of 40 percent from Lester Brown and Brian Halweil, "The Drying of China," *World Watch*, July/August 1998.

15. Seckler, Molden, and Barker, op. cit. note 13.

16. Ibid.

17. Ibid.

18. Postel, op. cit. note 12.

19. Ibid.

20. Seckler, Molden, and Barker, op. cit. note 13.

GROWTH IN FOSSIL FUEL BURNING SLOWS (pages 48–49)

1. The 1998 figure is a preliminary Worldwatch estimate based on British Petroleum (BP), *BP Statistical Review of World Energy 1997* (London: Group Media & Publications, 1998), on U.S. Department of Energy (DOE), Energy Information Administration (EIA), *Monthly Energy Review*, January 1999 (Washington, DC: 1999), on European Commission, *1998 Annual Energy Review* (Brussels: 1999), on Eurogas, "Natural Gas Consumption in Western Europe Sets a New Record in 1998," press release (Brussels: February 1999), on PlanEcon, Inc., *PlanEcon Energy Outlook: Regional Energy Update for 1997–98* (Washington, DC: 1998), on International Monetary Fund, *World Economic Outlook and International Capital Markets*, Interim Assessment (Washington, DC: December 1998), and on David Fridley, Lawrence Berkeley National Laboratory, Berkeley, CA, letter to author, 25 February 1999; 1950–97 data based on United Nations, *World Energy Supplies 1950–74* (New York: 1976), on BP, *BP Statistical Review of World Energy* (London: Group Media & Publications, various years), and on DOE, EIA, *International Energy Database*, May 1998.

2. DOE, *Monthly Energy Review*, op. cit. note 1.

3. Ibid.

4. Worldwatch Institute based on BP, *Statistical Review of World Energy* (various years), op. cit. note 1.

5. Michael R. Gordon, "Oil Price Drop Threatens to Squelch Russia's Economic Rebound," *New York Times*, 20 March 1998.
6. "Shell Losses Cut by Half," *Financial Times*, 12 February 1999.
7. Estrella Gutierrez, "1998 Will Live in Infamy for Oil Producers," *Global Information Network*, 25 January 1999.
8. "Tremors from Cheap Oil," *Business Week*, 14 December 1998.
9. Bob Williams, "Oil Producers Face Key Question: How Long Will Prices Stay Low?" *Oil and Gas Journal*, 28 December 1998; Ron Chernow, "No Funeral for OPEC Just Yet," *New York Times*, 5 January 1999.
10. Eurogas, op. cit. note 1; "Asia-Pacific Gas Projects Hit the Wall Amid Regional Economic Slump," *Oil and Gas Journal*, 8 February 1999.
11. Zhao Shaoqin, "Tarim Basin to Fuel China," *China Daily*, 12 October 1998.
12. Worldwatch Institute estimate based on sources cited in note 1.
13. Ibid.
14. Fridley, op. cit. note 1.
15. Ibid.
16. Mike R. Bowlin, "Clean Energy: Preparing Today for Tomorrow's Challenges," presented at Cambridge Energy Research Associates, 18th Annual Executive Conference: Globality & Energy: Strategies for the New Millennium, Houston, TX, 9 February 1999.

NUCLEAR POWER DECLINES SLIGHTLY (pages 50–51)

1. Installed nuclear capacity is defined as reactors connected to the grid as of 31 December 1998, and is based on Worldwatch Institute database complied from statistics from the International Atomic Energy Agency (IAEA) and press reports primarily from *Nucleonics Week, New York Times, Financial Times,* and Web sites. The previous decline in global capacity occurred in 1991.
2. Worldwatch Institute database, op cit. note 1.
3. Ibid.
4. Ibid.
5. Ibid.
6. Ibid. An additional two reactors in the United States that ceased operation in 1996 and 1997 were deemed permanently closed by their owner in early 1998; the resulting decreases in capacity are included in the 1996 and 1997 categories, however.
7. Worldwatch Institute database, op cit. note 1. Excluded from the list of operating reactors are seven in Canada that are officially "laid up" for repairs. Although not listed as permanently closed yet, it appears highly unlikely these reactors will ever operate again. Data for 1993 are from IAEA, *Nuclear Power Reactors in the World* (Vienna: 1994).
8. "Framatome: RHR Bypass Cracking Result of Bad Luck, Not Errors," *Nucleonics Week*, 29 October 1998.
9. "Schroeder to Preside Over January Phase-out Showdown," *Nucleonics Week*, 24 December 1998.
10. "New Government Won't Change Sweden's Nuclear Policy," *Nucleonics Week*, 8 October 1998.
11. "Swedish Supreme Court Delays N-Reactor Ruling," *Reuters*, 22 December 1998.
12. "Belgium Cancels Reprocessing, Orders Review of Nuclear Future," *Nucleonics Week*, 10 December 1998.
13. "France Cools Toward New Nuclear Plant Facilities," *The Electricity Daily*, 27 October 1998.
14. For example, GPU Energy's Oyster Creek is scheduled to close in 2000 due to its lack of economic competitiveness; "GPU to Close Oyster Creek," *Greenwire*, 7 July 1998.
15. "Nuclear Winter," *The Economist*, 10 January 1998.
16. "Korea Bracing for Chang to Trim Nuclear Buildup," *Nucleonics Week*, 19 November 1998.
17. "Japan Approves Nuclear Power Plant for First Time in 10 Years," *Agence France Press*, 31 August 1998.
18. Mika Ohbayashi, Citizens Nuclear Information Center, Tokyo, e-mail to author, 25 January 1999; "Tokai I Shutdown for Decommissioning: Legacy of Difficulties Waiting Ahead," *Nuke Info Tokyo*, March/April 1998.
19. "Nuclear Winter," op cit. note 15.
20. "India Starts Building Two New Nuclear Reactors—Agency," *Reuters*, 12 October 1998.
21. "Nationalist Indian Government Doubles Nuclear Power Funding," *Nucleonics Week*, 19 November 1998.
22. "India Starts Building," op cit. note 20.
23. Vladimir Sliviak, Socio-Ecological Union, Moscow, e-mail to author, 15 January 1999.
24. "K2/R4 Consultation Period Ends Amid Protests, Improving Prospects," *Nucleonics Week*, 17 December 1998.

WIND POWER BLOWS TO NEW RECORD (pages 52–53)

1. Worldwatch preliminary estimate based on Andreas Wagner, Fordergesellschaft Windenergie, Hamburg, Germany, e-mail to author, 20 January 1999, on Soren Krohn, Danish Wind Turbine Manufacturers Association, Copenhagen, Denmark, e-mail to author, 15 December 1998, on Jose Santamarta, Madrid, Spain, e-mail to author, 17 February 1999, on Kent Robertson, American Wind Energy Association, Washington, DC, e-mail to author, 26 February 1999, and on Birger Madsen, BTM Consult, Ringkobing, Denmark, letter to author, 26 February 1999.
2. Historical data from BTM Consult, *International Wind Energy Development: World Market Update 1997* (Ringkobing, Denmark: March 1998).
3. Estimate based on assumed capacity factor of 20 percent, an average electricity sales price of 7¢ per kilowatt-hour, and average use of 5,000 kilowatt-hours of electricity per home per year.
4. Worldwatch Institute estimate based on total installed costs of $1,000 per kilowatt on sales of 2.1 million kilowatts of capacity in 1998.
5. Wagner, op. cit. note 1.
6. Ibid.
7. Santamarta, op. cit. note 1.
8. Energia Hidroelectrica de Navarra, S.A., "Projects and Scope of Action of Energia Hidroelectrica de Navarra" (Pamplona, Spain: August 1998).
9. Robertson, op. cit. note 1.
10. Ibid.
11. Madsen, op. cit. note 1.
12. Ibid.
13. Krohn, op. cit. note 1.
14. Ibid.
15. Neelam Mathews, "Stimulation for Public Sector Investment," *Windpower Monthly*, October 1998.
16. Ibid.
17. Niall Martin, "First Commercial Wind Farm in China," *Windpower Monthly*, September 1998.
18. Electric Power Research Institute, *Renewable Energy Technology Characterizations* (Palo Alto, CA: 1997).

SOLAR CELLS CONTINUE DOUBLE-DIGIT GROWTH (pages 54–55)

1. Paul Maycock, "1998 World Cell/Module Shipments," *PV News*, February 1999.
2. Compound annual growth rate for 1990–98 based on Paul Maycock, *PV News*, various issues.
3. Maycock, op. cit. note 1.
4. Ibid.
5. Ibid.
6. Ibid.
7. Paul Maycock, *Photovoltaic Technology, Performance, Cost and Market Forecast: 1975–2010* (version seven) (Warrenton, VA: PV Energy Systems, 1998).
8. Ibid.
9. Ibid.
10. Anil Cabraal, Mac Cosgrove-Davies, and Loretta Schaeffer, *Best Practices for Photovoltaic Household Electrification Programs: Lessons from Experiences in Selected Countries* (Washington, DC: World Bank, 1996).
11. Ibid.
12. Christopher Flavin and Molly O'Meara, "Solar Power Markets Boom," *World Watch*, September/October 1998.
13. Paul Maycock, Photovoltaic Energy Systems, Inc., Warrenton, VA, discussion with author, December 1998.
14. Paul Maycock, "Japan Expands '70000 Roofs' Program," *PV News*, July 1998.
15. Ibid.
16. Maycock, op. cit. note 1.
17. U.S. Department of Energy, "Million Solar Roofs," Action Plan (draft, 27 April 1998), at < http://www.eren.doe.gov/millionroofs/ >, viewed 13 June 1998.
18. Paul Maycock, "Italian 10,000 Roofs Program Takes Shape," *PV News*, July 1998.
19. Paul Maycock, "German '100,000 Roofs' Program Details," *PV News*, March 1999.
20. U.S. Department of Energy, Energy Information Administration, *Renewable Energy Annual 1998* (Washington, DC: 1998).
21. U.S. Department of Energy, op. cit. note 17.
22. Paul Maycock, "Million Solar Roof Action Plan Launched at Soltech," *PV News*, June 1998.
23. Daniel McQuillen, "Harnessing the Sun: Building-Integrated Photovoltaics Are Turning Ordinary Roofs and Facades Into Producers of Clean, Green Energy," *Environmental Design and*

Construction, July/August 1998.

24. "Solarex and Japanese Partners Complete World's First Zero-Energy House," *Channels* (Solarex, Frederick, MD), Fall 1998.
25. Duncan Graham-Rowe, "Hello, Sunshine," *New Scientist,* 10 October 1998.
26. Mark C. Fitzgerald, "The PV Industry and Infrastructure Evolution," *Renewable Energy World,* July 1998.
27. PV GAP Secretariat, "PV GAP Enters Implementation Phase," press release, Geneva, 9 February 1998, < http://www.pvgap.org/ >, viewed 9 December 1998; Fitzgerald, op. cit. note 25.
28. "Loan Program to Back Solar Conversions," *Washington Post*, 25 June 1998; Japanese banks from Paul Maycock, "PV Home Systems Financing in Japan," *PV News,* October 1998.

GLOBAL TEMPERATURE GOES OFF THE CHART (pages 58–59)

1. James Hansen et al., Goddard Institute for Space Studies, Surface Air Temperature Analyses, "Global Land-Ocean Temperature Index," as posted at < http://www.giss.nasa.gov/Data/GISTEMP >, viewed 26 February 1999.
2. Ibid.; Joby Warrick, "1998 is Warmest On Record," *Washington Post*, 18 December 1998.
3. James Hansen et al., Goddard Institute for Space Studies, "Global Temperature Trends: 1998 Global Surface Temperature Smashes Record," as posted at < http://www.giss.nasa.gov/research/ >, viewed 21 December 1998.
4. Ibid.
5. Ibid.
6. Hansen et al., op. cit. note 1.
7. Hansen et al., op. cit. note 3.
8. Richard Monastersky, "Sea Change in the Arctic," *Science News*, 13 February 1999; Joby Warrick, "As Glaciers Melt, Talks On Warming Face Chill," *Washington Post*, 2 November 1998; Liu Jun, "Cold Comfort for Yangtze Glaciers," *China Daily*, 20 January 1999.
9. W. Krabill et al., "Rapid Thinning of Parts of the Southern Greenland Ice Sheet," *Science*, 5 March 1999.
10. Michael E. Mann, Raymond S. Bradley, and Malcolm K. Hughes, "Global-Scale Temperature Patterns and Climate Forcing Over the Past Six Centuries," *Nature*, 23 April 1998; William

K. Stevens, "New Evidence Finds This is Warmest Century in 600 Years," *New York Times*, 28 April 1998.
11. National Oceanic and Atmospheric Administration, "Climate of 1998, Annual Review: 1998 Overview" (Asheville, NC: National Climatic Data Center, 12 January 1999).
12. Joby Warrick, "Hot Year Was Killer for Coral," *Washington Post*, 5 March 1999.
13. R. Monastersky, "Satellites Misread Global Temperatures," *Science News*, 15 August 1998.
14. F.J. Wentz and M. Schabel, "Effects of Orbital Decay on Satellite-Derived Lower-Tropospheric Temperature Trends," *Nature*, 13 August 1998.
15. C.D. Keeling and Timothy Whorf, Scripps Institution of Oceanography, La Jolla, CA, letter to Seth Dunn, Worldwatch Institute, 26 January 1999.
16. C.D. Keeling and T.P. Whorf, "Atmospheric CO_2 Concentrations (ppmv) Derived From In Situ Air Samples Collected at Mauna Loa Observatory, Hawaii," Scripps Institution of Oceanography, La Jolla, CA, August 1998; Keeling and Whorf, op. cit. note 15.
17. Keeling and Whorf, op. cit. note 15.
18. Hadley Centre for Climate Prediction and Research, *Climate Change and Its Impacts* (London: November 1998).

CARBON EMISSIONS DIP
(pages 60–61)

1. 1998 figure is preliminary Worldwatch estimate based on emissions data (including gas flaring, but excluding cement production figures) from G. Marland et al., "Global, Regional, and National CO_2 Emission Estimates from Fossil Fuel Burning, Cement Production, and Gas Flaring: 1751–1996 (revised January 1999)," Carbon Dioxide Information Analysis Center, Oak Ridge National Laboratory, < http://cdiac.esd.ornl.gov >, viewed 26 January 1999, on British Petroleum (BP), *BP Statistical Review of World Energy 1997* (London: Group Media & Publications, 1998), on U.S. Department of Energy (DOE), Energy Information Administration, *Monthly Energy Review,* January 1999 (Washington, DC: 1999), on European Commission, *1998 Annual Energy Review* (Brussels: 1999), on Eurogas, "Natural Gas Consumption in Western Europe Sets a New

Record in 1998," press release (Brussels: February 1999), on PlanEcon, Inc., *PlanEcon Energy Outlook: Regional Energy Update for 1997–98* (Washington, DC: 1998), on International Monetary Fund, *World Economic Outlook and International Capital Markets, Interim Assessment* (Washington, DC: December 1998), and on David Fridley, Lawrence Berkeley Laboratory, letter to author, Berkeley, CA, 25 February 1999.

2. Data for 1950–96 are from Marland et al., op. cit. note 1; 1997 figure is Worldwatch estimate based on ibid. and on BP, op. cit. note 1.

3. Worldwatch estimate based on Marland et al., op. cit. note 1, on BP, op. cit. note 1, and on 1998 estimate cited in note 1.

4. Worldwatch estimate based on Marland et al., op. cit. note 1, and on BP, op. cit. note 1.

5. Worldwatch estimate based on Marland et al., op. cit. note 1, and on BP, op. cit. note 1; Martha M. Hamilton, "Greenhouse Gases' Increase Slows," *Washington Post*, 4 November 1998.

6. Worldwatch estimate based on Marland et al., op. cit. note 1, and on BP, op. cit. note 1.

7. Worldwatch estimate based on Marland et al., op. cit. note 1, and on BP, op. cit. note 1.

8. Worldwatch estimate based on Marland et al., op. cit. note 1, and on BP, op. cit. note 1.

9. Worldwatch estimate based on Marland et al., op. cit. note 1, and on BP, op. cit. note 1.

10. Earth Negotiations Bulletin (ENB), "Report of the Fourth Conference of Parties to the UN Framework Convention on Climate Change, 2–13 November 1998" (New York: International Institute for Sustainable Development, 16 November 1998).

11. Worldwatch estimate based on Marland et al., op. cit. note 1, and on BP, op. cit. note 1.

12. Worldwatch estimate based on Marland et al., op. cit. note 1, and on BP, op. cit. note 1.

13. Frederick A.B. Meyerson, "Population, Carbon Emissions, and Global Warming: The Forgotten Relationship at Kyoto," *Population and Development Review*, March 1998.

14. Worldwatch estimate based on Marland et al., op. cit. note 1, and on BP, op. cit. note 1.

15. Robert Engelman, *Profiles in Carbon: An Update on Population, Consumption and Carbon Dioxide Emissions* (Washington, DC: Population Action International, 1998).

16. Ibid.

17. John T. Houghton et al., eds., *Climate Change 1995: The Science of Climate Change* (New York: Cambridge University Press, 1996).

18. Carbon Dioxide Information Analysis Center, *Trends: A Compendium of Data on Global Change* (Oak Ridge, TN: Oak Ridge National Laboratory, 1998), < http://cdiac.esd.ornl.gov >, viewed 15 January 1999; C.D. Keeling and T.P. Whorf, "Atmospheric CO_2 Concentrations (ppmv) Derived From In Situ Air Samples Collected at Mauna Loa Observatory, Hawaii," Scripps Institution of Oceanography, La Jolla, CA, August 1998; C.D. Keeling and Timothy Whorf, Scripps Institution of Oceanography, La Jolla, CA, letter to author, 26 January 1999; Houghton et al., op. cit. note 17.

19. Houghton et al., op. cit. note 17; Robert T. Watson, Marufu C. Zinyowera, and Richard H. Moss, eds., *Climate Change 1995: Impacts, Adaptations and Mitigation of Climate Change, Scientific-Technical Analyses* (New York: Cambridge University Press, 1996).

20. T.M.L. Wigley, R.L. Smith, and B.D. Santer, "Anthropogenic Influence on the Autocorrelation Structure of Hemispheric-Mean Temperatures," *Science*, 27 November 1998.

21. David S. Schimel, "The Carbon Equation," *Nature*, 21 May 1998; Peter N. Spotts, "Are We Subduing Our Allies in Fight Against Climate Change?" *Christian Science Monitor*, 28 May 1998.

22. Jorge L. Sarmiento et al., "Simulated Response of the Ocean Carbon Cycle to Anthropogenic Climate Warming," *Nature*, 21 May 1998; Mingkui Cao and F. Ian Woodward, "Dynamic Responses of Terrestrial Ecosystem Carbon Cycling to Climate Change," *Nature*, 21 May 1998; Richard D. Boone, "Roots Exert A Strong Influence on the Temperature Sensitivity of Soil Respiration," *Nature*, 10 December 1998.

23. Cao and Woodward, op. cit. note 22; Jocelyn Kaiser, "Possibly Vast Greenhouse Gas Sponge Ignites Controversy," *Science*, 16 October 1998; S. Fan et al., "A Large Terrestrial Carbon Sink in North America Implied by Atmospheric and Oceanic Carbon Dioxide Data and Models," *Science*, 16 October 1998; Hanqin Tian, "Effect of Interannual Climate Variability on Carbon Storage in Amazonian Ecosystems," *Nature*, 17 December 1998.

24. ENB, op. cit. note 10.

25. William K. Stevens, "Deadline Set to Form Rules for Reducing Gas Emissions," *New York Times*, 15 November 1998.

26. Joby Warrick, "Argentina Fuels Talks With

Pollution Pledge," *Washington Post*, 12 November 1998; John H. Cushman, "U.S. Signs a Pact to Reduce Gases Tied to Warming," *New York Times*, 13 November 1998; Secretariat, U.N. Framework Convention on Climate Change, "List of Signatories to the Kyoto Protocol," (Bonn: 15 January 1999), < http://www.unfccc.de >, viewed 22 January 1999.

27. Martin E. Hoffert et al., "Energy Implications of Future Stabilization of Atmospheric CO_2 Content," *Nature*, 29 October 1998; David G. Victor, "Strategies for Cutting Carbon," *Nature*, 29 October 1998; Martin Parry et al., "Adapting to the Inevitable," *Nature*, 22 October 1998.

GLOBAL ECONOMIC GROWTH SLOWS (pages 64–65)

1. International Monetary Fund (IMF), *World Economic Outlook* (Washington, DC: December 1998).
2. Ibid.
3. Ibid.; U.S. Bureau of the Census, *International Data Base*, electronic database, Suitland, MD, updated 30 November 1998.
4. IMF, op. cit. note 1.
5. Worldwatch update of Angus Maddison, *Monitoring the World Economy 1820–1992* (Paris: Organisation for Economic Co-operation and Development, 1995), with updates and deflator indexes from IMF, *World Economic Outlook* tables.
6. Ibid.; Bureau of Census, op. cit. note 3.
7. IMF, op. cit. note 1.
8. Ibid.
9. Ibid.
10. Ibid.
11. Ibid.
12. Ibid.
13. Ibid.
14. Ibid.
15. Ibid.
16. Ibid.
17. Ibid; Population Reference Bureau (PRB), "1998 World Population Data Sheet," wall chart (Washington, DC: June 1998).
18. IMF, op. cit. note 1.
19. Ibid.; PRB, op. cit. note 17.
20. IMF, op. cit. note 1.
21. Ibid.
22. Ibid.
23. IMF, *World Economic Outlook, Interim Supplement* (Washington, DC: December 1997); IMF, op. cit. note 1.
24. IMF, op. cit. note 1; "I.M.F. Cuts World Growth Outlook to 2.2%," *New York Times*, 22 December 1998.

THIRD WORLD DEBT STILL RISING (pages 66–67)

1. World Bank, *Global Development Finance*, electronic database, Washington, DC, 1998.
2. World Bank, *Global Development Finance 1998* (Washington, DC: 1998).
3. Jubilee 2000 Coalition, "IMF Intervenes in Kenya's Teacher's Strike", 23 October 1998, < http://www.oneworld.org/jubilee2000/index.html >, viewed 9 November 1998.
4. World Bank, op. cit. note 1.
5. David Pearce et al., "Debt and the Environment," *Scientific American*, June 1995.
6. U.S. General Accounting Office (GAO), *Status of the Heavily Indebted Poor Countries Debt Relief Initiative* (Washington, DC: September 1998).
7. World Bank, HIPC Implementation Unit, "HIPC Debt Relief," information sheet (Washington, DC: April 1998).
8. Carole Collins, "Jubilee 2000 Debt Relief Campaign Targets G-8 Leaders," *Africa Recovery*, August 1998.
9. World Bank, op. cit. note 2.
10. European Network on Debt and Development, "The Heavily Indebted Poor Countries (HIPC) Debt Initiative: Any Impact on Poverty? Uganda, Mozambique, and Nicaragua," information sheet (Brussels: April 1998).
11. International Monetary Fund (IMF) and World Bank Development Committee, "HIPC Initiative: A Progress Report" (Washington, DC: 29 September 1998).
12. IMF, "Debt Relief Package of Nearly US$3 Billion Approved for Mozambique," press release (Washington, DC: 7 April 1998); Joseph Hanlon, "Mozambique Gains Little or Nothing from Debt 'Relief'," 4 June 1998, < http://www.oneworld.org/jubilee2000/fiasco.htm >, viewed 18 September 1998. Figures given in nominal terms.
13. Michael Camdessus, "Addressing Concerns for the Poor and Social Justice in Debt Relief and Adjustment Programs," speech at the Conference on the Ethical Dimensions of International Debt, Seton Hall University, South

Orange, NJ, 22 October 1998.

14. Jubilee 2000, "Why are People Demanding Debt Cancellation for Poor Countries?" e-mail to Hilary French, Worldwatch Institute, 9 September 1998.

15. Jo Marie Griesgraber, "Jubilee 2000: A Bold Call for Forgiveness of Debt," *News from the Center of Concern*, September 1998.

WORLD TRADE DECLINES
(pages 68–69)

1. Figures are Worldwatch estimates derived using export values and the export unit value index (EUVI) supplied by Neil Austriaco, Research Assistant, International Monetary Fund (IMF) Statistics Division, e-mails to Lisa Mastny, Worldwatch Institute, 25 January and 4 March 1999. Note that exports and EUVI figures for 1998 are preliminary. The EUVI reflects price changes over time in a typical basket of internationally traded goods.

2. Austriaco, op. cit. note 1.

3. World Trade Organization (WTO), *WTO Annual Report 1998—Special Topic: Globalization and Trade* (Geneva: 1998).

4. World Bank, *Global Economic Prospects for Developing Countries, 1998/99* (Washington, DC: 1999).

5. Ibid.

6. Historical information from WTO, op. cit. note 3.

7. Growth in exports is a Worldwatch Institute estimate based on Austriaco, op. cit. note 1; growth in world economy from Worldwatch data series for gross world product based on purchasing power parity, derived from Angus Maddison, *Monitoring the World Economy, 1820–1992* (Paris: Organisation for Economic Co-operation and Development (OECD), 1995), from Angus Maddison, *Chinese Economic Performance in the Long Run* (Paris: OECD, 1998), and from IMF, *World Economic Outlook and International Capital Markets Interim Assessment, December 1998* (Washington, DC: 1998).

8. Figures are derived from exports and gross world product times series documented in notes 1 and 7. The two series are deemed comparable based on the assumption that market exchange rates are a reasonable proxy for purchasing power in the tradable sector of the economy. It is worth noting, however, that the average price of tradable goods has risen more slowly over time than have prices throughout the economy. For this reason, the percentages obtained when measuring exports as a share of gross world product in constant dollars vary from those obtained in current dollars. Current price ratios have the effect of understating the change in relative volumes. Constant dollar ratios vary somewhat from year to year depending on the chosen base year.

9. Austriaco, op. cit. note 1; IMF, op. cit. note 7.

10. Figure for 1948 from WTO, op. cit. note 3; 1998 estimate from U.N. Conference on Trade and Development, "World Seaborne Trade Slows," press release (Geneva: 22 February 1999).

11. Energy used in shipping is a Worldwatch Institute estimate, based on Stacy C. Davis, *Transportation Energy Data Book: Edition 18* (Oak Ridge, TN: Oak Ridge National Laboratory, 1998), and on United Nations, *Review of Maritime Transport 1997* (New York: 1998); energy equivalents from British Petroleum, *BP Statistical Review of World Energy 1997* (London: Group Media & Publications, 1998).

12. Figures obtained from Attilio Costaguta, Statistics & Economic Analysis Section, International Civil Aviation Organization (ICAO), Montreal, e-mails to Lisa Mastny, Worldwatch Institute, 22 October 1998 and 5 March 1999.

13. Average energy intensity of shipping versus air freight is a Worldwatch Institute estimate based on Davis, op. cit. note 11, and on data supplied by Costaguta, op. cit. note 12. The estimate is based on energy intensities for shipping and air freight as of 1996, the most recent year for which comparable estimates could be obtained.

14. Energy used in shipping versus air freight is a Worldwatch Institute estimate based on Davis, op. cit. note 11, on data supplied by Costaguta, op. cit. note 12, and on United Nations, op. cit. note 11.

15. WTO, op. cit. note 3.

16. Ibid.

17. Ibid.

18. Services data obtained from Andreas Maurer, WTO, e-mail to Lisa Mastny, Worldwatch Institute, 20 January 1999; figures deflated using the export unit value index supplied by Austriaco, op. cit. note 1. Although the EUVI is based on prices of tradable goods rather than services, it is used here as a proxy for price shifts over time in international trade.

19. Worldwatch estimate, based on data provided by Austriaco, op. cit. note 1, and by Maurer, op. cit. note 17, as well as on IMF, op. cit. note 7.
20. "Border Battles" and "Time for Another Round," in *Where Next? A Survey of World Trade*, special issue of *The Economist*, 3 October 1998.
21. "WTO Members Raise Possible New Issues for Millennium Round," *Bridges Weekly Trade News Digest* (International Centre for Trade and Sustainable Development, Geneva), 8 February 1999.

WORLD AD SPENDING CLIMBS
(pages 70–71)

1. Data supplied by Robert J. Coen, senior vice-president, McCann-Erickson, Inc., New York, letter to author, 6 January 1999. Categories measured include all major media—television, newspapers, magazines, radio, and outdoor ads—as well as direct mail, the Yellow Pages, and various miscellaneous media. Global economic output from International Monetary Fund (IMF), *World Economic Outlook* (Washington, DC: October 1998).
2. Coen, op. cit. note 1; global economy from IMF, *World Economic Outlook* (Washington, DC: various years).
3. Ad spending data from Coen, op. cit. note 1; population from U.S. Bureau of the Census, *International Data Base*, electronic database, Suitland, MD, updated 30 November 1998.
4. *Advertising Age*, <www.adage.com/dataplace>, viewed 5 January 1999; Seth Dunn, "Automobile Production Sets Record," in Lester R. Brown, Christopher Flavin, and Michael Renner, *Vital Signs 1998* (New York: W.W. Norton & Company, 1998).
5. *Advertising Age*, op. cit. note 4.
6. Coen, op. cit. note 1.
7. McCann-Erickson, <http://www.mccann.com/res/detail.shtml>, viewed 27 December 1998; Coen, op. cit. note 1.
8. Regional data supplied by Adam Smith, Zenith Media, U.K., e-mail to author, 8 December 1998. Zenith's data measure only major media (television, print, radio, and outdoor advertising), which together account for about 70 percent of global ad spending measured by Coen, op. cit. note 1.
9. Smith, op. cit. note 8.
10. Ibid.
11. Ibid.
12. Ibid.; World Bank, *World Development Report 1997* (New York: Oxford University Press, 1997).
13. Smith, op. cit. note 8.
14. Ibid.
15. R. Bruce Hutton, "The Role and Potential of Marketing and Advertising on Global Human Development," 1998, study prepared for U.N. Development Programme, Human Development Report Office, New York.
16. Media Dynamics, Inc., *TV Dimensions '98* (New York: 1998).
17. Ibid.
18. Growth of television ads from McCann-Erickson, op. cit. note 7.
19. Forrester Research, Inc., *Media's Global Future* (Cambridge, MA: August 1998).
20. Hutton, op. cit. note 15.
21. U.N. Development Programme, *Human Development Report 1998* (New York: Oxford University Press, 1998).
22. Hutton, op. cit. note 15.

U.N. FINANCES DECLINE FURTHER   (pages 72–73)

1. U.N. General Assembly, "Budgetary and Financial Situation of Organizations of the United Nations System. Statistical Report by the Administrative Committee on Coordination," A/53/647 (New York: 6 November 1998), Table 1.
2. U.N. General Assembly, "Budgetary and Financial Situation of Organizations of the United Nations System. Statistical Report by the Administrative Committee on Coordination," A/51/505 (New York: 18 October 1996), Table 1; "Assessed Payments to the Regular Budget and Specialized Agencies: 1971–1995," in Tables and Charts, Global Policy Forum, <http://www.globalpolicy.org/finance/>, viewed 21 October 1997. The United Nations does not provide any inflation-corrected data, and there is no truly adequate deflator series to correct for inflation in U.N. budgets and expenditures. The U.S. gross national product deflator was applied here simply to provide a rough approximation of constant dollar budgets.
3. Actual expenditure trend calculated on the basis of data provided in Office of the Spokesman for the Secretary-General, United Nations, "Financial Tidbits," <http://www.un.org/News/

ossg/finance.htm >, viewed 31 January 1999.

4. Calculated from U.N. General Assembly, op. cit. note 1, Tables 7 and 8, and from Executive Board of the U.N. Development Programme and of the U.N. Population Fund, "Annual Report of the Administrator for 1997 and Related Matters," DP/1998/17/Add.7, 11 May 1998, Table 1.

5. Member states are assessed according to their ability to pay. Therefore, rich industrial countries cover the bulk of the budget. The United States, Japan, and the European Union together account for more than three quarters of the total. A short explanation of both history and current developments of the U.N. assessments is provided in Jeffrey Laurenti, "The New U.N. Assessment Scale," < http://www.unausa.org/programs/scale.htm >, viewed 2 February 1999.

6. "Outstanding Contributions to the Regular Budget, International Tribunals and Peacekeeping Operations as at 31 December 1998," from Jessica Jiji, Office of the Spokesman for the Secretary General, United Nations, New York, e-mail to author, 14 January 1999.

7. Number of countries calculated from ibid.

8. According to U.N. rules, annual budget contributions are due on 31 January, and members are considered to be in arrears if contributions have not been paid by 31 December; U.S. General Accounting Office (GAO), *United Nations: Financial Issues and U.S. Arrears* (Washington, DC: June 1998); 32 states from Jessica Jiji, Office of the Spokesman for the Secretary General, United Nations, New York, discussion with author, 1 February 1999; 22 states from Office of the Spokesman for the Secretary General, "The Honour Roll 1998," < http://www.un.org/News/ossg/hon98.htm >, viewed 23 November 1998.

9. "United Nations Financial Presentation," U.N. Under-Secretary-General for Management, New York, March 1998.

10. "Outstanding Contributions to the Regular Budget," op. cit. note 6.

11. Ibid.

12. Ibid.

13. Ibid.

14. Past arrears data from "Outstanding Debts to the UN Regular Budget at Yearend: 1971–1997," Global Policy Forum, < http://www.globalpolicy.org/finance/ >, viewed 31 January 1999; GAO, op. cit. note 8; "United Nations Financial Presentation," op. cit. note 9.

15. GAO, op. cit. note 8.

16. "Outstanding Contributions to the Regular Budget," op. cit. note 6.

17. GAO, op. cit. note 8.

18. "Congress Adjourns with No Resolution of Arrears to UN and International Organizations," *Washington Weekly Report* (UNA-USA, Washington, DC), 22 October 1998.

19. The committee is known as the Advisory Committee on Administrative and Budgetary Questions; GAO, op. cit. note 8; "US Not Elected Again to Key UN Budget Committee," *Washington Weekly Report* (UNA-USA, Washington, DC), 16 November 1998.

20. Laurenti, op. cit. note 5.

21. "Congress Adjourns with No Resolution," op. cit. note 18. Article 19 of the U.N. Charter states that members "shall have no vote in the General Assembly if the amount of its arrears equals or exceeds the amount of contributions due from it for the preceding two full years."

22. GAO, op. cit. note 8.

23. Ibid.

24. U.N. General Assembly, op. cit. note 1.

WEATHER-RELATED LOSSES HIT NEW HIGH (pages 74–75)

1. Number for 1998 from Munich Re, "Weather-Related Natural Disasters 1998" (Munich, Germany: 9 February 1999). All Munich Re data are strictly claims-related.

2. Data for 1950–97 from Munich Re database.

3. Munich Re, op. cit. note 1.

4. Munich Re, "Munich Re's Review of Natural Catastrophes in 1998," press release (Munich, Germany: 29 December 1998); Nick Nuttall, "World is a Far More Disastrous Place to Be," *The Times* (London), 30 December 1998.

5. Munich Re, op. cit. note 1.

6. Worldwatch estimate based on National Oceanic and Atmospheric Administration (NOAA), "Climate of 1998, Annual Review: Extreme Events of 1998" (Asheville, NC: National Climatic Data Center, 13 January 1999), and on International Federation of the Red Cross (IFRC), "Bangladesh: Floods," Situation Report No. 3, 16 October 1998.

7. Munich Re, op. cit. note 2; NOAA, "Climate of 1998, Annual Review: 1998 Overview," (Asheville, NC: National Climatic Data Center, 12 January 1999).

8. Munich Re, op. cit. note 4.

9. Ibid.
10. Ibid.; NOAA, op. cit. note 7.
11. Munich Re, op. cit. note 4.
12. Ibid.
13. NOAA, op. cit. note 6; IFRC, op. cit. note 6; Munich Re, op. cit. note 4.
14. Munich Re, op. cit. note 4.
15. Ibid.
16. NOAA, op. cit. note 6; Larry Rohter, "Now Ruined Economies Afflict Central America," *New York Times*, 13 November 1998.
17. NOAA, op. cit. note 6; Munich Re, op. cit. note 4.
18. Erik Eckholm, "Stunned By Floods, China Hastens Logging Curbs," *New York Times*, 27 September 1998.
19. Tina Rosenberg, "Trees and the Roots of a Storm's Destruction," *New York Times*, 26 November 1998.
20. John Ward Anderson, "Off Honduras, an Ecological Paradise Torn Asunder," *Washington Post*, 25 November 1998.
21. Robert T. Watson, Marufu C. Zinyowera, and Richard H. Moss, eds., *Climate Change 1995: Impacts, Adaptations, and Mitigation of Climate Change* (New York: Cambridge University Press, 1996); Thomas R. Karl, Neville Nichols, and Jonathan Gregory, "The Coming Climate," *Scientific American*, May 1997; Thomas R. Knutson, Robert E. Tuleya, and Yoshio Kurihara, "Simulated Increase of Hurricane Intensities in a CO_2-Warmed Climate," *Science*, 13 February 1998; R. Monastersky, "As Globe Warms, Hurricanes May Speed Up," *Science News*, 14 February 1998.
22. Nicholas R. Bates, "Contribution of Hurricanes to Local and Global Estimates of Air-Sea Exchange of CO_2," *Nature*, 3 September 1998; Robert C. Cowen, "How Hurricanes May Add to Global Warming," *Christian Science Monitor*, 3 September 1998.
23. Munich Re, op. cit. note 4.
24. Nick Nutall, "Climate Disaster Map Pinpoints 'No-Go' Areas for Insurers," *The Times* (London), 9 November 1998.
25. Ibid.

ROUNDWOOD PRODUCTION LEVELS OFF (pages 76–77)

1. U.N. Food and Agriculture Organization (FAO), *FAOSTAT Statistics Database*, < http://www.

apps.fao.org >, Rome, viewed 18 December 1998.
2. Ibid.
3. Ibid.
4. Ibid.
5. Ibid.
6. Ibid.
7. Birger Solberg et al., "An Overview of Factors Affecting the Long-Term Trends of Non-Industrial and Industrial Wood Supply and Demand," in Birger Solberg, ed., *Long-Term Trends and Prospects in World Supply and Demand for Wood and Implications for Sustainable Forest Management* (Joensuu, Finland: European Forestry Institute, 1996).
8. Peter J. Ince, "Recycling of Wood and Paper Products in the United States" (Madison, WI: U.S.Department of Agriculture, Forest Service, Forest Products Laboratory, January 1996).
9. FAO, op. cit. note 1.
10. Ibid.
11. Ibid.
12. James McIntire, ed., *The New Eco-Order: Economic and Ecological Linkages of the World's Temperate and Boreal Forest Resources* (Seattle, WA: Northwest Policy Center, University of Washington, 1995).
13. Worldwatch calculations based on FAO data.
14. Ibid.
15. FAO, *State of the World's Forests 1997* (Oxford, U.K.: 1997).
16. FAO, op cit. note 1.
17. International Institute for Environment and Development, *Towards a Sustainable Paper Cycle* (London: 1996).
18. FAO, op. cit. note 1.
19. Ibid.
20. Ibid.
21. Forest Stewardship Council, "Forests Certified by FSC-Accredited Certification Bodies," August 1998, < http://www.fscoa.org >, viewed 19 October 1998.

PAPER PRODUCTION INCHES UP (pages 78–79)

1. U.N. Food and Agriculture Organization (FAO), *FAOSTAT Statistics Database*, < http://apps. fao.org >, viewed 11 January 1999.
2. Figure for 1950 from International Institute for Environment and Development (IIED), *Towards a Sustainable Paper Cycle* (London: 1996); popu-

lation from U.S. Bureau of the Census, *International Data Base*, electronic database, Suitland, MD, updated 30 November 1998.

3. FAO, *Provisional Outlook for Global Forest Products Consumption, Production, and Trade to 2010* (Rome: 1997); Bureau of Census, op. cit. note 2.

4. FAO, op. cit. note 1.

5. Ibid.

6. Ibid.

7. FAO, op. cit. note 3.

8. FAO, op. cit. note 1.

9. Pulp and Paper International, *International Fact and Price Book 1997* (San Francisco, CA: Miller Freeman Inc., 1996).

10. FAO, op. cit., note 1.

11. Ibid.

12. FAO, *State of the World's Forests 1997* (Oxford, U.K.: 1997).

13. Greg McIvor, "Survey—World's Pulp and Paper: A Compelling Case on Paper," *Financial Times*, 7 December 1998.

14. Gary Mead, "Tough Year Ahead for Pulp and Paper," *Financial Times*, 31 January 1998.

15. Greg McIvor, "Commodities and Agriculture: Pulp Producers Still Waiting for a Rebound in Prices," *Financial Times*, 18 September 1998.

16. Calculated using 1993 data (the last time such an estimation was made) from Wood Resources International Ltd., *Fiber Sourcing Analysis for the Global Pulp and Paper Industry* (London: IIED, September 1996); IIED, op. cit. note 2.

17. FAO, op. cit. note 1.

18. Percentages calculated from IIED, op. cit. note 2.

19. Expanding production from FAO, op. cit. note 1.

20. Ibid.

21. FAO, op. cit. note 3.

22. Ibid.

23. FAO, op. cit. note 1.

24. Ibid.

25. U.S. Environmental Protection Agency (EPA), *1996 Toxics Release Inventory Public Data Release Report* (Washington, DC: 1996).

26. United States from Franklin Associates, Ltd., "Characterization of Municipal Solid Waste in the United States: 1997 Update," report prepared for EPA, Municipal and Industrial Solid Waste Division, Office of Solid Waste, 1998; Europe from IIED, op. cit. note 2.

AUTOMOBILE PRODUCTION DIPS (pages 82–83)

1. Production estimate for 1998 based on American Automobile Manufacturers Association (AAMA), *World Motor Vehicle Facts and Figures 1998* (Washington, DC: 1998), and on Standard & Poor's DRI, *World Car Industry Forecast Report, November 1998* (London: 1998); 1950–97 data from AAMA, *World Motor Vehicle Data, 1996* and *1998* eds. (Washington, DC: 1996, 1998), and on AAMA, *Facts and Figures*, op. cit. this note.

2. Standard & Poor's DRI, op. cit. note 1; fleet estimate for 1998 based on AAMA, *World Motor Vehicle Data, 1998*, op. cit. note 1, and on Standard & Poor's DRI, op. cit. note 1; 1950–97 numbers from AAMA, *World Motor Vehicle Data 1996* and *1998* op. cit. note 1, and from Standard & Poor's DRI, op. cit. note 1.

3. Figure for 1998 based on AAMA, *World Motor Vehicle Data, 1998*, op. cit. note 1, on Standard & Poor's DRI, op. cit. note 1, and on U.S. Bureau of the Census, *International Data Base*, electronic database, Suitland, MD, updated 30 November 1998.

4. AAMA, *Facts and Figures*, op. cit. note 1; Standard & Poor's DRI, op. cit. note 1.

5. Anne Swardson, "European Carmakers' Traffic Jam," *Washington Post*, 10 September 1998; AAMA, *Facts and Figures*, op. cit. note 1; Standard & Poor's DRI, op. cit. note 1.

6. Standard & Poor's DRI, op. cit. note 1; Nizhny Novgorod, "Turin Meets Detroit—On the Volga," *The Economist*, 7 March 1998; John Helmer, "Russian Auto Output Still Falling, Drops 13% in First 9 Months," *Journal of Commerce*, 16 November 1998.

7. AAMA, *Facts and Figures*, op. cit. note 1; Standard & Poor's DRI, op. cit. note 1.

8. Editorial, "Mercedes Goes To Motown," *The Economist*, 9 May 1998; Standard & Poor's DRI, op. cit. note 1; John Schnapp, "Korean Autos: Crash and Burn," *Journal of Commerce*, 10 June 1998; "On the Block," *The Economist*, 25 July 1998.

9. Standard & Poor's DRI, op. cit. note 1; Rodney Tasker, "Spinning Wheels," *Far Eastern Economic Review*, 16 April 1998.

10. AAMA, *Facts and Figures*, op. cit. note 1; Standard & Poor's DRI, op. cit. note 1.

11. Standard & Poor's DRI, op. cit. note 1.

12. Keith Bradsher, "Larger Vehicles Are Hampering Visibility," *New York Times*, 22

November 1998.

13. AAMA, *Facts and Figures*, op. cit. note 1; Standard & Poor's DRI, op. cit. note 1.

14. Standard & Poor's DRI, op. cit. note 1.

15. Ibid.

16. Robert L. Simison, "Fears of Overcapacity Continue to Grow," *Wall Street Journal*, 2 March 1998; "A New Kind of Car Company," *The Economist*, 9 May 1998.

17. Barrett Seaman and Ron Stodghill II, "Here Comes the Road Test," *Time*, 18 May 1998.

18. Anna Wilde Mathews, "Detroit to D.C.," *Wall Street Journal*, 27 November 1998.

19. "More Fuel-Efficient Vehicles Required As Part of Program to Cut Greenhouse Gases," *International Environment Reporter*, 5 August 1998.

20. Michael Smith, "Ministers Approve Deal on Emissions of CO_2," *Financial Times*, 7 October 1998.

21. John Tagliabue, "Europe Takes to the Road in a Small Way," *New York Times*, 21 April 1998; Haig Simonian, "Daimler-Benz Aims Small," *Financial Times*, 17 July 1998; Keith Bradsher, "European Auto Divisions Calling for Improved Fuel Economy," *New York Times*, 26 April 1998.

22. Keith Bradsher, "California to Toughen Its Emissions Standards," *New York Times*, 6 November 1998.

23. Matthew L. Wald, "Autos' Converters Increase Warming Even As They Cut Smog," *New York Times*, 29 May 1998.

24. Joby Warrick, "Diesel Deflated In Warming Battle," *Washington Post*, 3 May 1998.

25. "Toyota Plans Gas/Electric Hybrid for North America, Europe by 2000," *Wall Street Journal Interactive Edition*, 14 July 1998; Stacy C. Davis, "Center for Transportation Analysis, Oak Ridge National Laboratory, *Transportation Energy Data Book: Edition 18* (Oak Ridge, TN: September 1998).

26. Gregory L. White, "Honda Set to Sell Gas, Electric Car By Late Next Year," *Wall Street Journal*, 22 December 1998; Davis, op. cit. note 25.

BICYCLE PRODUCTION DOWN AGAIN (pages 84–85)

1. "World Market Report," *1999 Interbike Directory* (Laguna Beach, CA: Miller-Freeman, 1998); United Nations, *Industrial Commodity Statistics*

Yearbook 1996 (New York: 1998).

2. "World Market Report," op. cit. note 1; United Nations, op. cit. note 1.

3. Drop in output from "World Market Report," op. cit. note 1; reasons from Jay Townley, The Bicycle Council, Kent, WA, discussion with author, 9 February 1999.

4. "World Market Report," op. cit. note 1.

5. Frank Jamerson, Electric Battery Bicycle Company, Naples, FL, letter to author, 28 January 1999.

6. "World Market Report," op. cit. note 1; United Nations, op. cit. note 1.

7. Frank Jamerson, Electric Battery Bicycle Company, Naples, FL, discussion with author, 28 January 1999.

8. Anton G. Welleman, Cees J. Louisse, and Dirk M. Ligtermoet, "Theme Paper 5: Bicycles in Cities," in Stephen Stares and Liu Zhi, eds. *China's Urban Transport Development Strategy: Proceedings of a Symposium in Beijing*, 8–10 November 1995, World Bank Discussion Paper No. 352 (Washington, DC: World Bank, 1996).

9. Walter Hook, "Jakarta: A City in Crisis," *Sustainable Transport*, Winter 1998.

10. "Beijing Starts to Ban Cyclists in Busy Street," *China Daily*, 21 October 1998.

11. John Pucher, "Bicycling Boom in Germany: A Revival Engineered by Public Policy," *Transportation Quarterly*, fall 1997.

12. Cycle Import of Scandinavia Web Site, < http://www.cios.com/news.htm >, viewed 3 February 1999.

13. Herman Verhagen, Ecooperation, Amsterdam, Netherlands, letter to author, 8 February 1999.

14. John Pucher, "Let's Get Those Pedals Pumping!" *Conservation Matters*, autumn 1998.

15. Ibid.

16. U.S. Department of Transportation, Federal Highway Administration, *Nationwide Personal Transportation Survey* (Washington, DC: various years).

17. Ibid.

WORLD AIR TRAFFIC SOARING (pages 86–87)

1. Attilio Costaguta, Chief, Statistics & Economic Analysis Section, International Civil Aviation Organization (ICAO), Montreal, e-mail to author, 2 November 1998. Figures for 1950–69 do not include the 12 Commonwealth of

Independent States that are ICAO Contracting States. Figure for 1998 is an estimate based on projections in ICAO, "Mixed Regional Results Bring World Airline Traffic Growth to a Crawl in 1998," press release (Montreal: 23 December 1998).

2. ICAO, op. cit. note 1.

3. Costaguta, op. cit. note 1; ICAO, op. cit. note 1.

4. Costaguta, op. cit. note 1; Anu Vedantham and Michael Oppenheimer, "Long-term Scenarios for Aviation: Demand and Emissions of CO_2 and NO_x," *Energy Policy*, vol. 26, no. 8 (1998); Michael Oppenheimer, "Aircraft Emissions and the Global Atmosphere," *EDF Letter*, September 1994.

5. Air Transport Action Group (ATAG), *Air Transport and the Environment* (Geneva: 1992).

6. Martin Wright, Carl Frankel, and Dwight Holing, "Hot Air Space," *Tomorrow*, May-June 1997.

7. International Air Transport Association, "Challenges Ahead Despite Goldilocks Economy," press release (Montreal: 8 June 1998).

8. Costaguta, op. cit. note 1; ICAO, op. cit. note 1.

9. Boris Balashov and Andrew Smith, "ICAO Analyses Trends in Fuel Consumption by World's Airlines," *ICAO Journal*, August 1992; ATAG, op. cit. note 5.

10. Milieu Defensie, "The Right Price for Air Travel Campaign," < http://www.milieudefensie.nl/airtravel/info.htm >, viewed 23 December 1998.

11. Intergovernmental Panel on Climate Change (IPCC), *Special Report: Aviation and the Global Atmosphere* (Geneva: 1999); Keay Davidson, "Gossamer Jet Trails Tied to Global Warming," *San Francisco Examiner*, 15 March 1999.

12. G. Brasseur, G.T. Amanatidis, and G. Angeletti, eds., "European Scientific Assessment of the Atmospheric Effects of Aircraft Emissions," *Atmospheric Environment*, vol. 32, no. 13 (1998).

13. Tourism Working Group of the German NGO Forum on Environment and Development, "Position Paper on the Environmental and Social Responsibility of Tourism in the Context of Sustainable Development," prepared November 1998 for presentation at the Seventh Meeting of the Commission on Sustainable Development, New York, April 1999.

14. IPCC, op. cit. note 11.

15. Ibid. Figure for 2050 is based on a high-end scenario for total radiative forcing from aviation.

16. Wright, Frankel, and Holing, op. cit. note 6; General Electric (GE), "Advanced Technology Makes Jet Engines Cleaner and Quieter," press release (1995), GE Aircraft Engines, < http://www.ge.com/aircraftengines/cleaner.htm >, viewed 1 October 1998; Roger Bray, "Clean Air Turbulence," *Financial Times*, 3 September 1998.

17. Boeing, "Air Transportation Has an Unparalleled History of Improving Efficiency," < http://www.boeing.com/commercial/value/evImpeffncy_4.htm >, viewed 1 October 1998; ATAG, op. cit. note 5.

18. "Aircraft Pollution Threatens Planet," (London) *Evening Standard*, 13 July 1998.

19. Bray, op. cit. note 16; Milieu Defensie, *Airmail*, no. 2 (1997), < http://www.milieudefensie.nl/airtravel/airmail2.htm >, viewed 3 December 1998.

20. Milieu Defensie, *Airmail*, no. 1 (1997), < http://www.milieudefensie.nl/airtravel/airmail1.htm >, viewed 3 December 1998; Milieu Defensie, op. cit. note 10.

21. "Report of Impact of Aviation on Environment Released," *Airline Industry Information*, 8 September 1998.

22. Wright, Frankel, and Holing, op. cit note 6.

SATELLITE LAUNCHES GET A BOOST (pages 90–91)

1. Jos Heyman, *Spacecraft Tables 1957-1997* (Riverton, Australia: Tiros Space Information, 1998); Jos Heyman, Astronautical Society of Western Australia, e-mail to author, 4 January 1999.

2. The total does not include failed satellite launches or crewed, interplanetary, or lunar spacecraft.

3. John Bray, *The Communications Miracle: The Telecommunication Pioneers from Morse to the Information Superhighway* (New York: Plenum Press, 1995).

4. Heyman, *Tables*, op. cit. note 1; Heyman, e-mail, op. cit. note 1.

5. Heyman, *Tables*, op. cit. note 1; Heyman, e-mail, op. cit. note 1.

6. Theresa Foley, "Commercial Spacefarers," *Air Force Magazine*, December 1998; Jeff Zins-meister, "Private Space: A Free-Market Approach to Space Exploration," *Harvard International Review*, spring 1998.

7. Marco Caceres, "Commercial Satellites Surge Ahead," *Aerospace America*, November 1998.

8. Ibid.; Marco Caceres, Teal Group Corporation, Fairfax, VA, letter to author, 2 February 1999.

9. Heather E. Hudson, *Communication Satellites: Their Development and Impact* (New York: The Free Press, 1990).

10. "African Radio Satellite Launched," *Reuters*, 29 October 1998; Austin Bunn, "New Media: Information Affluence," *Wired*, February 1998.

11. John V. Evans, "New Satellites for Personal Communications," *Scientific American*, April 1998.

12. "Iridium Kicks Off Satellite Service," *PC Week*, 9 November 1998; David S. Bennahum, "The United Nations of Iridium," *Wired*, October 1998.

13. International Telecommunication Union, *World Telecommunication Development Report 1998* (Geneva: 1998).

14. Ibid.

15. Heyman, e-mail, op. cit. note 1; Claire L. Parkinson, *Earth From Above: Using Color-Coded Satellite Images to Examine the Global Environment* (Sausalito, CA: University Science Books, 1997).

16. "EU, Russia Team Up with Companies on Creation of Global Satellite Data Source," *International Environment Reporter*, 5 August 1998.

17. Charles F. Kennel, Pierre Morel, and Gregory J. Williams, "Keeping Watch on the Earth: An Integrated Global Observing Strategy," *Consequences*, vol. 3, no. 2 (1997); National Aeronautics and Space Administration (NASA), Goddard Space Flight Center, *The First EOS Satellite: NASA's Earth Observing System, EOS AM-1* (Greenbelt, MD: 1998).

18. NASA, op. cit. note 17.

19. J.M. Wallace and S. Vogel, *Reports to the Nation on Our Changing Planet: El Niño and Climate Prediction* (Boulder, CO: National Oceanic and Atmospheric Administration, 1994).

20. Lara Santoro, "Hunger Fight Takes Modern Twist in Sudan," *Christian Science Monitor*, 4 June 1998.

21. "Satellite Used to Detect Impending Volcanic Blast," *Associated Press*, 9 December 1998.

22. Liz Tynan, "Closing the Net on Coral Bleaching," *New Scientist*, 9 January 1999.

23. Foley, op. cit. note 6; "Pie in the Sky," *Total Telecom*, 1 January 1999.

TELEPHONE NETWORK KEEPS GROWING (pages 92–93)

1. Data for 1960–95 from International Telecommunication Union (ITU), *World Telecommunication Indicators on Diskette* (Geneva: 1996); 1996 from ITU, *Challenges to the Network: Telecoms and the Internet* (Geneva: September 1997); 1997 from ITU, "Telecommunications Industry at a Glance," <http://www.itu.int/ti/industryoverview/index.htm>, viewed 3 December 1998. The ITU collects information on telephone "main lines." These can be either exclusive or shared, so the number of telephone subscribers exceeds the number of lines. They can be used not only for telephone sets but also for fax machines or personal computers.

2. ITU, *World Indicators on Diskette,* op. cit. note 1.

3. Ithiel de Sola Pool, ed., *The Social Impact of the Telephone* (Cambridge, MA: The MIT Press, 1977).

4. ITU, *World Telecommunication Development Report 1998* (Geneva: 1998).

5. Ibid.

6. Ibid.

7. Ibid.

8. ITU, *World Indicators on Diskette,* op. cit. note 1; ITU, *Challenges to the Network,* op. cit. note 1; ITU, "Telecommunications Industry at a Glance," op. cit. note 1.

9. ITU, op. cit. note 4; "Telecommunications in Asia: Future on the Line," *Far Eastern Economic Review*, 4 June 1998.

10. "FT Telecoms: Financial Times Review of the Telecommunications Industry," *Financial Times*, 10 June 1998.

11. ITU, op. cit. note 4.

12. Ibid.

13. Joseph N. Pelton, "Telecommunications for the 21st Century," *Scientific American,* Wireless Technologies: Special Report, April 1998.

14. Alan Cane, "Operators Race to Surf 'Data Wave,'" *Financial Times*, 10 June 1998.

15. ITU, op. cit. note 4.

16. Ibid.

17. Alan Cane, "Millennium Forecast is for 1 bn Cellular Users," *Financial Times,* 18 November 1998.

18. ITU, *World Indicators on Diskette,* op. cit. note 1; ITU, *Challenges to the Network,* op. cit. note 1; ITU, "Telecommunications Industry at a Glance," op. cit. note 1.

19. ITU, *World Indicators on Diskette,* op. cit. note 1;

ITU, *Challenges to the Network,* op. cit. note 1; ITU, "Telecommunications Industry at a Glance," op. cit. note 1.

20. ITU, op. cit. note 4.

21. S. Kamaluddin, "Calling Countryfolk: Cellular-Phone Operator Targets Rural Bangladesh," *Far Eastern Economic Review,* 24 April 1997; ITU, "Phones for All the World?" <http://www.itu.int/newsarchive/press/WTDC98/Feature2.html>, viewed 16 December 1998.

22. Pernille Tranberg, "From Chickens to Cellphones, the New Face of Microcredit in Dhaka," *The Earth Times,* 1–15 August 1998.

23. Daniel B. Wood, "Rallying Cry: Indians Hear a High-Tech Drumbeat," *Christian Science Monitor,* 19 February 1998.

24. Yoichi Funabashi, *Asia Pacific Fusion: Japan's Role in APEC* (Washington, DC: Institute for International Economics, 1995).

INTERNET CONTINUES RAPID EXPANSION (pages 94–95)

1. Figure 1 and host computers from Network Wizards, "Internet Domain Surveys, 1981–1999," <http://www.nw.com>, updated January 1999. A single host computer can wire several computers to the Internet in the same way that one telephone line can plug in multiple phone extensions. Number of users is a Worldwatch estimate based on Nua Ltd., "How Many Online?" <http://www.nua.ie/>, updated February 1999, and on Computer Industry Almanac, Inc., *Internet User Forecast 1990–2005* (Arlington Heights, IL: 1999). Users are estimated in terms of individuals who use the Internet on a weekly basis. Because estimates for the number of users can vary, host computers provide a more reliable measure of the Internet's size.

2. Network Wizards, op. cit. note 1.

3. Computer Industry Almanac, Inc., op. cit. note 1.

4. U.S. military from International Telecommunication Union (ITU), *Challenges to the Network: Telecoms and the Internet* (Geneva: September 1997).

5. Figure for 1998 from Computer Industry Almanac, Inc., op. cit. note 1; 1997 from Nua, op. cit. note 1.

6. Computer Industry Almanac, Inc., op. cit. note 1.

7. Nua, op. cit. note 1; Figure 2 based on data from Network Wizards, op. cit. note 1, from ITU, op. cit. note 4, from ITU, *World Telecommunications Indicators on Diskette* (Geneva: 1996), and from U.S. Bureau of the Census, *International Data Base,* electronic database, Suitland, MD, updated 30 November 1998; U.S. share of <.com>, <.net>, and <.org> addresses is estimated using data provided by Nancy Huddleston, Network Solutions, Herndon, VA, e-mail to author, 3 March 1999.

8. Computer Industry Almanac, Inc., op. cit. note 1, Africa from Nua, op. cit. note 1.

9. Computer Industry Almanac, Inc., op. cit. note 1.

10. The International Data Corporation estimates China's online population will exceed 9 million in 2002, according to Barry Parr, Internet and E-Commerce Analyst, International Data Corporation, discussion with author, 23 February 1999, and to "China to Top Asian Net Use by 2001," *Reuters,* 28 October 1999; China's capacity expansion from "China Invests in Massive Internet Expansion," Nua Internet Surveys, 28 January 1999, <http://www.nua.ie>; lower fees from Bill Savadove, "China Rings in Lower Telephone, Internet Fees," *Reuters,* 1 March 1999.

11. Internet users from Parr, op. cit. note 11; car owners from Standard & Poor's DRI, *World Car Industry Forecast Report, November 1998* (London: 1998).

12. Network Wizards, op. cit. note 1; Figure 3 based on ibid., on ITU, op. cit. note 4, on ITU, op. cit. note 7, and on Bureau of Census, op. cit. note 7.

13. Network Wizards, op. cit. note 1.

14. Computer Industry Almanac, Inc., op. cit. note 1; Nua, op. cit. note 1.

15. Nua, op. cit. note 1.

16. Network Wizards, op. cit. note 1.

17. Laura Männistö, Tim Kelly, and Ben Petrazzini, "Internet and Global Information Infrastructure in Africa," in Terefe Ras-Work, ed., *Tam-Tam to Internet: Telecoms in Africa* (Johannesburg, South Africa: Mafube Publishing, 1998); Nua, op. cit. note 1.

18. Euro-marketing Associates, "Global Internet Statistics (By Language)," <www.euromktg.com/globstats/>, viewed 8 January 1999; Michael Marriott, "The Web Reflects a Wider World," *New York Times,* 18 June 1998.

19. Euro-marketing Associates, op. cit. note 18.

20. ITU, *World Telecommunication Development Report: Universal Access* (Geneva: 1998).

21. Brewster Kahle, President, Alexa Internet, San

Francisco, CA, discussion with author, 18 March 1999.

22. Alexa Internet, "Web Spawns 1.5 Million Pages Daily According to Findings from Alexa Internet," press release (San Francisco, CA: 31 August 1998).

23. Parr, op. cit. note 10.

24. Ibid.

25. The U.S. database is available at <http://www.epa.gov/opptintr/tri/>; Australian database at <http://www.environment.gov.au/epg/npi/home.html>; Canadian database at <http://www.pwc.bc.doe.ca/ep/npri/>.

26. Instituto Nacional de Ecología, "Registro de Emisiones y Transferencia de Contaminantes," <http://www.ine.gob.mx/retc/prtring.html>, viewed 12 January 1999.

27. ITU, op. cit. note 20.

28. Henry Chasia, "Internet in Africa: A Grassroots Perspective," in Ras-Work, op. cit. note 17.

29. Ibid.; University of South Africa, "Students On-line," <http://sol.unisa.ac.za/>, viewed 4 March 1999.

WORLD POPULATION SWELLS
(pages 98–99)

1. U.S. Bureau of the Census, *International Data Base,* electronic database, Suitland, MD, updated 30 November 1998.

2. United Nations, *World Population Prospects: The 1998 Revision* (New York: December 1998).

3. Bureau of Census, op. cit. note 1.

4. Ibid.

5. Population Reference Bureau (PRB), "1998 World Population Datasheet," wall chart (Washington, DC: June 1998).

6. Ibid.

7. Ibid.

8. Robert Engelman, "Human Population Prospects," Environmental Change and Security Project Report, Woodrow Wilson Center (Washington, DC: Spring 1997).

9. PRB, op. cit. note 5.

10. United Nations, op. cit. note 2.

11. Ibid.

12. World Health Organization, *World Health Report* (Geneva: 1998); United Nations Population Fund (UNFPA), *The State of World Population* (New York: 1998).

13. UNFPA, op. cit. note 12; United Nations, op. cit. note 2.

14. United Nations, op. cit. note 2.

15. Ibid.

16. Shapan Adnan, "Fertility Decline Under Absolute Poverty: Paradoxical Aspects of Demographic Change in Bangladesh," *Economic and Political Weekly,* 30 May 1998; United Nations, op. cit. note 2; PRB, op. cit. note 5.

17. United Nations, op. cit. note 2.

18. Nancy E. Riley, "Gender, Power, and Population Change," *Population Bulletin,* May 1997.

19. U.S. Agency for International Development, "U.S. AID/Egypt Status Report, 1998" (Washington, DC: 1998).

20. Craig Lasher, "U.S. Population Policy Since the Cairo Conference," Environmental Change and Security Project Report, Woodrow Wilson Center (Washington, DC: Spring 1998).

21. Ibid.; "Broken Promises: U.S. Public Funding for International and Domestic Reproductive Health Care" (draft), prepared by the Mobilizing Resources Task Force, U.S. NGOs in Support of the Cairo Consensus, Washington, DC, 15 July 1998.

22. "Broken Promises," op. cit. note 21; Sally Ethelston, Population Action International, Washington, DC, letter to author, 14 September 1998.

23. UNFPA, "Executive Director's Statement on the Withdrawal of U.S. Funding from UNFPA," New York, 20 October 1998.

LIFE EXPECTANCY EXTENDS TO NEW HIGH (pages 100–01)

1. United Nations, *World Population Prospects: The 1998 Revision* (New York: December 1998).

2. Ibid.

3. Ibid.; United Nations Population Fund (UNFPA), *The State of World Population* (New York: 1998).

4. World Health Organization (WHO), *The World Health Report 1998* (Geneva: 1998).

5. United Nations, op. cit. note 1.

6. Ibid.

7. Ibid.

8. Ibid.

9. Ibid.; Population Reference Bureau (PRB), "1998 World Population Datasheet," wall chart (Washington, DC: June 1998).

10. WHO, "Obesity: Preventing and Managing the Global Epidemic," Report of a WHO Consultation on Obesity, Geneva, 3–5 June 1997.

11. United Nations, op. cit. note 1; PRB, op. cit. note 9.
12. Thomas T. Perls and Ruth C. Fretts, "Why Women Live Longer Than Men," *Scientific American*, Summer 1998.
13. UNFPA, op. cit. note 3.
14. WHO, op. cit. note 4.
15. United Nations, op. cit. note 1.
16. "Russian Death Rate Almost Twice as High as in West," *Russia Today*, 13 November 1998.
17. UNAIDS, *Status of the Global HIV/AIDS Epidemic* (Geneva: June 1998).
18. Ross Nickson et al., "Arsenic Poisoning of Bangladesh Groundwater," *Nature*, 24 September 1998.
19. United Nations, op. cit. note 1.
20. "The Ageing of China," *The Economist*, 20 November 1998; John Authers, "Boomers Want to Work Forever," *Financial Times*, 30 October 1998; Theodore Roszak, "The Longevity Revolution," *Resurgence*, September/October 1998; UNFPA, op. cit. note 3; Dennis Pirages, "Demographic Change and Ecological Security," Environmental Change and Security Project Report, Woodrow Wilson Center (Washington, DC: Spring 1997).

HIV/AIDS PANDEMIC DECIMATES (pages 102–03)

1. Joint United Nations Programme on HIV/AIDS (UNAIDS), *AIDS Epidemic Update: December 1998* (Geneva: December 1998); annual HIV infection data since the beginning of the epidemic provided by Neff Walker, UNAIDS, Geneva, e-mail to author, 11 December 1998.
2. UNAIDS, op. cit. note 1.
3. Walker, op. cit. note 1.
4. UNAIDS, op. cit. note 1; Walker, op. cit. note 1.
5. UNAIDS, op. cit. note 1; Michael Specter, "Doctors Powerless as AIDS Rakes Africa," *New York Times*, 6 August 1998.
6. UNAIDS, *Report on the Global HIV/AIDS Epidemic* (Geneva: June 1998).
7. Ibid.; Lawrence K. Altman, "Parts of Africa Showing HIV in 1 in 4 Adults," *New York Times*, 24 June 1998.
8. Impact of AIDS on population growth from U.S. Bureau of the Census, *International Data Base*, electronic database, Suitland, MD, updated 30 November 1998.
9. UNAIDS, op. cit. note 1.
10. UNAIDS, op. cit. note 6; Christopher S. Wren, "Opium Puts Myanmar In Crisis Over AIDS," *New York Times*, 3 May 1998; Marcia R. Samson, "AIDS Threatens Asia's Promise," *ADB Review*, November-December 1997.
11. UNAIDS, op. cit. note 1.
12. Masako Iijima, "One Percent of Indians in Five States Have HIV," *Reuters*, 14 September 1998; number infected in India from UNAIDS, op. cit. note 6.
13. Myrna Watanabe, "China Faces Increased Spread of HIV," *Nature Medicine*, November 1998; Zhu Baoxia, "Fast Surge in AIDS Cases Seen for China," *China Daily*, 6 April 1998; Zhu Baoxia, "HIV Enters 'Fast Growth' Stage," *China Daily*, 26 June 1998; UNAIDS, op. cit. note 6.
14. David Brown, "AIDS Group Issues Alert on Parts of East Europe," *Washington Post*, 22 April 1998; "Drug-Taking Threatens Russian AIDS Explosion," *Reuters*, 8 June 1998; Laura Beil, "AIDS Cases Jump in Eastern Europe," *Dallas Morning News Online*, 3 July 1998; Andrew L. Ball et al., "HIV Prevention Among Injecting Drug Users: Responses in Developing and Transitional Countries," *Public Health Reports*, Supplement 1, June 1998.
15. UNAIDS, op. cit. note 1.
16. Ibid.; "Study: Drugs Cut European AIDS Deaths," *Washington Post*, 27 November 1998.
17. Tony Pugh, "AIDS Takes New Toll on Minorities," *Miami Herald*, 4 August 1998; "Study Says AIDS Rate Plummets in 4 Cities," *USA Today*, 19 November 1998; U.S. Centers for Disease Control and Prevention, "US HIV and AIDS Cases Reported Through December 1997," *HIV/AIDS Surveillance Report*, vol. 9, no. 2 (1998).
18. Donald G. McNeil, Jr., "AIDS Stalking Africa's Struggling Economies," *New York Times*, 15 November 1998.
19. Donald G. McNeil, Jr., "AIDS Takes a Toll on Africa, Even After Death," *New York Times*, 16 December 1998.
20. UNAIDS, op. cit. note 6.
21. "Drug-Taking Threatens Russian AIDS Explosion," op. cit. note 14.
22. Richard A. Knox, "Finding Ways to Help the Poorest Nations," *Boston Globe*, 13 July 1998.
23. Lawrence K. Altman, "AIDS Meeting Ends With Little Hope of Breakthrough," *New York Times*, 5 July 1998.
24. Ibid.
25. UNAIDS, op. cit. note 6.
26. UNAIDS, op. cit. note 1.

27. Ibid.; World Bank, *Confronting AIDS: Public Priorities in a Global Epidemic* (Oxford: Oxford University Press, 1997); Wiput Phoolcharoen, "HIV/AIDS Prevention in Thailand: Success and Challenges," *Science,* 19 June 1998.

28. Update of population of developing world where epidemic has not spread widely based on data from UNAIDS, op. cit. note 1, and provided by Martha Ainsworth, World Bank, e-mail to author, 9 November 1998.

POLIO NEARLY ERADICATED
(pages 104–05)

1. World Health Organization (WHO), "Case Counts," < http://whqsabin.who.int:8082/case.asp >, viewed 18 February 1999. Data for 1997 and 1998 are still incomplete because of delays in reporting.

2. Anthony Burton, Expanded Programme on Immunization, WHO, Geneva, e-mail to author, 22 September 1998.

3. WHO, "Polio Eradication Initiative at a Glance," information sheet, < http://whqsabin.who.int:8082/fact.htm >, viewed 19 November 1998.

4. "WHO Says Seven Fatal Diseases Could Be Gone Within Years," *The Japan Times,* 22 May 1998.

5. WHO, op. cit. note 3.

6. WHO, Expanded Programme on Immunization, "Global Eradication of Poliomyelitis," PowerPoint presentation provided by Burton, op. cit. note 2; 1998 figure as of July 1998.

7. Dave Rogers, "Ridding the World of Polio: Rotary International Has Raised Millions to Vaccinate Children," *Ottawa Citizen,* 13 September 1998.

8. WHO figures from September 1996, cited in The Rotary Fund of Rotary International's PolioPlus Program, *Annual Report on Operations 1996–7* (Evanston, IL: November 1997); 1997–98 figures from Anthony Burton, Expanded Programme on Immunization, WHO, Geneva, discussion with author, 20 December 1998.

9. WHO, op. cit. note 3.

10. WHO, op. cit. note 6.

11. Susan Okie, "Health Officials Aim for a Polio-Free 2000," *Washington Post,* 5 May 1998.

12. WHO, op. cit. note 6.

13. WHO, "The World on the Brink of Eradicating Polio, WHO Says," press release (Geneva: 30 January 1999).

14. WHO, "Polio—The Final Ascent," *Vaccine and Immunization News,* June 1998.

15. Ibid.

16. Jong Wook Lee, "Ending Polio—Now or Never?" in UNICEF, *The Progress of Nations* (New York: Oxford University Press, 1995); Susan Brink and Dana Coleman, "Global Epidemics, Close to Home," *U.S. News and World Report,* 28 October 1996.

REFUGEE NUMBERS DROP AGAIN (pages 106–07)

1. U.N. High Commissioner for Refugees (UNHCR), "UNHCR by Numbers," < http://www.unhcr.ch/un&ref/numbers/table1.htm >, viewed 6 January 1999.

2. Ibid.; comparison with 1995 from Jennifer D. Mitchell, "Refugee Flows Drop Steeply," in Lester R. Brown, Michael Renner, and Christopher Flavin, *Vital Signs 1998* (New York: W.W. Norton & Company, 1998).

3. UNHCR, "Refugees and Others of Concern to UNHCR—1997 Statistical Overview," Geneva, July 1998, posted in UNHCR's "RefWorld," < http://www.unhcr.ch/refworld/refbib/refstat/1998/98intro.htm >, viewed 6 January 1999.

4. UNHCR, op. cit. note 1.

5. Ibid.

6. UNHCR, "Populations of Concern to UNHCR—1997 Statistical Overview," < http://www.unhcr.ch/refworld/refbib/refstat/1998/98tab01.htm >, viewed 6 January 1999.

7. Ibid.

8. Ibid.

9. Ibid.

10. UNHCR, op. cit. note 1.

11. Ibid. The U.S. Committee for Refugees lists 37 countries with a population of internally displaced of 17 million, but points out that the total number worldwide may be much higher; U.S. Committee for Refugees, *World Refugee Survey 1998* (Washington, DC: 1998).

12. UNHCR, op.cit. note 1.

13. U.S. Committee for Refugees, op. cit. note 11.

14. The 56 million figure is arrived at by adding the populations of concern to UNHCR (excluding returnees: 18.9 million), those cared for by UNRWA (3.2 million), the internally displaced (some 30 million), and those in refugee-like situations (at least 3.9 million).

15. UNHCR, op. cit. note 3.

16. UNHCR, op. cit. note 1.

17. Ibid.

18. U.S. Committee for Refugees, op. cit. note 11.

19. UNHCR, op. cit. note 3.

20. Ibid.

21. U.S. Committee for Refugees, op. cit. note 11.

22. Ibid.; the other two donors were Guatemala and Argentina.

23. Ibid.

CIGARETTE PRODUCTION FALLS
(pages 108–09)

1. U.S. Department of Agriculture (USDA), Foreign Agricultural Service (FAS), *World Cigarette Database*, electronic database, Washington, DC, February 1999.

2. Ibid.

3. Ibid.; U.S. Bureau of the Census, *International Data Base*, electronic database, Suitland, MD, updated 30 November 1998.

4. USDA, op. cit. note 1; Bureau of Census, op. cit. note 3.

5. USDA, op. cit. note 1.

6. Ibid.

7. USDA, op. cit. note 1; Bureau of Census, op. cit. note 3.

8. USDA, op. cit. note 1; USDA, FAS, *World Cigarette Situation* (Washington, DC: November 1998).

9. USDA, Economic Research Service, "Cigarette Price Increase Follows Tobacco Pact," *Agricultural Outlook*, January-February 1999.

10. Ibid.

11. "US Tobacco Litigation Moving Ahead," *Associated Press*, 9 February 1999.

12. Kari Huus, "Lining Up At Tobacco's Door," MSNBC on-line, < http://www.msnbc.com >, viewed 28 January 1999.

13. Ibid.

14. Centers for Disease Control and Prevention (CDC), "History of the 1964 Surgeon General's Report," CDC's Tobacco Information & Prevention Sourcepage, < http://www.cdc.gov/nccdphp/osh >, viewed 27 October 1998.

15. Action on Smoking and Health (ASH), "News You Should Know," *ASH Newsletter*, January-February 1999.

16. World Health Organization, *The World Health Report 1998* (Geneva: 1998).

17. Joint United Nations Programme on HIV/AIDS, *AIDS Epidemic Update: December 1998* (Geneva: December 1998).

18. CDC, op. cit. note 14.

19. Jacqui Thornton, "WHO Looks to Ban Tobacco Advertising Worldwide," *Associated Press*, 30 January 1999.

WARS INCREASE ONCE AGAIN
(pages 112–13)

1. Arbeitsgemeinschaft Kriegsursachenforschung (AKUF), "Kriegesbilanz 1998," press release (Hamburg, Germany: Institute for Political Science, University of Hamburg, revised 11 January 1999); AKUF, "Kriege und Bewaffnete Konflikte 1997," < http://www.sozialwiss.uni-hamburg.de/Ipw/Akuf/kriege_text.html >, viewed 4 January 1999.

2. AKUF, "Kriegesbilanz 1998," op. cit. note 1.

3. AKUF defines a war as a violent conflict in which the regular armed forces of a state are involved at least on one side, where on both sides there is a minimum of central organization of fighting forces, and where there is a certain continuity of armed operations rather than isolated clashes; AKUF, "Kriegesbilanz 1998," op. cit. note 1. AKUF and other analysts of war trends also distinguish wars ("major armed conflicts") from more minor armed conflicts by requiring a minimum of 1,000 battle-related deaths over the course of the conflict; see Margareta Sollenberg, ed., *States in Armed Conflict 1997*, Report No. 49 (Uppsala, Sweden: Uppsala University, Department of Peace and Conflict Research, 1998).

4. The category "major armed conflicts" is subdivided into "wars" (1,000 or more battle-related deaths during any given year) and "intermediate armed conflicts" (more than 1,000 battle-related deaths during the course of the conflict, but fewer than that in any given year). "Minor armed conflicts" involve fewer than 1,000 deaths for the entire conflict duration. Sollenberg, op. cit. note 3.

5. Project Ploughshares, *Armed Conflicts Report '98* (Waterloo, Canada: Institute of Peace and Conflict Studies, Summer 1998).

6. AKUF, "Kriegesbilanz 1998," op. cit. note 1.

7. Ibid.

8. Sollenberg, op. cit. note 3.

9. Ibid.

10. Ibid.

11. Ibid.
12. Ian Fisher with Norimitsu Onishi, "Congo's Struggle May Unleash Broad Strife to Redraw Africa," *New York Times*, 12 January 1999.
13. Sollenberg, op. cit. note 3.
14. A.J. Jongman, "Contemporary Conflicts. A Global Survey of High and Lower Intensity Conflicts and Serious Disputes," *PIOOM Newsletter and Progress Report*, winter 1995 (Leiden, Netherlands: PIOOM Foundation).
15. High-intensity conflicts involve more than 1,000 deaths per year; low-intensity conflicts involve 100–1,000 deaths; violent political conflicts involve 25–100 deaths. A.J. Jongman and A.P. Schmid, "PIOOM's World Conflict Map 1997. A Comparison with Previous Years," *PIOOM Newsletter and Progress Report*, winter 1997 (Leiden, Netherlands: PIOOM Foundation); PIOOM, "World Conflict Map 1996," prepared for the Forum on Early Warning and Early Response, London.
16. Jongman and Schmid, op. cit. note 15.

U.N. PEACEKEEPING EXPENDITURES DROP MORE
(pages 114–15)

1. "Financial Tidbits," Office of the Spokesman for the Secretary-General, < http://www.un.org/News/ossg/finance.htm >, viewed 23 November 1998. (Beginning with July 1997, the United Nations switched its peacekeeping accounts from calendar years to July–June reporting periods.)
2. United Nations Department of Peacekeeping Operations, < http://www.un.org/Depts/dpko/troop/troop1.htm >, viewed 23 November 1998.
3. United Nations Department of Peacekeeping Operations, "1948–1998: 50 Years of United Nations Peacekeeping Operations," < http://www.un.org/Depts/DPKO/pk50_w.htm >, viewed 23 November 1998.
4. Ibid.
5. United Nations Department of Peacekeeping Operations, "Current Peacekeeping Operations," < http://www.un.org/Depts/DPKO/c_miss.htm >, viewed 23 November 1998.
6. Ibid.
7. Ibid.
8. Trevor Findlay, "Armed Conflict Prevention, Management and Resolution," in Stockholm International Peace Research Institute (SIPRI), *SIPRI Yearbook 1998: Armaments, Disarmament and International Security* (New York: Oxford University Press, 1998).
9. Ibid.
10. Paul Lewis, "Council Votes to Withdraw Peacekeepers from Angola," *New York Times*, 27 February 1999; Paul Lewis, "China Votes a U.N. Force Out of Balkans," *New York Times*, 26 February 1999.
11. United Nations Department of Peacekeeping Operations, op. cit. note 3.
12. Global Policy Forum, "Size of Individual Peacekeeping Operations by Month: 1998," < http://www.globalpolicy.org/security/peacekpg/pkoms98.htm >, viewed 23 November 1998.
13. "Status of Contributions to the Regular Budget, International Tribunals and Peacekeeping Operations as at 31 December 1998," United Nations, Office of the Spokesman for the Secretary-General, New York.
14. Ibid.
15. United Nations Department of Peacekeeping Operations, op. cit. note 3.
16. SFOR from International Institute for Strategic Studies, *The Military Balance 1998/99* (London: Oxford University Press, 1998).
17. International Institute for Strategic Studies, "The 1998 Chart of Armed Conflict," wall chart, issued in conjunction with *The Military Balance 1998/99*.
18. Susanna Eckstein, "Multilateral Peace Missions," in SIPRI, op. cit. note 8.
19. Ibid.

NUCLEAR ARSENALS SHRINK
(pages 116–17)

1. Robert S. Norris and William M. Arkin, "Global Nuclear Stockpiles, 1945–1997," Nuclear Notebook, *Bulletin of the Atomic Scientists*, November/December 1997.
2. William M. Arkin, Robert S. Norris, and Joshua Handler, *Taking Stock: Worldwide Nuclear Deployments 1998* (Washington, DC: Natural Resources Defense Council, March 1998).
3. Norris and Arkin, op. cit. note 1.
4. Ibid.
5. Ibid.
6. "US and USSR/Russian Total Strategic Launchers (Force Loadings), 1945–1996," NRDC Nuclear Program, Natural Resources Defense Council, < http://www.nrdc.org/

nrdcpro/nudb/dafig1.html>, viewed 31 July 1998.

7. Arkin, Norris, and Handler, op. cit. note 2.

8. Ibid. For annual U.S. dismantlement numbers since 1980, see "Summary of Declassified Nuclear Stockpile Information," >http://www.osti.gov/html/osti/opennet/document/press/pc26tab1.html>, viewed 4 August 1998.

9. Robert S. Norris and William M. Arkin, "U.S. Nuclear Weapons Stockpile, July 1998," Nuclear Notebook, *Bulletin of the Atomic Scientists*, July/August 1998.

10. Arkin, Norris, and Handler, op. cit. note 2.

11. Robert S. Norris and William M. Arkin, "Known Nuclear Tests Worldwide, 1945–1998," Nuclear Notebook, *Bulletin of the Atomic Scientists*, November/December 1998.

12. Ibid.

13. Signatures as of 29 October 1998, from the Web site of the Preparatory Commission for the Comprehensive Nuclear Test Ban Treaty Organization, <http://www.ctbto.org/ctbto/sig_rat.shtml>, viewed 23 November 1998.

14. Norris and Arkin, op. cit. note 11.

15. Stephen I. Schwartz, ed., *Atomic Audit: The Costs and Consequences of U.S. Nuclear Weapons* (Washington, DC: Brookings Institution Press, 1998). Original data in 1996 dollars.

16. Ibid.

17. Ibid.

18. Ruth Leger Sivard, *World Military and Social Expenditures 1996* (Washington, DC: World Priorities, 1996).

TRANSGENIC CROPS PROLIFERATE (pages 122–23)

1. Clive James, *Global Review of Commercialized Transgenic Crops: 1998 (Preliminary Executive Summary and Principal Tables)*, ISAAA Briefs No. 8 (Ithaca, NY: International Service for the Acquisition of Agri-biotech Applications (ISAAA), 1998).

2. U.S. Department of Agriculture (USDA), *Production, Supply, and Distribution*, electronic database, Washington, DC, updated February 1999.

3. Jane Rissler and Margaret Melon, *The Ecological Risks of Engineered Crops* (Cambridge, MA: The MIT Press, 1996).

4. Ibid.

5. James, op. cit. note 1.

6. Ibid.

7. Ibid.

8. Ibid.

9. Ibid.

10. Ibid.

11. Ibid.; cotton share is Worldwatch calculation based on ibid. and on USDA, op. cit. note 2.

12. James, op. cit. note 1; rapeseed share is Worldwatch calculation based on ibid. and on USDA, op. cit. note 2.

13. James, op. cit. note 1.

14. Stephen Nottingham, *Eat Your Genes: How Genetically Modified Food is Entering Your Diet* (London: Zed Books, 1998).

15. USDA, op. cit. note 2; Dennis R. Henderson et al., eds., *Globalization of the Processed Foods Market*, Agricultural Economics Report No. 742 (Washington, DC: USDA, Economic Research Service, September 1996).

16. James, op. cit. note 1.

17. Ibid.

18. Ibid.

19. Ibid.

20. Ibid.

21. Alan Gersten, "Seed Firm Works to Tailor Crops to Users," *Journal of Commerce*, 6 February 1998; James, op. cit. note 1.

22. Johnathon Friedland and Scott Kilman, "As Geneticists Develop an Appetite for Greens Mr. Romo Flourishes," *Wall Street Journal*, 28 January 1999.

23. James, op. cit. note 1; Monsanto Corporation, <http://www.monsanto.com>, viewed 5 January 1999.

24. Nottingham, op. cit. note 14.

25. Julie A. Nordlee et al., "Identification of a Brazil-Nut Allergen in Transgenic Soybeans," *New England Journal of Medicine*, 14 March 1996.

26. Angelika Hilbeck et al., "Toxicity of *Bacillus thuringiensis* Cry1Ab Toxin to the Predator *Chrysoperla carnea* (Neuroptera: Chrysopidae)," *Environmental Entomology*, August 1998; A.N.E. Birch et al., "Interactions Between Plant Resistance Genes, Pest Aphid Populations and Beneficial Aphid Predators," *Scottish Crop Research Institute Annual Report* (Dundee, Scotland: 1996/97); Rissler and Melon, op. cit. note 3.

27. Allison A. Snow and Pedro Moran Palma, "Commercialization of Transgenic Plants: Potential Ecological Risks," *BioScience*, February 1997; Rissler and Melon, op. cit. note 3.

28. Mary MacArthur, "GE Canola Crossbreeds

Create Tough Weed Problem," *Western Producer*, 15 October 1998.

29. Rural Advancement Foundation International (RAFI), "Seed Industry Consolidation: Who Owns Whom?" *RAFI Communique*, July/August 1998.

30. Ibid.

31. RAFI, "Terminator Technology Targets Farmers," *RAFI Communique*, April 1998.

32. "Report of BSWG-5," *Earth Negotiations Bulletin*, August 1998.

33. "Efforts to Adopt UN Biosafety Protocol Fail," *Financial Times*, 25 February 1999.

PESTICIDE-RESISTANT SPECIES FLOURISH (pages 124–25)

1. Insect and mite data from Mark Whalon, Pesticide Research Center, Michigan State University, Lansing, MI, e-mail to author, 26 January 1999; plant disease data from Wolfram Koeller, Plant Pathology Department, Cornell University, Ithaca, NY, e-mail to author, 21 December 1998; weed data from Ian Heap, "The Occurrence of Herbicide-Resistant Weeds Worldwide," *Pesticide Science*, November 1997, with update from Ian Heap, Weed Sciences, Oregon State University, Corvallis, OR, e-mail to author, 12 January 1999.

2. Mark L. Winston, *Nature Wars: People vs. Pests* (Cambridge, MA: Harvard University Press, 1997).

3. Ibid.

4. Ibid.

5. Ibid.

6. George P. Georghiou and Angel Lagunes-Tejeda, *The Occurrence of Resistance to Pesticides in Arthropods* (Rome: U.N. Food and Agriculture Organization, 1991).

7. Edward J. Grafius, "Managing Insecticide Resistance in the Colorado Potato Beetle," presented at annual meeting of Entomological Society of America, Las Vegas, NV, 9–12 November 1998.

8. Koeller, op. cit. note 1.

9. Montague Yudelman et al., "Pest Management and Food Production: Looking to the Future," Food, Agriculture, and the Environment Discussion Paper 25 (Washington: International Food Policy Research Institute, September 1998).

10. Grafius, op. cit. note 7.

11. Heap, op. cit. note 1; Ian Heap, Weed Sciences, Oregon State University, Corvallis, OR, e-mail to author, 25 January 1999.

12. George N. Agrios, *Plant Pathology* (New York: Academic Press, 1997).

13. Ibid.

14. Ibid.; Miguel Altieri, "Escaping the Treadmill," *Ceres*, July/August 1995.

15. Altieri, op. cit. note 14.

16. Chris Bright, *Life Out of Bounds* (New York: W.W. Norton & Company, 1998).

17. David Pimentel, "Protecting Crops," in Walter C. Olsen, ed., *The Literature of Crop Science* (Ithaca, NY: Cornell University Press, 1995).

18. Yudelman et al., op. cit. note 9; Sandra Postel, *Pillar of Sand* (New York: W.W. Norton & Company, in press).

19. Yudelman et al., op. cit. note 9.

20. Ibid.

21. Ibid.

22. Ibid.

23. Jane Rissler and Margaret Mellon, *The Ecological Risks of Engineered Crops* (Cambridge, MA: The MIT Press, 1996).

24. Margaret Mellon and Jane Rissler, eds., *Now or Never: Serious New Plans to Save a Natural Pest Control* (Cambridge, MA: Union of Concerned Scientists, 1998).

25. Mary MacArthur, "GE Canola Crossbreads Create Tough Weed Problem," *Western Producer*, 15 October 1998.

26. Helmut F. Van Emden and David B. Peakall, *Beyond Silent Spring: Integrated Pest Management and Chemical Safety* (London: Chapman & Hall, 1996).

27. Ibid.

28. Ibid.

29. Ibid.; U.S. Department of Agriculture, *Production, Distribution and Supply*, electronic database, Washington, DC, updated February 1999.

30. Hasan Bolkan, "Integrated Pest Management of Processing Tomatoes Grown in Mexico: A Food Processor Success Story," Annex 4 from Organisation for Economic Co-operation and Development, "Report of the OECD/FAO Workshop on Integrated Pest Management and Pesticide Risk Reduction," Neuchâtel, Switzerland, 28 June–2 July 1998.

31. Van Emden and Peakall, op. cit. note 26.

HARMFUL ALGAE BLOOMING WORLDWIDE (pages 126–27)

1. G. M. Hallegraeff, "A Review of Harmful Algal Blooms and Their Apparent Increase," *Phycologia*, vol. 32, no. 2 (1993).
2. Liu Yinglang, "Pollution to Blame for Sea Scourge," *China Daily*, 12 October 1998.
3. Theodore Smayda, University of Rhode Island, Graduate School of Oceanography, "The Toxic Sea: The Global Epidemic of Harmful Algal Blooms," presentation at Naval War College, Newport, RI, 11 August 1998.
4. Julian Robbins, "Harmful Algae Blooms: A Short Introduction," *IMS Newsletter* (Intergovernmental Oceanographic Commission, UNESCO), 16 October 1998.
5. S.W. Jeffrey, M. Vesk, and R.F.C. Mantoura, "Phytoplankton Pigments: Windows into the Pastures of the Sea," *Nature & Resources*, vol. 33, no. 2 (1997).
6. Theodore J. Smayda, "Harmful Algal Blooms: Their Ecophysiology and General Relevance to Phytoplankton Blooms in the Sea," *Limnology and Oceanography*, vol. 42, no. 5, suppl. (1997).
7. Christine Mlott, "The Rise in Toxic Tides: What's Behind the Ocean Blooms?" *Science News*, 27 September 1997.
8. David Malakoff, "Death by Suffocation in the Gulf of Mexico," *Science*, 10 July 1998.
9. Ibid.
10. Ibid.
11. Adriatic and Black Seas from Tim Beardsley, "Death in the Deep," *Scientific American*, November 1997; Baltic from E. Rantajärvi et al., "Phytoplankton Blooms in the Baltic Sea in 1997," Finnish Institute of Marine Research, < http://www2.fimr.fi/algaline/ARC97/SUM97.HTM >, viewed 7 December 1998.
12. Smayda, op. cit. note 3.
13. Scott W. Nixon, "Enriching the Sea to Death," *Scientific American Presents*, fall 1998.
14. Hallegraeff, op. cit. note 1.
15. Donald M. Anderson and Alan W. White, "Marine Biotoxins at the Top of the Food Chain," *Oceanus*, fall 1992.
16. Dick Russell, "Underwater Epidemic," *Amicus Journal*, spring 1998.
17. Table 1 from the following: Theodore J. Smayda, "Novel and Nuisance Phytoplankton Blooms in the Sea: Evidence for a Global Epidemic," *Toxic Marine Phytoplankton: Proceedings of the Fourth International Conference on Toxic Marine Phytoplankton, Held June 26-30 in Lund, Sweden* (New York: Elsevier Science Publishers, 1990); Maine and New England from Linda Kanamine, "Scientists Sounds Red Alert Over Harmful Algae," *USA Today International*, 15 November 1996; Puget Sound and Washington State from Donald F. Boesch et al., *Harmful Algal Blooms in Coastal Waters: Options for Prevention, Control and Mitigation*, National Oceanic and Atmospheric Administration (NOAA) Coastal Ocean Program, Decision Analysis Series No. 10 (Silver Spring, MD: NOAA, February 1997); Texas from "Growing Red Tide Imperils Shellfishing Along Texas Gulf Coast," *New York Times*, 13 October 1996; Brian Morton, "Hong Kong: Wonders Never Cease," *Marine Pollution Bulletin*, July 1998.
18. John Tibbetts, "Toxic Tides," *Environmental Health Perspectives*, July 1998.
19. Morton, op. cit. note 17; John Ridding, "HK Fishermen Fear Drowning in 'Red Tide'," *Financial Times*, 15 April 1998.
20. John Harwood, "What Killed the Monk Seals?" *Nature*, 7 May 1998; one third from J. Raloff, "Endangered Seals Suffer Massive Die-Off," *Science News*, 30 August 1997.
21. Hallegraeff, op. cit. note 1.
22. Ibid.
23. Ibid.
24. Indrani Karunasagar et al., "Another Outbreak of PSP in India," *Harmful Algae News* (Intergovernmental Oceanographic Commission, UNESCO), April 1998.
25. Hallegraeff, op. cit. note 1; Donald M. Anderson, "Red Tides," *Scientific American*, August 1994.
26. Hallegraeff, op. cit. note 1.
27. Ibid.
28. Rita A. Horner, David L. Garrison, and F. Gerald Plumley, "Harmful Algal Blooms and Red Tide Problems on the U.S. West Coast," *Limnology and Oceanography*, vol. 42, no. 5, suppl. (1997).
29. Joby Warrick, "Tiny Plants Threaten Bounty of Seas," *Washington Post*, 23 September 1997.
30. JoAnn M. Burkholder et al., "New 'Phantom' Dinoflagellate Is the Causative Agent of Major Estuarine Fish Kills," *Nature*, 30 July 1992.
31. Edward D. Levin et al., "Persisting Learning Deficits in Rats After Exposure to Pfiesteria piscicida," *Environmental Health Perspectives*, December 1997.
32. Eugene L. Meyer, "Pfiesteria Torpedoes Sales of Md. Seafood," *Washington Post*, 25 September 1997.

33. Health, Ecological and Economic Dimensions of Global Change Program, *Marine Ecosystems: Emerging Diseases as Indicators of Change* (Cambridge, MA: Harvard University, December 1998).

34. Boesch et al., op. cit. note 17.

URBAN AIR TAKING LIVES
(pages 128–29)

1. World Resources Institute (WRI) et al., *World Resources 1998–99* (New York: Oxford University Press, 1998); United Nations Environment Programme (UNEP) and World Health Organization (WHO), *City Air Quality Trends,* GEMS/AIR Data Vol. 3 (Nairobi: UNEP, 1995); WHO and UNEP, *Urban Air Pollution in Megacities of the World* (Oxford, U.K.: Blackwell, 1992); UNEP and WHO, *Assessment of Urban Air Quality* (Nairobi: Global Environment Monitoring System (GEMS), 1998).

2. Problems with data verification and funding led to the program's termination in 1996.

3. Jack M. Hollander and Duncan Brown, "Air Pollution," in Jack M. Hollander, ed., *The Energy-Environment Connection* (Washington, DC: Island Press, 1992).

4. Ibid.

5. UNEP and WHO, *City Air Quality Trends,* op. cit. note 1.

6. Derek Elsom, *Smog Alert: Managing Urban Air Quality* (London: Earthscan, 1996).

7. WHO, "WHO Guidelines for Air Quality," Fact Sheet No. 187 (Geneva: December 1997); J. Raloff, "Clues Hint How Particulates Harm Lungs," *Science News,* 24 October 1998.

8. Hollander and Brown, op. cit. note 3; John Harte, "Acid Rain," in Hollander, op. cit. note 3.

9. Figures 1 and 2 from the following sources: 1985 data for all cities and 1995 data for Tehran and Cairo from WHO and UNEP, GEMS/AIR database, available through the U.S. Environmental Protection Agency (EPA), < http://www.epa.gov/airs/aewin/ >; 1985 data for Beijing are an average of 1984 and 1986; 1995 data for Tehran and Cairo are from 1993; 1995 data for most cities are from WRI et al., op. cit. note 1; 1995 sulfur dioxide data for Calcutta are from 1994; 1995 particulates data for Calcutta are from Priti Kumar et al., "Death is In the Air," *Down to Earth,* 15 November 1997.

10. WHO and UNEP, *City Air Quality Trends,* op. cit. note 1; WHO and UNEP, *Urban Air Pollution in Megacities,* op. cit. note 1; UNEP and WHO, op. cit. note 1; WHO and UNEP, op. cit. note 9.

11. Dieter Schwela, WHO, Geneva, e-mail to author, 3 March 1999.

12. Dieter Schwela, "Assessing Urban Air Pollution—The GEMS/AIR Programme Revitalized," *Environmental Health Newsletter,* October 1996.

13. UNEP and WHO, *City Air Quality Trends,* op. cit. note 1; Schwela, op. cit. note 11.

14. "UN/ECE's Sulfur Protocol to Treaty on Long-Range Air Pollution Goes Into Force," *International Environment Reporter,* 19 August 1998.

15. "Official Says Canada Will Seek Deeper Cuts in U.S. Emissions in Upcoming Negotiations," *International Environment Reporter,* 4 February 1998; Office of Air Quality Planning and Standards, Emissions Monitoring and Analysis Division, Air Quality Trends Analysis Group, *National Air Pollutant Emission Trends Update: 1970–1997* (Research Triangle Park, NC: EPA, 1998).

16. Elsom, op. cit. note 6.

17. Hollander and Brown, op. cit. note 3.

18. David Stanners and Philippe Bourdeau, eds., *Europe's Environment: The Dobris Assessment* (Copenhagen: European Environment Agency, 1995).

19. Office of Air Quality Planning and Standards, Emissions Monitoring and Analysis Division, Air Quality Trends Analysis Group, *National Air Quality and Emissions Trends Report, 1997* (Research Triangle Park, NC: EPA, 1998).

20. Anthony J. McMichael and Kirk R. Smith, "Seeking a Global Perspective on Air Pollution and Health," *Epidemiology,* January 1999.

21. China from World Bank, *Clear Water, Blue Skies: China's Environment in the New Century* (Washington, DC: 1997), and from WRI et al., op. cit. note 1; Tata Energy Research Institute, *Looking Back to Think Ahead: Green India 2047* (New Delhi: Tata Energy Research Institute, 1998).

22. WRI et al., op. cit. note 1.

23. Figure of 1.8 million from WHO, op. cit. note 7; 2.8 million from WHO, *Health and Environment in Sustainable Development: Five Years after the Earth Summit* (Geneva: 1997), cited in WRI et al., op. cit. note 1.

24. Peter Gaupp, "Air Pollution in the Third World," *Swiss Review of World Affairs,* February 1997;

Utpal Chatterjee, "Expert Paints Gloomy Picture of Pollution," *The Times of India*, 27 April 1998.

25. WHO, op. cit. note 7; Molly Moore, "Mexico City Gasping in Quest of Fair Air," *Washington Post*, 25 November 1996; Anthony Faiola, "Santiago's Children Gasp for Cleaner Air," *Washington Post*, 12 July 1998.

26. WRI et al., op. cit. note 1.

27. Hollander and Brown, op. cit. note 3.

28. "Delhi Children Have High Level of Lead in Blood," *The Statesman* (India), 9 July 1998; Chanda Handa, "Umbilical Discord," *Down to Earth*, 31 May 1998; Shanghai from X.M. Shen et al., "Childhood Lead Poisoning in Children," *Science of the Total Environment*, vol. 181, 1996, cited in World Bank, op. cit. note 21.

29. Howard Schneider, "Colossal Gridlock on the Nile," *Washington Post*, 20 January 1999; "36 Stations Monitor Lead Pollution in Cairo," *Agence France Presse*, 28 January 1999.

30. United Nations, *World Urbanization Prospects: The 1996 Revision* (New York: 1998).

31. Figure for 1995 from Kumar et al., op. cit. note 9. Kumar's estimate is based on the model used in Carter Brandon and Kirsten Hommann, "The Cost of Inaction: Valuing the Economy-Wide Cost of Environmental Degradation in India," presented at the Modeling Global Sustainability conference, United Nations University, Tokyo, October 1995. Brandon and Hommann used air pollution data for 36 cities in either 1991 or 1992 to obtain an estimate of annual air pollution-related deaths.

32. "China Adopts Effective Measures to Curb Pollution," *Xinhua News Agency*, 14 October 1996; "Authorities Reveal 3 Million Deaths Linked to Illness from Urban Air Pollution," *International Environment Reporter*, 30 October 1996.

33. World Bank, op. cit. note 21.

34. Devra Davis et al., "Children at Risk from Current Patterns of Global Air Pollution" (draft), presented at the Annual Meeting of the American Association for the Advancement of Science, Anaheim, CA, 24 January 1999.

35. "Study Reports Children Globally Facing Major Health Risks from Air Pollution," press release (Washington, DC: WRI, 24 January 1999).

BIOMASS ENERGY USE GROWING SLOWLY (pages 130–31)

1. International Energy Agency (IEA), *Biomass Energy: Data, Analysis, and Trends* (Paris: Organisation for Economic Co-operation and Development (OECD/IEA, 1998). Final energy use reflects energy reaching consumers, which is distinct from primary energy use figures that appear elsewhere in *Vital Signs*.

2. Vaclav Smil, *Energy in World History* (Oxford, U.K.: Westview Press, 1994).

3. IEA, op. cit. note 1.

4. Ibid.

5. Ibid.

6. Ibid.

7. Ibid.

8. IEA, *Energy Statistics and Balances of Non-OECD Countries, 1995–96* (Paris: OECD/IEA, 1998).

9. IEA, op. cit. note 1.

10. Ibid.

11. Ibid.

12. IEA, *World Energy Outlook 1998* (Paris: OECD/IEA, 1998); Marian Radetzki, "The Economics of Biomass in Industrialized Countries: An Overview," *Energy Policy*, May 1997.

13. D.O. Hall, "Biomass Energy in Industrialized Countries—A View of the Future," *Forest Ecology and Management*, vol. 91, pp. 17–45 (1997); IEA, op. cit. note 1.

14. IEA, op. cit. note 1; European Commission, *Energy For the Future: Renewable Sources of Energy* (White Paper for a Community Strategy and Action Plan) (Brussels: 1997).

15. World Bank, *Rural Energy and Development: Improving Energy Supplies for Two Billion People* (Washington, DC: 1996).

16. IEA, op. cit. note 1.

17. Ibid.; Daniel Kammen, "Cookstoves for the Developing World," *Scientific American*, July 1995.

18. IEA, op. cit. note 1.

19. D.O. Hall and J.I. Scrase, "Will Biomass Be the Environmentally Friendly Fuel of the Future?" *Biomass and Bioenergy*, vol. 15, nos. 4–5 (1998).

20. Ibid.

21. Ibid.

22. Ibid.

23. Ibid.

24. Ibid.; David O. Hall et al., "Biomass Energy for Energy: Supply Prospects," in Thomas B. Johansson et al., eds., *Renewable Energy: Sources for Fuels and Electricity* (Washington, DC: Island

Press, 1993); Robert Williams, "Roles for Biomass Energy in Sustainable Development," in R. Socolow et al., eds., *Industrial Ecology and Global Change* (New York: Cambridge University Press, 1997).

25. IEA, op. cit. note 12.

26. President's Committee of Advisors on Science and Technology, Report of the Energy Research and Development Panel, *Energy Research and Development for the Challenges of the Twenty-First Century* (Washington, DC: November 1997).

27. Ibid.

28. Mario Giampietro, Sergio Ulgiati, and David Pimentel, "Feasibility of Large-Scale Biofuel Production," *BioScience*, October 1997.

TRANSPORTATION SHAPES CITIES (pages 134–35)

1. Peter Newman and Jeff Kenworthy, *Sustainability and Cities: Overcoming Automobile Dependence* (Washington, DC: Island Press, 1999).

2. Ibid.

3. Ibid.; for Figure 1, the U.S. cities are Boston, Chicago, Denver, Detroit, Houston, Los Angeles, New York, Phoenix, San Francisco, and Washington; Australian cities are Adelaide, Brisbane, Melbourne, Perth, and Sydney; Canadian cities are Calgary, Montreal, Ottawa, Toronto, Vancouver, and Winnipeg; West European cities are Amsterdam, Brussels, Copenhagen, Frankfurt, Hamburg, London, Munich, Paris, Stockholm, Vienna, and Zurich; wealthy Asian cities are Hong Kong, Tokyo, and Singapore; and developing Asian cities are Jakarta, Kuala Lumpur, Manila, and Surabaya (Indonesia).

4. Newman and Kenworthy, op. cit. note 1.

5. Ibid.; Joel Garreau, *Edge City: Life on the New Frontier* (New York: Doubleday, 1991).

6. U.S. Department of Transportation, Federal Highway Administration, *Our Nation's Travel: 1995 Nationwide Personal Transportation Survey Early Results Report* (Washington, DC: September 1997).

7. Newman and Kenworthy, op. cit. note 1.

8. Ibid.

9. Gui Nei, "Traffic Accidents Soaring," *China Daily*, 10 November 1998; Jane Seymour, "Trafficking in Death," *New Scientist*, 14 September 1996; Eduardo A. Vasconcellos,

"Transport and Environment in Developing Countries: Comparing Air Pollution and Traffic Accidents as Policy Priorities," *Habitat International*, vol. 21, no. 1 (1997).

10. Newman and Kenworthy, op. cit. note 1; see also Matthew Wald, "Pedestrian Death Risk is Seen as Major Public Health Crisis," *New York Times*, 9 April 1997, and Anna Wilde Mathews, "Motorists, Bike Riders Clash, With Mounting Casualties," *Wall Street Journal*, 31 August 1998. For Table 1, cities are those listed in footnote 3 plus Portland, Sacramento, and San Diego in the United States; Canberra in Australia; Edmonton in Canada; and Bangkok, Beijing, and Seoul in developing Asia.

11. World Health Organization, *The World Health Report 1995* (Geneva: 1995).

12. Walter Hook, "Hurdles to Easing Congestion in Asia," *Habitat Debate* (newsletter of the United Nations Centre for Human Settlements), vol. 4, no. 2 (1998); Texas Transportation Institute, *Mobility Study*, summary at < http://www. mobility.tamu.edu/ study/ >, viewed 24 August 1998.

13. Texas Transportation Institute, op. cit. note 12.

14. Surface Transportation Policy Project, *An Analysis of the Relationship Between Highway Expansion and Congestion in Metropolitan Areas: Lessons from the 15-Year Texas Transportation Institute Study* (Washington, DC: 1998), at < http://www.transact.org >; Alan Sipress, "Widen the Roads, Drivers Will Come," *Washington Post*, 4 January 1999.

15. Car exhaust from Jack Hollander, ed., *The Energy-Environment Connection* (Washington, DC: Island Press, 1992).

16. Gywneth Howells, *Acid Rain and Acid Waters*, 2nd ed. (London: Ellis Horwood Limited, 1995); J.T. Houghton et al., eds., *Climate Change 1995: The Science of Climate Change*, Contribution of Working Group I to the Second Assessment Report of the Intergovernmental Panel on Climate Change (Cambridge, U.K.: Cambridge University Press, 1996).

17. Walter Hook and Michael Replogle, "Motorization and Non-Motorized Transport in Asia," *Land Use Policy*, vol. 13, no. 1 (1996).

18. Graham Haughton and Colin Hunter, *Sustainable Cities*, Regional Policy and Development Series 7 (London: Jessica Kingsley Publishers, 1994).

19. Chester Arnold and James Gibbons, "Impervious Surface Coverage: The Emergence of a Key Environmental Indicator," *Journal of the*

American Planning Association, March 1996.

20. Jeff Kenworthy et al., *Indicators of Transport Efficiency in 37 Global Cities* (Washington, DC: World Bank, 1997).

21. PriceWaterhouse Coopers Lend Lease Ratings, cited in Neal Peirce, "Investment Market Message to Atlanta: Grow Smarter," *Sacramento Bee,* 3 January 1999.

22. Netherlands Ministry of Housing, Physical Planning and the Environment, *Fourth Report (EXTRA) on Physical Planning in the Netherlands: Comprehensive Summary, On the Road to 2015* (The Hague: 1991).

23. H. William Batt, "Motor Vehicle Transportation and Proper Pricing: User Fees, Environmental Fees, and Value Capture," *Ecological Economics Bulletin,* first quarter 1998.

24. David Weller, "For Whom the Road Tolls: Road Pricing in Singapore," *Harvard International Review,* summer 1998.

25. Donald Shoup, "Congress Okays Cash Out," *Access,* Fall 1998.

26. Ibid.

27. Ibid.

28. Todd Litman, "The Costs of Automobile Dependency" (Victoria, BC, Canada: Victoria Transport Policy Institute, 1996).

29. Mary Williams Walsh, "Instant Mobility, No Headaches," *The Sun,* 3 August 1998.

30. European Academy of the Urban Environment, "Berlin: Stattauto-Germany Largest Car-Sharing Company," *SURBAN-Good Practice in Urban Development* (Berlin: June 1997). The SURBAN database is available at < http://www.eaue.de/ >.

31. Susanna Jacona Salafia, "Italy Shares Electric Cars to Cut Emissions," *Environmental News Service,* 11 December 1998.

32. United Nations, *World Urbanization Prospects: The 1996 Revision* (New York: 1998).

33. Ibid.

CORPORATIONS DRIVING GLOBALIZATION (pages 136–37)

1. Joshua Karliner, *The Corporate Planet* (San Francisco, CA: Sierra Club Books, 1997).

2. U.N. Conference on Trade and Development (UNCTAD), *World Investment Report 1998* (New York: United Nations, 1998).

3. Ibid.

4. "Fortune 500: The World's Largest Corporations," *Fortune,* 3 August 1998.

5. "Multinationals: Back in Fashion," *The Economist,* 27 March 1993.

6. UNCTAD refers to wholly or partially owned subsidiaries as "affiliates." UNCTAD, op. cit. note 2.

7. Ibid.

8. Ibid.

9. UNCTAD, *World Investment Report 1994* (New York: United Nations, 1994).

10. David C. Korten, *When Corporations Rule the World* (West Hartford, CT: Kumarian Press, 1995).

11. Ibid.

12. UNCTAD, op. cit. note 2.

13. Faster growth of sales over exports from "Worldbeater, Inc.," *The Economist,* 18 January 1998; 1997 figure from UNCTAD, op. cit. note 2.

14. UNCTAD, op. cit. note 2.

15. UNCTAD, *World Investment Report 1997* (New York: United Nations, 1997); "Worldbeater, Inc.," op. cit. note 13.

16. UNCTAD, op. cit. note 2.

17. Carrie Smith, Securities Data Co., e-mails to author, 4 and 11 January 1999.

18. Ibid.

19. "Megamergers," *Fortune,* 11 January 1999; "How to Merge," *The Economist,* 9 January 1999.

20. Allen R. Myerson, "Exxon and Mobil Announce $80 Billion Deal to Create World's Largest Company," *New York Times,* 2 December 1998.

21. "The Top 10 Deals of 1998," *Fortune,* 11 January 1999; Stephen Labaton, "Merger Wave Spurs a New Scrutiny," *New York Times,* 13 December 1998.

22. Smith, op. cit. note 17.

23. UNCTAD, op. cit. note 2.

24. Ibid.

25. "How to Make Mergers Work," *The Economist,* 9 January 1999.

26. Karliner, op. cit. note 1; Korten, op. cit. note 10; William Greider, *One World, Ready or Not* (New York: Simon & Schuster, 1997).

GOVERNMENT CORRUPTION WIDESPREAD (pages 138–39)

1. Johann Graf Lambsdorff, Göttingen University, "Transparency International (TI) 1998 Corruption Perceptions Index: Framework Document" (Göttingen, Germany: 14 September 1998).

2. Transparency International (TI), "1998 Corruption Perceptions Index" (Berlin: 22 September 1998).

3. TI, "Transparency International (TI) 1998 Corruption Perceptions Index: Questions & Answers" (Göttingen, Germany: 22 September 1998).

4. "Who Will Listen to Mr Clean?" *The Economist*, 2 August 1997.

5. James D. Wolfensohn, President, World Bank Group, speech given at the World Bank Group annual meeting, Washington, DC, 1 October 1996.

6. Papua New Guinea from Abby Yadi, "World Bank Axes Loan," *The Independent* (Port Moresby), 2 August 1996; other nations from Paul Lewis, "2 Global Lenders Use Leverage to Combat Corruption," *New York Times*, 11 August 1997.

7. Nathaniel Leff, "Economic Development through Bureaucratic Corruption," *American Behavioral Scientist*, pp. 8–14 (1964), and Samuel P. Huntington, *Political Order in Changing Societies* (New Haven, CT: Yale University Press, 1968), both cited in Paolo Mauro, "Corruption and Growth," *Quarterly Journal of Economics*, August 1995.

8. Mauro, op. cit. note 7.

9. Shang-Jin Wei, *How Taxing Is Corruption on International Investors?* Working Paper 6030 (Cambridge, MA: National Bureau of Economic Research, 1997).

10. TI, op. cit. note 2.

11. Paulo Mauro, "Essays on Country Risk, Asset Markets and Growth," Ph.D. thesis, Harvard University, Cambridge, MA, November 1993, cited in Mauro, op. cit. note 7.

12. Frank Vogl, "The Supply Side of Global Bribery," *Finance & Development*, June 1998.

13. William W. Bevis, *Borneo Log: The Struggle for Sarawak's Forests* (Seattle: University of Washington Press, 1995).

14. See, for example, Charles Victor Barber, Nels C. Johnson, and Emmy Hafild, *Breaking the Logjam* (Washington, DC: World Resources Institute, 1994).

15. Susan Rose-Ackerman, *Redesigning the State to Fight Corruption*, Viewpoint Note No. 75 (Washington, DC: World Bank, 1996).

16. Robin Broad, with John Cavanagh, *Plundering Paradise: The Struggle for the Environment in the Philippines* (Berkeley: University of California Press, 1993).

17. Rose-Ackerman, op. cit. note 15.

18. Ibid.

19. TI, "Greater Access to Official Information and Containing Conflicts of Interest, 'Key To Containing Corruption'," press release (London: 3 December 1998).

20. Bevis, op. cit. note 13.

21. Center for Responsive Politics, *The Big Picture: Where the Money Came from in the 1996 Elections* (Washington, DC: 1997).

22. Johann Graf Lambsdorff, "An Empirical Investigation of Bribery in International Trade," *European Journal of Development Research*, June 1998.

23. Ibid.

24. Ibid.; Organisation for Economic Co-operation and Development, "Convention on Combating Bribery of Foreign Officials in International Business Transactions" (Paris: 1997).

25. Vogl, op. cit. note 12.

26. TI, "Bribery of Foreign Officials Will Become A Crime in February: Last Hurdle for Entry into Force of OECD Convention Removed," press release (Berlin: 9 December 1998).

UNEMPLOYMENT PLAGUES MANY NATIONS (pages 142–43)

1. International Labour Office (ILO), *World Employment Report 1998–99* (Geneva: 1998).

2. Ibid.

3. Ibid.

4. Ibid.

5. Press Information of the German Federal Government, "Sieben Millionen Arbeitsplatze Fehlen," 13 November 1998, 'Newsticker-Archiv,' < http://195.143.20.53/01/0108/02225/index.html >.

6. ILO, op. cit. note 1; ILO, "Economically Active Population 1950–2010," STAT Working Papers No. 96–5 (Geneva: 1996).

7. Lester R. Brown, Gary Gardner, and Brian Halweil, *Beyond Malthus: Sixteen Dimensions of the Population Problem*, Worldwatch Paper 143 (Washington, DC: Worldwatch Institute, September 1998).

8. ILO, op. cit. note 1.

9. Richard J. Barnet, "Lords of the Global Economy," *The Nation*, 19 December 1994; U.N. Research Institute for Social Development (UNRISD), *States of Disarray: The Social Effects of Globalization* (Geneva: 1995).

10. BBC News, "Japan Sees Record Unemployment," 30 June 1998; Japan Statistics Bureau and Statistics Center, "Employed Persons and Unemployment Rate," <http://www.stat.go.jp/1603.htm>, viewed 24 January 1999.

11. ILO, op. cit. note 1; "The Main EU Statistical Indicators On-Line," EUROSTAT (Statistical Office of the European Communities) Web site, <http://europa.eu.int/en/eurostat/indic/indic14.htm>, viewed 23 December 1998.

12. Economic Policy Institute (EPI), "Real Average Weekly and Hourly Earnings of Production and Non-Supervisory Workers, 1967–97," *The Datazone*, <http://epinet.org/datazone/>, viewed 2 February 1999.

13. Lawrence Mischel, Jared Bernstein, and John Schmitt, "The State of American Workers," *Challenge*, November/December 1996.

14. EPI, "Share of Employment of All Workers by Wage Multiple of Poverty Wage, 1973–97," *The Datazone*, op. cit. note 12.

15. ILO, op. cit. note 1.

16. United Nations, *Monthly Bulletin of Statistics* (New York: October 1998).

17. ILO, op. cit. note 1.

18. "Asian Labour Market Woes Deepening," press release (Geneva: ILO, 2 December 1998); ILO, op. cit. note 1; Seth Mydans, "Bad News, Silver Lining for Indonesian Laborers," *New York Times*, 6 February 1998.

19. "Asian Labour Market Woes Deepening," op. cit. note 18; Sheryl WuDunn, "South Korea's Mood Swings from Bleak to Bullish," *New York Times*, 24 January 1999.

20. "Asian Labour Market Woes Deepening," op. cit. note 18; ILO, op. cit. note 1.

21. ILO, op. cit. note 1.

22. Ibid.

23. Erik Eckholm, "Joblessness: A Perilous Curve on China's Capitalist Road," *New York Times*, 20 January 1998.

24. ILO, op. cit. note 1.

25. "China: Streamlining Mines," *New York Times*, 9 January 1999.

26. Eckholm, op. cit. note 23.

27. Elisabeth Rosenthal, "In China, 35+ and Female = Unemployable," *New York Times*, 13 October 1998.

28. Ibid.

29. ILO, op. cit. note 1.

30. Ibid.

31. Ibid.

32. Ibid.

33. ILO, *World Labour Report 1993* (Geneva: 1993).

34. ILO, op. cit. note 1.

35. Ibid.

36. Ibid.

37. Population Reference Bureau, "1998 World Population Data Sheet," wallchart (Washington, DC: June 1998).

38. Calculated from ILO, op. cit. note 6.

NGOS PROLIFERATE WORLDWIDE (pages 144–45)

1. Lester M. Salamon and Helmut K. Anheier, *The Emerging Sector Revisited: A Summary of Initial Estimates* (Baltimore, MD: The Johns Hopkins University Center for Civil Society Studies, 1998).

2. P.J. Simmons, "Learning to Live with NGOs," *Foreign Policy*, fall 1998.

3. Commission on Global Governance, *Our Global Neighborhood* (New York: Oxford University Press, 1995).

4. Lester M. Salamon and Helmut K. Anheier, *Defining the Nonprofit Sector: A Cross-National Analysis* (New York: Manchester University Press, 1997).

5. Union of International Organizations, *Yearbook of International Organizations 1996–1997* (Munich: K.G. Saur Verlag, 1997).

6. Ibid.; John Boli and George M. Thomas, "World Culture in the World Polity: A Century of International Non-Governmental Organization," *American Sociological Review*, April 1997.

7. Frederick Starr, "The Era of Civil Society in Perspective," *Give & Take* (Initiative for Social Action and Renewal in Eurasia, Washington, DC), summer 1998.

8. Salamon and Anheier, op. cit. note 4.

9. Alan B. Durning, *Action at the Grassroots: Fighting Poverty and Environmental Decline*, Worldwatch Paper 88 (Washington, DC: Worldwatch Institute, January 1989); Starr, op. cit. note 7.

10. Salamon and Anheier, op. cit. note 1; Starr, op. cit. note 7.

11. Simmons, op. cit. note 2.

12. Salamon and Anheier, op. cit. note 1. The countries examined were Argentina, Australia, Austria, Belgium, Brazil, Colombia, the Czech Republic, Finland, France, Germany, Hungary, Ireland, Israel, Japan, Mexico, the Netherlands, Peru, Romania, Spain, Slovakia, the United Kingdom, and the United States. These num-

bers do not include religious congregations.

13. Salamon and Anheir, op. cit. note 1.
14. Ibid.
15. Alex Demirovic, "NGOs and Social Movements: A Study in Contrasts," *CNS* (Capitalism, Nature, and Socialism, New York), September 1998.
16. David Rieff, "The False Dawn of Civil Society," *The Nation*, 22 February 1999.
17. Jessica T. Mathews, "Power Shift," *Foreign Affairs*, January/February 1997.
18. Ibid.
19. Salamon and Anheier, op cit. note 1.
20. Demirovic, op. cit. note 15.
21. Mathews, op. cit. note 17. This estimate excludes funds from the World Bank and the International Monetary Fund.
22. Mathews, op. cit. note 17.
23. John Bray, ed., *No Hiding Place: Business and the Politics of Pressure* (London: Control Risks Group, July 1997).
24. Salamon and Anheier, op. cit. note 1.
25. Commission on Global Governance, op cit. note 3.
26. Mark Megali and Andy Friedman, "Fronting for Business," *Multinational Monitor*, March 1992.
27. Salamon and Anheier, op. cit. note 1.
28. Megali and Friedman, op. cit. note 26.
29. Michael Clough, "Reflections on Civil Society," *The Nation*, 22 February 1999; Simmons, op. cit. note 2.
30. Salamon and Anheier, op. cit. note 1.
31. Ibid.

MALNUTRITION STILL PREVALENT (pages 146–47)

1. Figure of 1 billion chronically hungry from U.N. Food and Agriculture Organization (FAO), *The State of Food and Agriculture* (Rome: 1998); nutrient deficiencies from World Health Organization (WHO), *The World Health Report 1998* (Geneva: 1998).
2. Figure of 600 million is Worldwatch Institute estimate based on rates of overweight from WHO, op. cit. note 1, from WHO, "Obesity: Preventing and Managing the Global Epidemic," Report of a WHO Consultation on Obesity, Geneva, 3–5 June 1997, and from populations of industrial nations and several large developing nations from Population Reference Bureau (PRB), "1998 World Population Datasheet," wall chart (Washington, DC: June 1998). The technical definitions of overweight and obese are linked to the body mass index (BMI), a measure of a person's weight relative to their height; overweight is defined as a BMI between 25 and 30, while obese is defined as a BMI above 30. More generally, overweight is defined as being 15 percent over normal body weight, while obesity is defined as 20 percent above normal.
3. WHO, op. cit. note 1.
4. Ibid.
5. Ibid.
6. FAO, op. cit. note 1; unlike the "nearly 1 billion" mentioned earlier, this figure includes only developing nations, and not the hungry in Eastern Europe and the former Soviet bloc, or those who go hungry in industrial nations.
7. FAO, op. cit. note 1.
8. Ibid.
9. Ibid.; PRB, op. cit. note 2.
10. WHO, *WHO Global Database on Child Growth and Malnutrition* (Geneva: 1997); M. de Onis et al., "The Worldwide Magnitude of Protein-Energy Malnutrition: An Overview from the WHO Global Database on Child Growth" (Geneva: WHO, January 1998).
11. FAO, op. cit. note 1.
12. Ibid.
13. Per Pinstrup-Andersen and Marc J. Cohen, "An Overview of the Future Global Food Situation," paper prepared for the Millennial Symposium on Feeding the Planet, Cosmos Club, Washington, DC, 12 February 1999; Frances Moore Lappe et al., *World Hunger: 12 Myths* (New York: Grove Press, 1998).
14. FAO, op. cit. note 1.
15. Ibid.
16. WHO, op. cit. note 1.
17. Ibid.
18. Ibid.
19. WHO, op. cit. note 10.
20. Ibid.
21. De Onis et al., op. cit. note 10.
22. WHO, op. cit. note 1; WHO, op. cit. note 2.
23. National Heart, Lung, and Blood Institute (NHLBI), "Clinical Guidelines on the Identification, Evaluation, and Treatment of Overweight and Obesity in Adults" (Bethesda, MD: National Institutes of Health, 17 June 1998); WHO, op. cit. note 2.
24. WHO, op. cit. note 2; Michael R. Gordon, "Facing Severe Shortage of Food, Russia Seeks Foreign Relief Aid," *New York Times*, 10 October 1998.
25. Jane E. Brody, "Persuading Potatoes to Get Off

the Couches," *New York Times*, 2 February 1999; Adam Drewnowski and Barry M. Popkin, "The Nutrition Transition: New Trends in the Global Diet," *Nutrition Reviews*, February 1997; NHLBI, op. cit. note 23; Shannon Dortch, "America Weighs In," *American Demographics*, June 1997.

26. WHO, op. cit. note 2.
27. Ibid.
28. WHO, op. cit. note 1; WHO, op. cit. note 2; FAO, *The Sixth World Food Survey* (Rome: 1996).
29. WHO, op. cit. note 2.
30. NHLBI, op. cit. note 23; WHO, op. cit. note 2.
31. WHO, op. cit. note 2.
32. Ibid.
33. Walter Willet, Department of Nutrition, Harvard School of Public Health, discussion with author, 12 January 1999; Laura Shapiro, "In Sugar We Trust," *Newsweek*, 13 July 1998.
34. WHO, op. cit. note 1.
35. WHO, op. cit. note 2.
36. Ibid.
37. Ibid.; WHO, op. cit. note 10; Ginger Thompson, "With Obesity in Children Rising, More Get Adult Type Diabetes," *New York Times*, 14 December 1998.
38. Drewnowski and Popkin, op. cit. note 26; Philip T. James et al., "Diet-Related Diseases Shift Global Burden," *Global Health & Environment Monitor*, winter 1998.
39. Colin Campbell et al., "Association of Diet and Disease: A Comprehensive Study of Health Characteristics in China," presented at Fairbank Center on East Asian Studies, Harvard University, Cambridge, MA, 23–24 May 1997; Junshi Chen, "Change in Diet Sparks Chronic Disease Surge in China," *Global Health & Environment Monitor*, winter 1998.
40. WHO, op. cit. note 1.

SPERM COUNTS DROPPING
(pages 148–49)

1. Shanna H. Swan et al., "Have Sperm Densities Declined? A Reanalysis of Global Trend Data," *Environmental Health Perspectives*, November 1997.
2. T. Colborn, Dianne Dumanoski, and John Peterson Myers, *Our Stolen Future* (New York: Penguin Books, 1996).
3. Swan et al., op. cit. note 1.
4. Ibid.
5. Shanna H. Swan, Department of Family and Community Medicine, University of Missouri, Columbia, MO, discussions with author, 5 January and 4 February 1999; Michael D. Lemonick, "What's Wrong With Our Sperm?" *Time*, 18 March 1996.
6. Swan et al., op. cit. note 1; Elisabeth Carlsen et al., "Evidence for Decreasing Quality of Semen During the Past 50 Years," *British Medical Journal*, 12 September 1992.
7. Jacques Auger et al., "Decline in Semen Quality Among Fertile Men in Paris During the Past 20 Years," *New England Journal of Medicine*, 2 February 1995; Stewart Irvine et al., "Evidence of Deteriorating Semen Quality in the United Kingdom: Birth Cohort Study in 577 Men in Scotland Over 11 Years," *British Medical Journal*, 24 February 1996; Edward V. Younglai et al., "Canadian Semen Quality: An Analysis of Sperm Density Among Eleven Academic Fertility Centers," *Fertility and Sterility*, July 1998; K. Van Waeleghem et al., "Deterioration of Sperm Quality in Young Healthy Belgian Men," *Human Reproduction*, February 1996; Carlsen et al., op. cit. note 6.
8. Shanna H. Swan and Eric P. Elkin, "Declining Semen Quality: Can the Past Inform the Present?" unpublished, letter to author, 5 December 1998.
9. Larry I. Lipshultz, "The Debate Continues—The Continuing Debate over the Possible Decline in Semen Quality" (editorial), *Fertility and Sterility*, May 1996; Harry Fisch and Erik T. Goluboff, "Geographic Variations in Sperm Counts: A Potential Cause of Bias in Studies of Semen Quality," *Fertility and Sterility*, May 1996.
10. Swan, op. cit. note 5.
11. C.A. Paulsen et al, "Data from Men in the Greater Seattle Area Reveals No Downward Trend in Semen Quality: Further Evidence That Deterioration in Semen Quality Is Not Geographically Uniform," *Fertility and Sterility*, May 1996; H. Fisch et al., "Semen Analyses in 1,283 Men from the United States over a 25-Year Period: No Decline in Quality," *Fertility and Sterility*, May 1996.
12. J. Ginsburg et al., "Residence in the London Area and Sperm Density," *Lancet*, 22 January 1994.
13. J. Toppari et al., "Male Reproductive Health and Environmental Xenoestrogens," *Environmental Health Perspectives*, August 1996.
14. Ibid.; R. Bergstrom et al., "Increase in Testicular Cancer Incidence in Six European Countries: a Birth Cohort Phenomenon," *Journal of the*

National Cancer Institute, vol. 88, pp. 727–33 (1996).

15. Colborn, Dumanoski, and Myers, op. cit. note 2.
16. Richard M. Sharpe and Niels E. Skakkebaek, "Are Oestrogens Involved in Falling Sperm Counts and Disorders of the Male Reproductive Tract?" *Lancet*, 29 May 1993; T. Colborn and C. Clement, *Chemically Induced Alterations in Sexual and Functional Development: The Wildlife/Human Connection* (Princeton, NJ: Princeton Scientific Publishing, 1992); T. Colborn, F.S. vom Saal, and A.M. Soto, "Developmental Effects of Endocrine Disrupting Chemicals in Wildlife and Humans," *Environmental Health Perspectives*, March 1993.
17. J. Toppari et al., "Male Reproductive Health and Environmental Xenoestrogens," *Environmental Health Perspectives*, August 1996; Thomas M. Crisp et al., "Environmental Endocrine Disruption: An Effects Assessment and Analysis," *Environmental Health Perspectives*, February 1998.
18. L.E. Gray Jr. et al., "Exposure to TCDD During Development Permanently Alters Reproductive Function in Male Long Evans Rats and Hamsters: Reduced Ejaculated and Epididymal Sperm Numbers and Sex Accessory Gland Weights in Offspring with Normal Androgenic Status," *Toxicology and Applied Pharmacology*, vol. 131, pp. 108–18 (1995).
19. Richard M. Sharpe et al., "Gestational and Lactational Exposure of Rats to Xenoestrogens Results in Reduced Testicular Size and Sperm Production," *Environmental Health Perspectives*, December 1995; Betsy Carpenter, "Investigating the Next 'Silent Spring'," *U.S. News & World Report*, 11 March 1996.
20. Sharpe et al., op. cit. note 19.
21. Crisp et al., op. cit. note 17.
22. W.B. Gill et al., "Association of Diethylstilbestrol Exposure in Utero with Cryptorchidism, Testicular Hypoplasia and Semen Abnormalities," *Journal of Urology*, March 1979; A.J. Wilcox et al., "Fertility in Men Exposed Prenatally to Diethylstilbestrol," *New England Journal of Medicine*, 25 April 1995.
23. R.Z. Sokol, "Toxicants and Infertility: Identification and Prevention," in E.D. Whitehead and H.M. Nagler, eds., *Management of Impotence and Infertility* (Philadelphia: J.B. Lippincott Company, 1994); R.L. Garcia-Rodriguez et al., "Exposure to Pesticides and Cryptochidism: Geographical Evidence of a Possible Association," *Environmental Health Perspectives*, October 1996.
24. Theo Colborn, "The Wildlife/Human Connection: Modernizing Risk Decisions," *Environmental Health Perspectives*, December 1994.
25. Colborn, Dumanoski, and Myers, op. cit. note 2.
26. Peter M. Vonier et al., "Interaction of Environmental Chemicals with the Estrogen and Progesterone Receptors from the Oviduct of the American Alligator," *Environmental Health Perspectives*, December 1996; Louis J. Guillette, Jr., et al., "Developmental Abnormalities of the Gonad and Abnormal Sex Hormone Concentrations in Juvenile Alligators from Contaminated and Control Lakes in Florida," *Environmental Health Perspectives*, August 1994.
27. Marla Cone, "River Pollution Linked to Sex Defects in Fish," *Los Angeles Times*, 22 September 1998; Crisp et al., op. cit. note 17.
28. Crisp et al., op. cit. note 17.
29. Frederick S. Vom Saal and Daniel M. Sheehan, "Challenging Risk Assessment," *Forum for Applied Research and Public Policy*, Fall 1998.
30. Colborn, Dumanoski, and Myers, op. cit. note 2; 2.4-D and endosulfan from Janet Raloff, "That Feminine Touch," *Science News*, 22 January 1994.
31. B. Field et al., "Reproductive Effects of Environmental Agents," *Series in Reproductive Endocrinology*, vol. 8 (1990), as quoted in Sharpe and Skakkebaek, op. cit. note 16.
32. Colborn, Dumanoski, and Myers, op. cit. note 2.
33. Swan and Elkin, op. cit. note 8.
34. "Japan Studies Drop in Sperm Counts," *Nature*, 29 October 1998.
35. Colin Macilwain, "US Panel Split on Endocrine Disruptors," *Nature*, 29 October 1998.

PEOPLE EVERYWHERE EATING MORE FAST FOOD (pages 150–51)

1. Gale Business Resources, "Restaurants," overview analysis of the global restaurant industry viewed at <http://galenet.gale.com/a/acp/n...acp/db/gbrd/expert.html>, viewed 5 January 1999.
2. Brian Breuhaus, "Risky Business?" *Restaurant Business*, 1 November 1998. Tricon Global Restaurants, the parent company for Kentucky Fried Chicken, Pizza Hut, and Taco Bell, is often cited as the industry leader, with nearly 30,000 restaurants.

3. McDonald's Corporation, *1997 Annual Report*, at < http://www.mcdonalds.com >, viewed 23 January 1999.

4. Breuhas, op. cit. note 2. Burger King was founded and is headquartered in the United States, but is now owned by a U.K. company.

5. Figure 1 is a Worldwatch compilation of data from annual reports and Web sites of 10 fast-food companies.

6. McDonald's Corporation, op. cit. note 3.

7. Figure of 900 units, which includes some non-fast-food outlets, from Charlene C. Price, "The U.S. Food Service Industry Looks Abroad," *FoodReview*, May-August, 1996; 32,000 units, which is all fast food, from Chris Urban, Technomic Inc. Food Industry Group, letter to author, 3 February 1999.

8. Breuhaus, op. cit. note 2.

9. John F. Love, *McDonald's: Behind the Arches* (New York: Bantam Books, 1986).

10. Ibid.

11. Ibid.

12. Gale Business Resources, op. cit. note 1.

13. Outside home from Eric Schlosser, "Meat and Potatoes," *Rolling Stone*, 26 November 1998; food in the car from National Restaurant Association, *Takeout Foods: A Consumer Study of Carryout and Delivery* (Washington, DC: May 1998).

14. Gale Business Resources, op. cit. note 1; advertising from *Advertising Age*, < http://www.adage.com/dataplace >, viewed 3 February 1999.

15. Office of the Minnesota Attorney General, "Fast Food Facts," at < http://www.olen.com/food/book.html >, viewed 12 February 1999.

16. Philip T. James and Karen A. McColl, "Diet-Related Diseases Shift Global Burden," *Global Health and Environment Monitor*, winter 1998.

17. National Institutes of Health, "Statement on First Federal Obesity Clinical Guidelines," press release (Bethesda, MD: 3 June 1998).

18. Kamala Krishnaswamy, "Urbanization Promotes Obesity Among India's Middle Class," *Global Health and Environment Monitor*, Winter 1998.

19. Amy Zuber, "Hamburger University Beefs Up Program with Global Curriculum," *Nation's Restaurant News*, 27 October 1997; Ed Rubinstein, "Tricon Global's Toolkit Organizes and Disseminates Marketing Data Globally," *Nation's Restaurant News*, 9 February 1998.

20. "Burger King Corporation Internet Press Kit" (Miami: Burger King Corporation, 1998).

21. Louise Kramer, "McD's, Disney: Year-old Pact is a Happy Deal," *Advertising Age*, 11 May 1998.

22. Ibid.

23. Estimate of 28 percent is a Worldwatch calculation based on "Potatoes: 1997 Summary," U.S. Department of Agriculture (USDA), Economic Research Service (ERS), at < http://usda.mannlib.cornell.edu/reports/nassr/field/ppo-bbp/potatoes_09.22.98 >, viewed 16 January 1999; use by fast-food restaurants from "Potatoes Briefing Room," USDA, ERS, < http://www.econ.ag.gov/ briefing/potato/ >, viewed 16 January 1999.

24. Schlosser, op. cit. note 13.

25. Gale Business Resources, op. cit. note 1.

26. Slow food Web site at < http://www.slowfood.com/main.html >, viewed 23 January 1999.

SMALL ARMS FOUND IN ALL NATIONS (pages 154–55)

1. The term "small arms and light weapons" encompasses such items as pistols and revolvers, hunting rifles and assault rifles, machine guns and submachine guns, hand grenades, light mortars, light anti-tank weapons like grenade launchers and recoilless rifles, and portable, shoulder-fired surface-to-air missiles.

2. The 500 million estimate is from Jasjit Singh, ed., *Light Weapons and International Security* (Delhi: Indian Pugwash Society and British American Security Information Council, December 1995).

3. Swadesh Rana, *Small Arms and Intra-State Conflicts*, UNIDIR Research Paper No. 34 (Geneva and New York: United Nations Institute for Disarmament Research, 1995).

4. Ibid.

5. Terry J. Gander, ed., *Jane's Infantry Weapons 1998–99* (Coulsdon, U.K.: Jane's Information Group Ltd., 1998). This number does not include Iraq and North Korea, where state factories produce small arms. The Jane's listing includes manufacturers of related equipment such as "sighting equipment," "suppressors," "mortar fire control," and "pyrotechnics."

6. Ibid.

7. Calculated from ibid.

8. Michael T. Klare, "Light Weapons Diffusion and Global Violence in the Post–Cold War Era," in Singh, op. cit. note 2; Gander, op. cit. note 5.

9. Estimate of 50 million from Gander, op. cit. note 5; 70 million estimate from "Russia:

Kalashnikov Anniversary," *Omri Daily Digest*, 21 February 1997 (includes a number of subsequent versions of the Kalashnikov, designated AK-47, AK-74, AKS-74, and AKM).

10. Calculated from Terry J. Gander, ed., *Jane's Infantry Weapons 1996–97* (Coulsdon, U.K.: Jane's Information Group Ltd., 1996). The 1998–99 edition lists a substantially smaller number of countries as having the Kalashnikov in their arsenal. It is possible that some have retired older versions of this weapon in favor of newer rifles.

11. Gander, op. cit. note 5.

12. Ibid.

13. Ibid.

14. Ibid.

15. Ibid.

16. Estimate of 100 million assault rifle from Bonn International Center for Conversion, *Conversion Survey 1997: Global Disarmament and Disposal of Surplus Arms* (New York: Oxford University Press, 1997).

17. Calculated from Gander, op. cit. note 5.

18. Ibid.

19. Ibid.

20. Ibid.

21. Ibid.

22. Ibid.

23. Organization of American States, "Inter-American Convention Against the Illicit Manufacturing of and Trafficking in Firearms, Ammunition, Explosives, and Other Related Materials," Washington, DC, 13 November 1997.

24. Arms Monitoring Project of the Federation of American Scientists, "Regional, International, and Governmental Efforts to Combat the Illicit Traffic in Small and Light Arms," posted on the Prep Com Web site, at < http://www.prepcom. org/low/pc2/pc2a11.html >.

25. Geraldine O'Callaghan and Brian Wood, "Wheeling and Dealing," and Daniel N. Nelson, "Damage Control," both in *Bulletin of the Atomic Scientists*, January/February 1999.

26. Jim Wurst, "The U.N. Gears Up," *Bulletin of the Atomic Scientists*, January/February 1999.

27. Rachel Stohl, "Weapons Collection Program in Albania to Begin with U.N. Support," *The Weekly Defense Monitor* (Center for Defense Information, Washington, DC), 21 January 1999.

28. Rachel Stohl, "West African Small Arms Moratorium Adopted," *The Weekly Defense Monitor* (Center for Defense Information, Washington, DC) 12 November 1998.

29. Stephen Laufer, "Tenders Called to Destroy Arms," *Business Day* (South Africa), 1 March 1999.

30. See in particular "Message from Prep Com Administrator Ed Laurance," < http://www. prepcom.org/low/pc10/pc10index.htm >, 1 November 1998; "International NGO Action Network on Small Arms (IANSA)," < http:// www.prepcom.org/low/pc2/pc2a40.htm >; *Prep Com Newsletter*, 29 January 1999.

31. "Message from Prep Com Administrator," op. cit. note 30.

THE VITAL SIGNS SERIES

Some topics are included each year in Vital Signs; *others, particularly those in Part Two, are included only in certain years. The following is a list of the topics covered thus far in the series, with the year or years each appeared indicated in parentheses.*

Part One: KEY INDICATORS

FOOD TRENDS
Grain Production (1992–99)
Soybean Harvest (1992–99)
Meat Production (1992–99)
Fish Catch (1992–99)
Grain Stocks (1992–99)
Grain Used for Feed (1993, 1995–96)
Aquaculture (1994, 1996, 1998)

AGRICULTURAL RESOURCE TRENDS
Grain Area (1992–93, 1996–97, 1999)
Fertilizer Use (1992–98)
Irrigation (1992, 1994, 1996–99)
Grain Yield (1994–95, 1998)

ENERGY TRENDS
Oil Production (1992–96, 1998)
Wind Power (1992–99)
Nuclear Power (1992–99)

Solar Cell Production (1992–99)
Natural Gas (1992, 1994–96, 1998)
Energy Efficiency (1992)
Geothermal Power (1993, 1997)
Coal Use (1993–96, 1998)
Hydroelectric Power (1993, 1998)
Carbon Use (1993)
Compact Fluorescent Lamps (1993–96, 1998)
Fossil Fuel Use (1997, 1999)

ATMOSPHERIC TRENDS
CFC Production (1992–96, 1998)
Global Temperature (1992–99)
Carbon Emissions (1992, 1994–99)

ECONOMIC TRENDS
Global Economy (1992–99)
Third World Debt (1992–95, 1999)
International Trade (1993–96, 1998–99)
Steel Production (1993, 1996)

Paper Production (1993, 1994, 1998–99)
Advertising Expenditures (1993, 1999)
Roundwood Production (1994, 1997, 1999)
Gold Production (1994)
Television Use (1995)
Storm Damages (1997–99)
U.N. Finances (1998–99)

TRANSPORTATION TRENDS
Bicycle Production (1992–99)
Automobile Production (1992–99)
Air Travel (1993, 1999)
Motorbike Production (1998)

ENVIRONMENTAL TRENDS
Pesticide Resistance (1994)
Sulfur and Nitrogen Emissions (1994–97)
Environmental Treaties (1995)
Nuclear Waste (1995)

COMMUNICATION TRENDS
Satellite Launches (1998–99)

Telephones (1998–99)
Internet Use (1998–99)

SOCIAL TRENDS
Population Growth (1992–99)
Cigarette Production (1992–99)
Infant Mortality (1992)
Child Mortality (1993)
Refugees (1993–99)
HIV/AIDS Incidence (1994–99)
Immunizations (1994)
Urbanization (1995–96, 1998)
Life Expectancy (1999)
Polio (1999)

MILITARY TRENDS
Military Expenditures (1992, 1998)
Nuclear Arsenal (1992, 1994–96, 1999)
Arms Trade (1994)
Peace Expenditures (1994–99)
Wars (1995, 1998–99)
Armed Forces (1997)

Part Two: SPECIAL FEATURES

ENVIRONMENTAL FEATURES
Bird Populations (1992, 1994)
Forest Loss (1992, 1994–98)
Soil Erosion (1992, 1995)
Steel Recycling (1992, 1995)
Nuclear Waste (1992)
Water Scarcity (1993)
Forest Damage from Air Pollution (1993)
Marine Mammal Populations (1993)
Paper Recycling (1994, 1998)
Coral Reefs (1994)

Energy Productivity (1994)
Amphibian Populations (1995)
Large Dams (1995)
Water Tables (1995)
Lead in Gasoline (1995)
Aquatic Species (1996)
Environmental Treaties (1996)
Ecosystem Conversion (1997)
Primate Populations (1997)
Ozone Layer (1997)
Subsidies for Environmental Harm (1997)

Tree Plantations (1998)
Vertebrate Loss (1998)
Organic Waste Reuse (1998)
Nitrogen Fixation (1998)
Acid Rain (1998)
Transgenic Crops (1999)
Pesticide Resistance (1999)
Algal Blooms (1999)
Urban Air Pollution (1999)
Biomass Energy (1999)

AGRICULTURAL FEATURES
Pesticide Control (1996)
Organic Farming (1996)

ECONOMIC FEATURES
Wheat/Oil Exchange Rate (1992, 1993)
Trade in Arms and Grain (1992)
Cigarette Taxes (1993, 1995, 1998)
U.S. Seafood Prices (1993)
Environmental Taxes (1996, 1998)
Private Finance in Third World (1996, 1998)
Storm Damages (1996)
Aid for Sustainable Development (1997)
Food Aid (1997)
R&D Expenditures (1997)
Urban Agriculture (1997)
Electric Cars (1997)
Arms Production (1997)
Fossil Fuel Subsidies (1998)
Metals Exploration (1998)
Pollution Control Markets (1998)
Urban Transportation (1999)
Transnational Corporations (1999)
Government Corruption (1999)

SOCIAL FEATURES
Income Distribution (1992, 1995, 1997)
Maternal Mortality (1992, 1997)
Access to Family Planning (1992)
Literacy (1993)
Fertility Rates (1993)
Traffic Accidents (1994)
Life Expectancy (1994)
Women in Politics (1995)
Computer Production and Use (1995)
Breast and Prostate Cancer (1995)
Homelessness (1995)
Hunger (1995)
Access to Safe Water (1995)
Infectious Diseases (1996)
Landmines (1996)
Violence Against Women (1996)
Voter Turnouts (1996)
Aging Populations (1997)
Noncommunicable Diseases (1997)
Extinction of Languages (1997)
Female Education (1998)
Sanitation (1998)
Unemployment (1999)
Nongovernmental Organizations (1999)
Malnutrition (1999)
Sperm Count (1999)
Fast-Food Use (1999)

MILITARY FEATURES
Nuclear Arsenal (1993)
U.N. Peacekeeping (1993)
Small Arms (1998–99)

Now you can import all the tables and graphs from *Vital Signs 1999* and other recent Worldwatch publications into your spreadsheet program, presentation software, or word processor with the . . .

1999 WORLDWATCH DATABASE DISK

The Worldwatch Database Disk Subscription gives you current data from all Worldwatch publications, including the *State of the World* and *Vital Signs* annual book series, WORLD WATCH magazine, Worldwatch Papers, and Environmental Alert Series books.

Your subscription includes: a disk (IBM or Macintosh) with all current data and a FREE copy of *Vital Signs 1999*. In January 2000, you will receive a six-month update of the disk with a FREE copy of *State of the World 2000*. This disk will include updates of all long-term data series in *State of the World*, as well as new data from WORLD WATCH and all new Worldwatch Papers.

The disk covers trends from mid-century onward . . . much not readily available from other sources. All data are sourced, and are accurate, comprehensive, and up-to-date. Researchers, students, professors, reporters, and policy analysts use the disk to—

- ◆ *Design graphs to illustrate newspaper stories and policy reports*
- ◆ *Prepare overhead projections on trends for policy briefings, board meetings, and corporate presentations*
- ◆ *Create specific "what if?" scenarios for energy, population, or grain supply*
- ◆ *Overlay one trend onto another, to see how they relate*
- ◆ *Track long-term trends and discern new ones*

To order the 1999 Worldwatch Database Disk for just $89 plus $4 shipping and handling:
Phone: (202) 452-1999 (credit cards accepted: Mastercard, Visa, or American Express);
Fax: (202) 296-7365; E-mail: wwpub@worldwatch.org; Web site: http://www.worldwatch.org
Or send your request to:

1776 Massachusetts Ave., NW
Washington, DC 20036
www.worldwatch.org